A WAR BETWIXT
ENGLISHMEN

Also available from I.B.Tauris:

INDEPENDENCE OR DEATH
British Sailors and Brazilian Independence, 1822–1825
Brian Vale
ISBN 1 86064 060 5

A WAR BETWIXT ENGLISHMEN

Brazil against Argentina
on the River Plate
1825–1830

BRIAN VALE

I.B.Tauris *Publishers*
LONDON • NEW YORK

Published in 2000 by I.B.Tauris & Co Ltd
Victoria House, Bloomsbury Square, London WC1B 4DZ
175 Fifth Avenue, New York NY 10010
Website: http://www.ibtauris.com

In the United States and Canada distributed by St. Martin's Press
175 Fifth Avenue, New York NY 10010

ISBN 1 86064 456 2

A full CIP record for this book is available from the British Library
A full CIP record for this book is available from the Library of
Congress

Library of Congress catalog card: available

Typeset in Garamond by A. & D. Worthington, Newmarket
Printed and bound in Great Britain by WBC Ltd, Bridgend

CONTENTS

MAPS

vii

PREFACE

One glance at the map will show the strategic importance of the River Plate. Cutting into the side of South America like a great gash, the river systems of the Uruguay and the Paraná which flow into it provide a back door to the continent, penetrating northwards for thousands of miles between the Andes and the coastal mountains as far as Paraguay and Bolivia. In colonial times, it was this route that enabled the interior to be settled and exploited, and its mineral wealth and agricultural products to be exported. The fact that inland Brazil depended on these rivers as frontiers and major transportation routes, while the Argentinian provinces dominated the mouth and the exit to the sea, set the scene for centuries of conflict.

At the end of 1825, the newly independent Empire of Brazil went to war with the newly independent Republic of Argentina – then called the United Provinces of the River Plate – over control of the north bank of the Plate Estuary and consequently over the river itself. It was a replay of the long-standing dispute inherited from the old Portuguese and Spanish colonial empires over what is confusingly called the 'Banda Oriental' (properly the 'Banda Oriental del Uruguay'). The war lasted for three years. On land, Argentina drove Brazil onto the defensive and steadily gained the upper hand. At sea the situation was reversed. The Brazilian Navy concentrated on strangling the trade of Buenos Aires by blockade, and on containing the audacious attacks of a small Argentinian squadron under Commodore William Brown. The United Provinces replied by unleashing a swarm of privateers on Brazil's seaborne commerce. The war ended in stalemate and the creation of the state of Uruguay as a buffer between the two sides.

This book describes the naval side of the war and its international impact. Set against the politics and intrigues of the time, its theme is the struggle between a maritime power – Brazil – with an extensive sea-borne commerce and a large and experienced navy, and a continental country – Argentina – which at the time had few maritime pretensions, tiny naval forces but an enormous international trade carried principally in British, American and French vessels. It is a story of cat and mouse amid the shallows and fogs of the River Plate as the might of the Imperial Navy enforced the blockade in the face of lightning strikes by its small but daring Argentinian counterpart, and of single ship actions in the blue rollers of the South Atlantic as Argentinian privateers took on both merchant vessels and Brazilian cruisers. A major casualty of the maritime strategy of both sides was foreign trade, and the book describes the reaction of the three powers whose ships were seized – on the one hand the determination of the United States and France to weaken the Brazilian blockade, and on the other, the relentless pressure of local British diplomats in favour of peace.

The book is also about the men who fought the naval war. A remarkable feature was that both Brazil and Argentina relied heavily on foreign officers and sailors – notably British and Americans – to man and fight their ships. These men, whether veterans of the Wars of Independence, short-term opportunists or long-term immigrants, brought experience, leadership and fighting spirit to the navies they served. And when Ambassador Robert Gordon complained in 1827 that the conflict between Brazil and Argentina which was ruining British trade was essentially 'a war betwixt Englishmen' (in which definition Gordon – a Scot himself – included all subjects of King George whether English, Scottish or Irish), he was not far from the truth. At that time, one-third of officers at sea in the Brazilian Navy, including Commodore James Norton who masterminded the blockade, and over one-sixth of the seamen were British. On the opposing side, the situation was even more striking in that two-thirds of the Argentinian Navy's officers – including its legendary commander, William Brown – and half of its sailors were men of Anglo-Saxon origin. Most were British, but the republican hue of the regime also appealed to large numbers of North Americans. There were also representatives of more individualistic nationalities, such as Frenchmen, Italians, Spaniards, and Latin Americans, but these by and large preferred the more free and easy life of the privateer to the discipline of the naval service.

The aim of this book is to illuminate a hitherto hidden corner of naval history for British and American readers. It is the first detailed study of the war in English, and is based on Brazilian, Argentinian and British sources. Hopefully, its tri-national base will provide insights for South American historians as well. In Brazil, interest in maritime history is accelerating, but little has been done on this topic since Boiteux's exhaustive but unfocused study of 1956. And the studies produced in Argentina since the reprint of Carranza's pioneering work in 1962 have inevitably concentrated on the detailed records which exist locally.

The Portuguese and Spanish languages have changed slightly in spelling over the last 150 years. For simplicity I have therefore used the modern variants. Likewise during the early eighteenth century the Brazilian Navy used naval ranks inherited from the old Portuguese service, whereas the Argentinians still employed military titles. For the sake of consistency I have therefore translated both in the terms of contemporary British Navy usage. Thus, the Brazilian *Capitão-de-Mar-e-Guerra*, *Capitão-Tenente* and *1º Tenente* and their Argentinian equivalents of *Coronel*, *Sargento-Mayor* and *Teniente/Capitan* are translated respectively as Captain, Commander and Lieutenant. Following normal practice, the term 'Captain' is also sometimes used to mean an officer commanding a ship irrespective of his actual rank.

I would like to thank the many people and institutions whose work and assistance have made this book possible. In Brazil, Vice Admiral Luiz Edmundo Bittencourt of the Serviço de Documentação da Marinha for the supply of much material, my old friend Rear Admiral Max Justo Guedes of the Patrimônio Histórico a Cultural da Marinha, and the Director of the Arquivo Nacional, Rio de Janeiro. Also to Reginaldo da Siva Bacchi, Brazilian representative of Asociación de Historia Marítima y Naval Iberoamericana, for valuable suggestions. In Argentina, Edwin Haines of the British Council for the supply of crucial material, and the Directors of the Instituto Browniano and the Departamento de Estudios Históricos Navales for their excellent publications. In Britain, the Directors of the National Maritime Museum, the Public Record Office and the Hydrographic Office, Taunton which supplied contemporary charts. But particularly I must pay tribute to the fathers of Brazilian and Argentinian naval history, Lucas Boiteux and Angel Carranza, who not only produced pioneering studies on the period but reproduced a host of important contemporary documents.

Brian Vale
Greenwich 1999

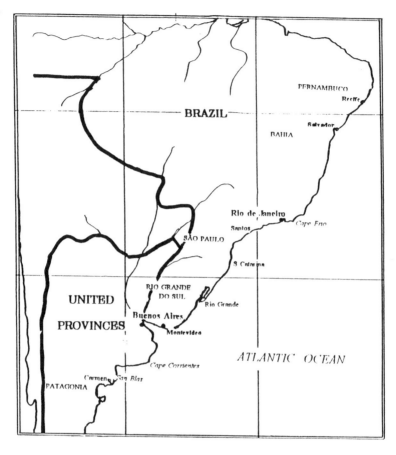

THE EMPIRE OF BRAZIL
AND THE UNITED PROVINCES OF THE RIVER PLATE 1826

PART I: OPENING MOVES

CHAPTER 1

REBELLION IN THE RIVER PLATE

On 19 April 1825, a small sailing launch could be seen battling its way across the broad mouth of the Uruguay where it flows into the western end of the River Plate. Its destination was a small inlet near the tiny port of Las Vacas in what is now the state of Uruguay, but was then part of Brazil. It was a bright autumnal day, and a historic moment in South American history, for the vessel carried the Uruguayan patriot, General Juan Lavalleja, and 33 companions. In a now legendary adventure, they had come to the Banda Oriental to raise the standard of revolt and to seize for their homeland the same independence which other South American countries had won in the wake of the Napoleonic Wars.

Lavalleja and his 33 companions had left their supporters in Buenos Aires the previous day and had first sailed north, avoiding Brazilian naval patrols by keeping to the shallows formed by the muddy tributaries of the Paraná, then headed east to the narrows where the clear waters of the River Uruguay flowed briskly into the Plate Estuary. There, guided by signal fires lit by confederates and driven by a south-westerly wind, the vessel thrashed its way across the current, took in sail and grounded on the eastern bank. Its occupants climbed eagerly ashore, then, with the taking of oaths and the unfurling of flags, they declared war on the Empire of Brazil.

1

Originally part of the Spanish Viceroyalty of the River Plate, the Banda Oriental had been in Brazilian hands for nine years. In 1816, the Portuguese Government, then based in Rio de Janeiro, had taken advantage of the chaos caused by the Napoleonic Wars to realize its long-held dream of extending the frontiers of Brazil to the banks of the River Plate. In June, a Portuguese army, its numbers recently augmented by veterans of Wellington's victories in the Peninsular War and led by General Carlos Frederico Lecor, had marched into the Banda Oriental. A short, dapper figure with waxed moustaches in the French fashion, Lecor's guiding military principle was caution. Proceeding slowly and methodically, it took him six months to take the major port towns of Montevideo and Colonia, and to occupy the smaller settlements along the valleys of the Rio Negro and the Uruguay which formed the frontier with the western Argentinian provinces.

Then, equally slowly, Lecor began to extend his authority over the rolling, treeless pampas which formed the rest of the country. Typically, he avoided any major encounter with the resistance forces led by the patriot José Artigas, but in time effectively eliminated them in a series of small but remorseless local pushes. Some of the patriots fled into exile, others submitted to the inevitable and switched their allegiance. Indeed, one of these, Fructuoso Rivera, who had been Artigas' principal lieutenant, displayed his loyalty to the new regime so ostentatiously that he was promoted to the rank of general by the Brazilians and made Inspector of Imperial Troops in the province. Lecor too was rewarded. His slow and systematic movements were hailed as brilliant examples of Fabian tactics, and he was raised to the nobility as Barão de Laguna. So complete was his success that in 1821, the Banda Oriental was incorporated into Brazil as its Cisplatine Province.

The situation there was hardly affected by Brazil's own struggle for independence in 1823. The occupying army found itself split on the issue, the Portuguese units withdrawing to Montevideo where they were blockaded for a year by their erstwhile Brazilian comrades commanded by General Lecor. But with the rest of the country brought rapidly under Brazilian control, and a Brazilian

naval squadron dominating the River Plate, the Portuguese bowed
to the inevitable and quietly left. With Lecor still in charge, the process of assimilation continued. Many of his officers and men married locally to become
integrated into Uruguayan society. Merchants and ranchers were
won over by the new prosperity which peace brought to commerce and the beef industry. Any thoughts of resistance by the
scattered and apathetic rural population were nullified by the
presence of some 6000 Imperial troops, many of whom were by
now local recruits. Montevideo and Colonia had garrisons of 2500
and 1100 respectively, and there were another 1500 men distributed among the small settlements along the Uruguay and the Rio
Negro. It was these last units which were to receive the first
impact of Juan Lavalleja's invasion.

Lavalleja paused at his landing point for four days, gathering
support and awaiting the arrival of a second group of 200 men
from Buenos Aires. That done, he moved boldly northwards,
scattering the smaller Brazilian detachments as he went or sub-
verting those made up of local troops. The Imperial commanders
were confident in their ability to contain the outbreak, and General
Fructuoso Rivera was ordered to deal with it at the head of 500
men. Unfortunately for Brazil, the restless and inconstant Rivera
had a talent for treachery. He caught up with Lavalleja, but instead
of fighting, promptly broke his oath and changed sides in a second
act of betrayal in what was to become a long and troublesome
career. With his forces now augmented, Lavalleja struck inland. As
his army marched it mushroomed in size as wild *gaucho* irregulars
flocked to join the ranks. The Brazilians fell back before them. In
September, they suffered their first serious reverse at Rincon de las
Gallinas, by the confluence of the Uruguay and the Rio Negro.
Then, in October, an Imperial army stood, fought and was roundly
defeated at Sarandí, in the centre of the province. Within six
months of his landing, the bulk of the Banda Oriental had fallen
into Lavalleja's hands. Supplied by sea and invulnerable except by
regular assault by land, only the garrison towns of Montevideo and
Colonia and their surrounding areas remained under Imperial

control. Lavalleja was so confident of his position that on 25 August he had been able to call an Uruguayan Assembly which had promptly denounced Brazilian rule, declared the Banda Oriental independent, and demanded reunion with the United Provinces.

The United Provinces of the River Plate – as Argentina was then styled – was a huge, empty country of rich plains and small provincial centres, with a scattered population of only 650,000, one-fifth of whom were nomadic Indians. Its economy was based upon a primitive export industry based on beef and hides and the only town of significance was Buenos Aires whose position enabled it to act as a trading centre for the interior of the continent. In Buenos Aires and elsewhere there had been bitter hostility to the Portuguese-Brazilian occupation of the Banda Oriental from the beginning, and an unconcealed desire to see the area reunited with the United Provinces. News of Lavalleja's rising was therefore received with enthusiasm. Uruguayan successes and Brazilian reverses were the cause of widespread public rejoicing, and Buenos Aires became the unofficial base for the supply of volunteers, munitions and supplies. At the official level, however, the Government was too weak to be able to give open support, however much its members may have shared the popular enthusiasm for the cause of freedom. Indeed, the revolutionary credentials of Buenos Aires were impeccable. From 1810 onwards, it had been Buenos Aires which had led the regional struggle for freedom against Spain whether in terms of the revolutionary doctrines or military and naval action. It was Buenos Aires which had ejected the Viceroy, abolished the restrictions on international trade, proclaimed the equality of all citizens, and inspired the formation of the United Provinces in 1813. It was likewise Buenos Aires which, in support of Artigas in the Banda Oriental, had sent its army and a newly formed navy to attack, besiege and ultimately topple the last Royal Governor in Montevideo.

And Buenos Aires had not only been the powerhouse of independence in the River Plate: it had also been the springboard for a series of unsuccessful revolutionary expeditions against the royalist governments in Chile, Peru and Bolivia northwards through the valleys of the Paraná system. Then in 1817, General José de San

Martin had switched the line of attack, and had led an army out of the United Provinces and across the High Andes to the west. There, he had won the battles of Chacabuco and Maipú, seized control of Chile and then, ferried by Lord Cochrane's navy, had attacked Peru. There were early rebuffs, but with Bolivar advancing victoriously from the north, the fate of Spanish rule across the Andes was sealed by their defeat at Ayacucho in 1824.

The official impotence of Buenos Aires in the face of the turmoil in the Banda Oriental was not therefore because of any lack of republican enthusiasm or military experience. Before 1820, the obstacle had been a paralysing struggle for power between the urban, liberal, modernizers of Buenos Aires who saw prosperity in terms of international trade, and the reactionary, xenophobic *caudillos* in the provinces who controlled the cattle industry on which the country's economy was based. It was only the intervention of General Manuel Dorrego in 1820, a man whose personal dignity, education, military skills and courage had won the confidence of both sides, that restored the situation. A new constitution in 1819 had proposed a compromise system of government, midway between the 'unitary' and 'federal' models advocated by the two sides. Dorrego masterminded its implementation, then handed over the governorship of Buenos Aires to General Martin Rodrigues, a hero of the resistance to the British invasion of 1806. In the three years that followed, the new Government laid the foundations of the modern Argentine state.

The driving force behind these changes was a young minister called Bernadino Rivadavia. Overweight and swarthy, Rivadavia was not physically impressive. Indeed, his bulk, heavy jowls and bulging eyes led hostile satirists to portray him as a frog! But there was nothing wrong with his intellect. Vivacious and intelligent, he saw Argentina's future as a liberal secular state, modernized by free trade, foreign investment and European immigration. In power he moved rapidly to realize his vision. Church powers were restricted, secular schools were opened, and freedom of worship permitted. A bank was established, import duties slashed, military expenditure cut, and a system devised for settling the crippling debts caused by the war. And, most significantly, in 1823, Spain recognized the country's independence, followed by Britain, the United States and France. The result of all this was a dramatic expansion in foreign investment and commerce. By 1824, Rivadavia had made himself unpopular with the Church and the Army, but the level of foreign trade had risen to £2 million a year, half of which was with Britain and one-tenth with, respectively, Brazil and the United States.[1] The British community was also thriving. Standing at 3000, it continued to be enlarged by individuals drawn by commercial opportunities, good wages, cheap living and the diverse attractions of worship in a specially licensed Anglican Church or high jinks in the numerous taverns and billiard halls.[2]

In April 1824, Governor Rodrigues stepped down and was replaced by General Gregorio Las Heras. Another liberal intellectual, Manuel José Garcia, replaced Rivadavia who was sent to London as Argentinian Minister in exchange for Woodbine Parish, who had arrived to be the first British Consul-General complete with three handsome gold presentation snuff boxes bearing the likeness of King George IV. These were so highly sought after by potential recipients that Parish had to send for more. Meanwhile, in London, Rivadavia threw himself with single-minded energy into his new role, successfully concluding deals for further investment and immigration and raising a massive loan with Baring Brothers. He was less successful in convincing British ministers that they should take the side of Buenos Aires in the dispute over the Banda Oriental.

Back home, the Government of Las Heras had to deal with the situation created by Lavalleja's rebellion. It had one advantage, for it had now been given authority to act as an executive government on behalf of all of the United Provinces, but its freedom of action was limited by a chronic shortage of funds and a lack of military muscle. Its navy had been effectively disbanded, and its small army was heavily engaged on the frontier. Garcia in particular, was reluctant to see Argentina's recent progress destroyed by becoming involved in a war over the Banda Oriental, and foreign observers reported that the Government, in defiance of public opinion, was following a policy of strict neutrality.[3] Nevertheless, precautions had to be taken. Laws were passed laying down conditions for a reorganized national army, and the old war-horse Martin Rodrigues was sent with troops to the Uruguay to watch over Argentina's sensitive frontier with the Banda Oriental.

CHAPTER 2

THE DRIFT TO WAR

In comparison to the United Provinces, the Empire of Brazil was strong and stable. It was a giant of a country with vast resources stretching from the tropical forests of the Amazon to the temperate grasslands of the River Plate. Its population was four and a half million – of which one and a half million were white, one million slaves of African descent, a quarter of a million Indians, and nearly two million semi-free, mixed race *mulatos* and *caboclos*. Brazil's struggle for independence from Portugal had been no revolutionary conflict, but had been led by the Prince Regent and his royalist ministers in Rio de Janeiro. The new Empire had therefore inherited an established system of government and had been spared the internal strife which had been the bane of the newly independent Spanish American republics. True, there were regional tensions and some hostility to the authoritarian style of the young and charismatic Emperor Pedro, but the system of government was not disrupted, and the mystique of monarchy served to bind the huge and diverse country together. The independence campaign had also left Brazil with a large though ramshackle army and a formidable navy whose audacious performance, under the inspired leadership of Lord Cochrane, had been decisive in the struggle. On the surface, Brazil was a powerful and dangerous enemy.

The reaction of the Imperial Government to the rising in the Banda Oriental was uncomplicated. Ignoring the region's Spanish American roots, the Emperor denounced the rebels as simple traitors and took immediate action to bring them to heel. As early as March 1825, 1500 extra men had been sent south as a result of Argentinian threats and reports that Bolivar had been asked to intervene.[1] At the end of April, the small Brazilian squadron in the

8

River Plate was reinforced with the corvette *Maria da Glória*, the brigs *Rio da Plata* and *Real João*, and ten gunboats and schooners.[2] They were followed a month later by the armed ship *Jurujuba* and the brig *Caboclo* commanded by a young British hero of the independence campaign, John Pascoe Grenfell, convoying half a dozen transports with 1200 troops. But more significantly, the *Jurujuba* carried a new commander for the Brazilian Navy in the River Plate, the veteran Vice Admiral Rodrigo Ferreira Lobo.

Lobo's appointment was a signal that the Brazilian Government was taking the rebellion seriously and would stand no nonsense from Buenos Aires. It was clearly felt that the United Provinces presented no military problem and that the threat of the Imperial Navy in the Plate would be enough to keep them in check. So confident were the Brazilians that Lobo was ordered to mount a naval demonstration off Buenos Aires and to convey to that Government in almost threatening tones 'the justified resentment of HIM the Emperor for its comportment towards the Empire; to demand ... explanations for its actions ... and to order any of its subjects involved in the revolution to desist.'[3]

Vice Admiral Lobo made his appearance in the shallow brown waters off the port of Buenos Aires on 4 July 1825, flying his flag in the corvette *Liberal*. To make his show of force as impressive as possible, he had gathered together almost every sizeable Brazilian warship in the Plate and was accompanied by the corvette *Maria da Glória*, the brigs *Pirajá*, *Caboclo* and *Rio da Plata*, the schooner *Maria Theresa* and two gunboats. In accordance with his orders, the following day he addressed a sharp note to Manuel Garcia, cataloguing Brazilian complaints and demanding explanations. There was clear evidence, he claimed, of Buenos Aires' support for the revolt in the Banda Oriental: money had being collected, arms and munitions were being supplied, armed ships had been prepared to attack Imperial vessels off Colonia, and local newspapers had not only openly advocated union with the Banda Oriental, but had referred to the Emperor in insulting terms. Nevertheless, he concluded, the Emperor would not resort to hostilities if adequate explanations were given and if all assistance to the rebels now ceased.

Affronted by Lobo's tone and the scarcely concealed threat of force, Garcia at first evaded the issue by claiming that the Vice Admiral lacked the necessary credentials. But on 8 July he was forced to respond. Beginning his letter with a statement that although the Republic was 'unaccustomed to give diplomatic explanations to a military chief … presenting himself at the head of a clearly hostile force' he nevertheless had been authorized to reply. Courteously and at length, Garcia explained that the revolt in the Banda Oriental was entirely the work of its inhabitants, and that the Government of Buenos Aires had neither inspired it nor was supporting it. Private citizens were, however, entitled to take what action they wished, and if arms were being supplied, it was being done on a purely commercial basis. The United Provinces wanted friendly relations with Brazil, and was willing to send an emissary to Rio de Janeiro to show its amicable intentions. Lobo, in reply, thanked Garcia for his explanation, and assured him in return that the Imperial squadron was there solely to prevent the flow of arms to the Banda Oriental and posed no threat whatsoever to Buenos Aires or its commerce.[4]

Lobo was sceptical about Garcia's assurances, but felt that the veiled treat posed by the squadron had been salutary. Nevertheless, on the surface, the exchange seemed to have defused the situation and in July and August, officers and men from the Brazilian ships could be seen in the streets and taverns of Buenos Aires taking shore leave and fraternizing with the inhabitants. In some cases relations became too cordial, and Lobo was forced to complain that men were being tempted to desert by generous Argentinian bounties – not only from the *Caboclo* and the *Pirajá* which were commanded and manned predominantly by British seamen, but from the Brazilian-manned *Rio da Plata*.[5]

In reality however, Lobo's appearance had provoked anger among the population and the growing war party in Buenos Aires. There were demonstrations outside the Brazilian Consulate. In Congress, Garcia was forced to give a full explanation of the Government's thinking, revealing that he believed that Brazil was fully prepared to blockade Buenos Aires, that only national weakness had prevented him from defying Lobo's demands, and that half a million pesos had now been allocated to preparing for war. Cruising off the port, the Brazilian commander was perfectly aware from the newspapers as to what was going on, and his despatches detailed the Argentinian preparations. In August he reported that they were fortifying the port, building six gunboats armed with heavy cannon, fitting out two disarmed brigs of war and a schooner, and had sent emissaries to Chile to buy three frigates.[6]

At the same time Lobo began to make contingency plans in case it came to war. His principal objectives would be to blockade Buenos Aires, and to prevent the supply of reinforcements and munitions reaching the Banda Oriental across the estuary and the River Uruguay. To do this, he estimated that he would need a force of 40 vessels – two frigates, six corvettes, a dozen brigs and schooners drawing less than ten feet of water, eight sailing gunboats or armed yachts, and eight oared gunboats which could remain on station whatever the wind. If it was decided to bombard Buenos Aires, four additional ships armed with mortars and drawing eight feet would be required.[7] In Rio de Janeiro, the Ministry of Marine took him at his word. More reinforcements were hurried south. The corvette *Carioca*, the brigantine *Pará* and the schooner *Conceição* sailed at the end of July. The frigates *Thetis*, *Imperatriz* and *Paraguassú* were prepared for sea, additional brigs and gunboats were sought and orders were sent to Rio Grande do Sul to build six armed yachts.

But in Buenos Aires, the Brazilian threat of force had clearly backfired. As Garcia later explained to Consul-General Woodbine Parish, public reaction to Lobo's arrival had forced the Government to change its policy of neutrality in the Banda Oriental. But it was the news of the victory at Sarandí that brought matters to a head. The Brazilian Consulate was stoned by a mob and sailors of the Imperial Navy were attacked in the streets. On 20 October, Bernadino Rivadavia returned from London, keen to use the situation to his advantage. Five days later, in a wave of patriotic enthusiasm and antipathy to Brazil, the Argentinian Congress reviewed the situation, applauded the Uruguayan declaration of 25 August and decreed the incorporation of the Banda Oriental into the United Provinces. There were tentative attempts to ask the British to mediate, but it was too late. General Rodrigues' army crossed the Uruguay in support of Lavalleja's forces, and Buenos Aires prepared to face the inevitable conflict. On 10 December 1825, the Imperial Government responded by declaring war on the United Provinces. The same day, Brazilian diplomatic agents overseas were ordered to inform their host governments of the beginning of hostilities and were issued with a lengthy printed memorandum which justified Brazil's action and showed why it had been forced into a defensive war by Argentinian provocation. On 1 January 1826, Buenos Aires responded with a counter declaration. The die was cast.

CHAPTER 3

THE NAVY OF BRAZIL

On the brink of war in 1825, the Brazilian Navy was the most powerful naval force in the Americas. It possessed no fewer than 65 sizeable fighting vessels carrying 690 guns, and another 31 small armed launches, mail packets and transports. There was one 74-gun ship, 6 frigates, 5 corvettes, 18 brigs and brigantines, 19 schooners-of-war and 16 small gunboats.[1] Its nucleus was made up of ships seized from the old Portuguese Navy at the time of independence but in the succeeding three years, the Brazilian Navy had doubled in size by purchasing foreign vessels and converting prizes taken by Lord Cochrane during the war. Inevitably these ships varied widely in age and strength. None of its frigates were older than eight years, but they varied in size from the smaller 12-pounder vessels *Niterói* and *Thetis*, to the massive 1500-ton 24-pounder *Piranga*. Its force of corvettes and brigs was much more variable, consisting both of veterans of the Napoleonic Wars like the *Itaparica*, *Liberal* and *Cacique* and brand new modern vessels such as the American-built *Maria da Glória* and the *Maceió*. There were also a number of converted merchantmen, mostly prizes, like the *Carioca*, *Pirajá* and *29 de Agosto*. These were perfectly service-able, but to make up for their weaker build the Brazilians armed them – and the smaller frigates *Niterói* and *Thetis* – with light weight but short-range carronades. This was to prove a handicap when they faced the longer range guns of their Argentinian oppo-nents in the River Plate.

Brazil had also inherited from the colonial period a ready-made machinery for naval administration. This comprised the Ministry of Marine made up of a chief secretary and seven clerks; the Intendencia run by the veteran Vice Admiral José de Almeida and

a staff of 45 divided into departments for accounting, pay and
stores; eight arsenals, five smaller shipyards, naval hospitals, and a
Naval Academy. Foreign observers were critical of the apparent
clumsiness of the bureaucracy, pointing out that to repair a boat or
move a man needed a ponderous *Portaria* beginning 'HIM the
Emperor through his Secretary of State for the Navy commands…',[2] but a detailed examination of records and letter books
shows an efficient and well run machine. From the Ministry
flowed a smooth stream of orders for victualling, paying off, naval
movements, manning and promotions, and sets of regulations for
pensions, prizes, pay and uniforms. Brazilian officers at the time
were expected to wear a rich uniform consisting of white panta-
loons and a blue coat with a single row of gilt buttons, epaulettes
on the shoulder and more buttons on the cuff. The coats of flag
officers were additionally embroidered with thick sprigs of golden
oak leaves across the chest.

From the beginning, the Imperial Government had decided to
invest in a large and impressive navy. Indeed, as well as the 65
warships already afloat in 1825, a second ship-of-the-line, two
frigates and two corvettes were being built in the arsenals of Rio,
Pará and Bahia, while numerous gunboats and yachts were being
constructed at the smaller yards in Rio Grande do Sul, Ilha Grande
and Santos. There were also two massive 1700-ton frigates, *Príncipe
Imperial* and *Isabela*, being built in the United States.[3] Opposition
politicians, keen to embarrass the Emperor's ministers under any
pretext, were highly critical of what they described as a naval policy
of ostentation and waste, and argued that instead of buying heavy
modern frigates, they should have concentrated on shallow
draught schooners suitable for service in the shallow waters of the
Plate. This criticism was unjustified. For coastal and river policing,
small ships had an important role, but as the Argentinian war was
to show, it was big ships which won battles and outgunned
privateers. Likewise, as a glance at the map will show, Brazil's
enormous coastline and its position across the trade routes of
South America required a mixed naval force of both large and
small naval units. And this is what the Imperial Government, led
by the Minister of Marine, Francisco Vilela Barbosa, Marquis of

Paranaguá, provided. Unfortunately for his reputation, the strictures of the opposition were repeated by foreign observers, notably the English merchant and historian John Armitage, and have since been accepted uncritically at their face value by too many historians.

Brazil's abundance of natural resources ensured that there was no shortage of woods and material for ship construction and repair, but the lack of any local manufacturing industry made naval stores and munitions a problem. The Brazilians, however, solved it by buying huge quantities of both from Great Britain. During 1825, no fewer than 25 ships sailed from British ports, their holds packed with supplies for the arsenals and dockyards of Brazil. The range of goods was enormous, varying from anchors, spars, cables, cordage, canvas, steam pumps and cannon to uniforms, buttons, surgeons' instruments, bayonets, ramrods and muskets. The cost to the Brazilian Government was £93,000 even with generous discounts.[4]

The Brazilian Navy may have lacked nothing in terms of ships and supplies, but it had a critical manpower problem. To command its warships and to staff its shore establishments, the Navy needed over 200 officers – 6 flag officers, 30 captains, 15 commanders and 150 lieutenants of various grades. In 1826, Brazil was unable to find enough men. At the beginning of the War of Independence the Imperial Government had faced the same problem, but had solved it by signing on 59 British officers. Most of these had been recruited secretly in London during 1823, but the rest – including Lord Cochrane and a group of officers disenchanted with their experiences in Chile – had been found locally.[5] Although numerically in the minority, these men had proved of enormous value to the development of the infant Brazilian Navy. Not only had they filled the vacancies in the lower commissioned ranks but they had brought with them a high level of technical experience, aggression and a confidence in victory derived from years of unquestioned British supremacy at sea. The result had been a series of spectacular engagements in which the Imperial Navy had first swept the Portuguese from the seas and guaranteed Brazil's independence, then gone on to suppress a dangerous northern rebellion which had threatened to destroy the unity of the new country.

This is not to say that all British officers were outstanding as either seamen or as leaders of men. Inevitably they were a mixed bunch. Many served usefully but undramatically during the War of Independence and returned home at the end of their five-year contracts. Others distinguished themselves by their skill and bravery – men like John Pascoe Grenfell who had secured the evacuation of Pará with an audacious bluff; John Taylor who, in command of the *Niterói* had chased a Portuguese convoy across the Atlantic in an epic voyage in which he had taken 17 prizes; and James Norton who had stormed Recife during the rebellion. More were to do so in the war against the United Provinces. But some had careers which were spectacularly unsuccessful, very often caused by excessive drinking, and either abandoned the service or were dismissed.

Between their arrival and the declaration of war against Buenos Aires two years later, the original group of British officers had inevitably been depleted by sickness or departure, but their numbers had been replenished by further recruitment in London and by promoting many of the volunteers who had signed on in the hope of eventually reaching the quarterdeck. Thus, by the beginning of 1825, one-third of Imperial officers employed at sea were British – 1 commodore, 4 captains, 6 commanders, 34 lieutenants and 12 midshipmen or volunteers.[6] Of these, 13 were in command of ships. Woodbine Parish was not far from the truth when, gloomily contemplating the menacing sails of Lobo's squadron, he commented that 'the Brazilian Navy appears so formidable to the Buenos Aireans because it is largely commanded and manned by Englishmen'.[7] But in spite of these British recruits – and of another 16 officers of American, French and Scandinavian origin – the Imperial Navy still had severe shortages in the middle ranks. Since its creation, many Brazilian young men had eagerly joined their country's naval service as junior officers, but few had yet had time to acquire much experience at sea. Nevertheless, the rapid expansion of the Imperial Navy meant that many of them had to be employed in command of its smaller vessels. At the first battle of the war at Corales for example, Vice Admiral Lobo blamed his lack of success on the fact that six of his ships were commanded by inexperienced young sublieutenants. Likewise, the schooners and gunboats which formed the Flotilla of the Uruguay were so short of officers that many were commanded by Army officers or sergeants of the Marine Artillery.

But Brazil was not only short of officers. It was also afflicted by a chronic shortage of sailors. To man and fight its ships the Navy needed 10,500 men – 8000 sailors and 2500 marines from the newly formed Marine Artillery. The latter were not difficult to find, but it proved impossible to recruit enough seamen. There were constant complaints throughout the war from both Lobo and his successor, Admiral Pinto Guedes, about shortages of men. The authorities resorted to every device. Criminals were sent on board. Deserters were continually pardoned. The pay of Able Seamen was increased to 10 milreis (£2) a month and they were offered a bounty of the same amount. But neither recruiting campaigns nor the press gang did the trick. In spite of its extensive coastline, Brazil remained essentially a continental country of mines and plantations with no reserve of seamen to draw on in time of war. Its merchant marine consisted of tiny coasters often manned by slaves, and its fishermen plied their trade by going to sea in primitive rafts. Neither bred either the skills or the numbers of men needed to man a modern navy.

The Brazilian Government once more fell back on foreign recruitment. In 1823, it had successfully found 500 men in London and Liverpool. In 1825 it tried again and raised another 300. This was supplemented by recruiting in Brazilian ports. The generous pay offered to foreigners – 15 milreis (£3) a month for Able Seamen – was an enormous temptation, being double that paid in the Royal Navy. Desertion from foreign merchantmen and men-of-war promptly increased, provoking angry complaints from consuls and naval officers. By 1827, British Ambassador Robert Gordon estimated that there were 1200 British subjects serving in the Brazilian Navy, adding 'no ship enters here which does not lose many of its ablest seamen, nor can it be prevented for they are enticed away by their own countrymen.'[8] At the other end of the spectrum, the Brazilian Government had to find a suitable commander-in-chief for the River Plate. Lord Cochrane, although a quarrelsome menace in port, had been a genius at sea. But now he had left to try his fortunes in Greece. Who could take his place? The choice fell on 62-year-old Vice Admiral Rodrigo Lobo. Although highly experienced and known to be a competent administrator, Lobo had a reputation for timidity as a sea commander. He was chosen simply because no-one else was available. Nevertheless, the Government hoped to stiffen his sinews by appointing a younger and more active figure as second-in-command. The man they wanted was Captain John Taylor, a former Royal Navy lieutenant who had been the hero of the voyage of the *Niterói* in 1823, and the man who had blockaded Pernambuco with consummate political and tactical skill the following year. Unfortunately, Taylor had been serving as an officer in the British South America Squadron when he had been offered the post of captain-of-frigate in the Brazilian Navy, and the authorities had refused to accept his resignation. Ignoring the advice of the commander-in-chief, Sir Thomas Hardy, that the matter be treated with moderation, the Admiralty had branded Taylor a deserter, threatened a court martial and exerted strong diplomatic pressure to get him dismissed from the Imperial Navy. The Brazilians had prevaricated for 18 months before they had reluctantly agreed, but when Taylor married locally and became a Brazilian citizen he was promptly reinstated and promoted.

At the end of November 1825, Taylor, in the uniform of a commodore, hoisted his broad pennant in the frigate *Dona Paula*. Wild rumours began to circulate. It was whispered that he was about to be appointed as admiral and sent to command in the Plate. On hearing the news, Consul-General Chamberlain and naval commander-in-chief Sir George Eyre were furious. Diplomatic protests were sent from Rio and London claiming that his appointment was an insult to every British officer.[9] The Imperial Government tried once more to temporize. But Eyre become increasingly irate and, writing from HMS *Wellesley* on his way to

Montevideo, told the Brazilian authorities bluntly that 'I shall consider the ship which bears Mr Taylor's flag or pennant, whatever may be its size, as in a state of hostility with His Majesty's Government and will act accordingly'.[10] Not even the Imperial Government could ignore such a brutal threat. Taylor's appointment was cancelled.

The Imperial Government then approached American-born Commodore David Jewitt to see if he would accept the job. Unfortunately, before joining the Brazilian service in 1822, Jewitt had served as a privateer and an officer in the navy of Buenos Aires. There in 1820, he had had the distinction of raising the Argentinian flag over the Malvinas – or Falkland Islands – as an early demonstration of sovereignty. Jewitt was naturally reluctant to fight his erstwhile friends and declined the offer. The Government then turned to its third choice, Commodore Diogo Jorge de Brito, then in command of the Naval Academy in Rio de Janeiro. De Brito had had 26 years' experience at sea but had seen little action either before or during the War of Independence. However he was keen, promptly accepted the offer, and sailed south on 13 January 1826 with the brig *Caboclo* and the schooners *Itaparica* and *Alcantara*. De Brito's first act was to produce an analysis of the strategic problem posed by the position of Buenos Aires.[11] And he was right to do so for the geography of the River Plate was to be the major factor which determined Brazil's conduct of the naval war.

The Plate Estuary is like a great funnel penetrating deep into the side of the South American continent. The distance between its western extremity at the confluence of the Uruguay to its easternmost points at Cape Santa Maria to the north and Cape Santo Antonio to the south is 275 miles, and between the two capes is a stretch of water 200 miles wide. Exploring it in the 1830s, Charles Darwin was to write, 'the Plate looks like a noble estuary on the map; but it is in truth a poor affair. A wide expanse of muddy water that has neither grandeur nor beauty.'[12] He was right. In spite of its extent, the River Plate was a shallow and treacherous stretch of water dominated by four extensive muddy

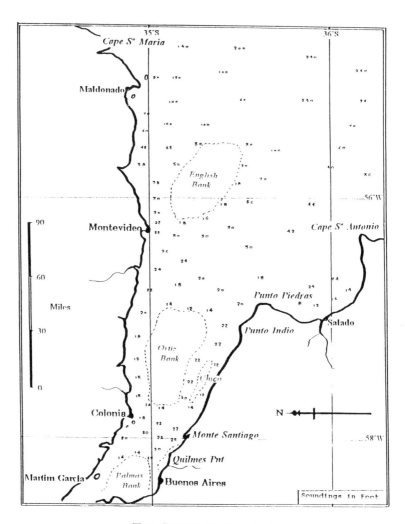

THE RIVER PLATE 1826

shoals. These were the English Bank, south-east of Montevideo; the huge Ortiz Bank between Montevideo and Buenos Aires; its smaller companion, the Chico; and the Palmas Bank north-west of Buenos Aires which effectively restricted entry to the Uruguay and the Paraná to a channel along the northern shore. The only open water in the river wide enough for naval manoeuvres lay at each end of the Ortiz Bank between Montevideo and Punto Indio to the east, and between Colonia and Buenos Aires to the west.

At no point was the estuary deeper than 22 feet – an obvious difficulty for Brazilian warships when even a medium-sized frigate like the *Imperatiz* needed 17 feet in which to float. And the depth of the three channels between the banks was even less. At its deepest point, the safest passage between the Chico and the Ortiz contained only 20 feet of water; the channel between the northern shore and the Ortiz had only 15 feet, effectively restricting its use to schooners and small brigs; while the passage between the Chico and the southern bank was even less, with only 13 feet. And if this were not enough, strong winds from the south could suddenly reduce the water level on that side by as much as six feet and pile it up on the opposite shore.

Navigation was also made difficult by the absence of clear landmarks. The major towns were recognizable enough – Buenos Aires with its cupolas and steeples, Colonia on its rocky crag, and Montevideo with its conical hill, the Cerro, dominating the bay – but the treeless shores on both sides of the river were low and difficult to see from the deck of a ship, and the only aids to navigation were the occasional church or clump of Ombu trees.[13] In these conditions, navigation was so tricky that few shipping movements took place at night, giving rise to the old mariners' saying 'Down sun, down anchor.'

The task of the Brazilian Navy in dominating the Plate was difficult enough, but the geography of Buenos Aires also gave a clear advantage to the Argentinians. The main approach to the city's anchorage was a shallow channel two miles in length, 1500 yards in width, and with a maximum depth of 12 feet which could easily be defended by a small force. Any Brazilian attack would also be compromised by the fact that its smaller frigates and larger corvettes drew 15 feet of water and could get no nearer than five miles from the city; while the shallow draught brigantines and schooners which were able to enter the channel ran the risk of being outgunned by the bigger Argentinian ships or overwhelmed by its heavily manned gunboats on the first foggy night. Likewise, even if the Argentinians could be tempted to leave their anchorage in order to fight, any damaged ships would find a refuge only an hour away to leeward, while Brazilian casualties were a hundred miles away from a friendly port and could fall easy prey to the Argentinian oared gunboats with their heavy cannon. Whatever its size and strength, the Brazilian Navy would face enormous problems in the Plate if confronted by a resolute enemy.

CHAPTER 4

THE ARGENTINIAN
CHALLENGER

Compared with the maritime power of Brazil, the naval forces of
the United Provinces were insignificant and consisted of little
more than a handful of small vessels left over from the independence campaign. The sight of the sails of Lobo's squadron anchored
jauntily off Buenos Aires was a constant reminder of Argentina's
weakness, and in the middle of 1825, the Government began to do
something about it. The first act of the new Minister of War and
Marine, General Marcus Balcarte, was to create the administrative
framework which the Navy would need. In August, José Zapiola –
an old soldier of the independence war who had previously served
at sea with the Spanish Navy – was appointed as Commandant-
General with the rank of Colonel Major (that is, Commodore)[1]
and Benito de Goyena, was given the post of Commissioner of the
Navy, with responsibility for the civil departments handling pay,
personnel, stores, supplies and construction. Goyena, who had
done the same job during the independence campaign, was a
sound administrator and it is the excellence of his records that
makes it possible to gain such a comprehensive account of the
workings of the Argentinian Navy at this time.[2] With the help of a
small staff of clerks, the two men issued articles of war, privateering regulations, and instructions which lay down the size of the
naval establishment, rates of pay, ration scales and uniforms.
These specified that Argentinian officers should wear a simple
uniform comprising blue trousers and a matching jacket with
anchor pattern buttons, the coat trimmed with gold lace appropri-

ate to the rank of the wearer and worn with the lapels turned back to show a lighter blue facing.[3]

Balcarte's second priority was to find ships and munitions. Orders were immediately sent to the Captain of the Port, Juan Azopardo, to fit-out the two 14-gun brigs *General Belgrano* and *General Balcarce* and the launch *Correntina* which had lain disarmed off Buenos Aires for years, and to build six – later eleven – gunboats for port defence. The dockyard facilities of Buenos Aires were minuscule and were incapable of building anything larger, but with minimum crews of 25 and carrying an 18-pounder cannon in their bow, the gunboats were ideal for their purpose. Foreign vessels on offer in the port were surveyed for their suitability as warships and, in January 1826, the Government purchased the ship-rigged *Comercio de Lima*, the brigs *Upton* and *Mohawk* and the schooner *Gracie Ann*. The first was converted to a 36-gun corvette and renamed *25 de Mayo*. The others became the 16-gun brigs-of-war *República Argentina* and *Congresso Nacional*, and the armed schooner *Sarandí* carrying eight tiny 4-pounders and a 16-pounder gun in the bow. United with its existing vessels, these ships were to provide the backbone of the squadron with which the United Provinces would bravely challenge the Brazilian supremacy at sea. Fortunately, the Artillery Park in Buenos Aires was able to furnish the guns that were needed – a miscellaneous collection, many of them left over from the War of Independence. Modern carronades were lacking, but this proved to be an advantage for it meant that Argentinian ships were equipped with medium and long Spanish calibre cannon which gave them a superiority of range over many of their Brazilian opponents.[4]

Like the Brazilians, the Government in Buenos Aires had to find a naval commander-in-chief. While acting as Argentinian Minster in London, Rivadavia had met, and been impressed by, a short, red-haired Royal Navy captain called Robert Ramsay. Ramsay was a veteran of the American War of 1812 and had also served in command of the British corvette *Mistletoe* in the River Plate. His enthusiasm for the Republic was so marked and his naval expertise so impressive, that Rivadavia brought him back to Buenos Aires when he returned in October 1825. Ramsay's views on the strategic problems facing the United Provinces were perceptive. Seeing that the majority of Brazilian ships able to reach the western River Plate were small corvettes, brigs and schooners, he recommended that the Argentinians arm their existing ships, all of which were of similar size, with light cannon of superior range to keep the enemy at bay, and to concentrate temporarily on defending Buenos Aires with well manned gunboats and fast shallow-draught schooners which could overwhelm the blockaders in a calm. In the longer term however, he advised Argentina to acquire two good frigates 'which if manned with experienced crews and intelligently commanded will be able to capture, destroy or disperse the whole Brazilian squadron found in the river because their smaller ships with their short guns ... cannot operate effectively against real ships of war.'[5]

Impetuous as ever, and without considering alternatives, Rivadavia was sure that Ramsay was the man to lead the new Argentinian Navy. There was an obvious problem, since he would need British Government permission to take up the appointment, but discussions began on the form of Ramsay's contract and on his terms of service. However it soon began to dawn on the authorities – and on Ramsay – that an ideal candidate for the job of commander-in-chief was already available. He was an audacious red-haired Irishman called William Brown.

Born in the town of Foxford in County Mayo in 1776, Brown's early career is uncertain. It is said that, like so many other young men with a maritime background, he fought with the Royal Navy during the Napoleonic Wars – a theory which is made more likely by the fact that his brother, Michael, served as a senior warrant officer rising to the rank of Master RN. Arriving in Buenos Aires with his wife, Elizabeth Chitty of Deal, before the end of the war as captain of his own vessel, Brown devoted himself to a trading career on the river and became an expert in the tricky navigation of the Plate. But with the climax of the struggle for independence in 1814, he volunteered for, and later became the commander of, the small navy which the patriots had formed to challenge the Spanish command of the river. Rapidly gaining a reputation for daring, skill, impetuosity but also impatience, Brown challenged the blockade of Colonia, crippled his enemy's fighting capacity at an engagement off Martim Garcia, then led the Argentinian sea forces in the blockade of Montevideo which finally ended Spanish rule in the Plate. In 1815, flying the flag of the United Provinces – a blue and white ensign emblazoned with a golden sunburst – he sailed in command of the *Hercules* to the Pacific on a privateering expedition which was to begin in triumph and end in tragedy. His exploits caused panic along the whole coast of Chile and Peru but then, ignoring orders to return to Buenos Aires, Brown carried his campaign against the Spanish flag to the West Indies. Unfortunately for him, the British authorities there refused to recognize the republic under whose colours he fought, arrested Brown and confiscated his ship. Worse was to follow. On his return to Buenos Aires in 1818, he was jailed, court martialled for failure to obey orders and disgraced. Brown spent the next seven years as a commercial seafarer living in comparative obscurity in his new homeland.[6]

At the end of 1825, when the Government of Buenos Aires was looking for an experienced commander, the name of William Brown was suddenly remembered. Former comrades who had been recalled to the colours began to speak of his achievements and powers of leadership. Balcarce was enthusiastic. Ramsay promptly stood down and, on 12 January 1826, William Brown was rehabilitated and appointed commander-in-chief of the Navy of the United Provinces with the rank of Commodore. He lost no time. The following day he led the squadron into the river for exercises and artillery practice before the approach of a strong Imperial force sent him back to his anchorage. A week later, he was out again, falling on an unsuspecting Brazilian convoy and capturing one of the Empire's newest gunboats, the *Araçatuba*. It was a good start.

The establishment of the Argentinian Navy in its first year was set at 56 sea officers – 2 commodores, 1 captain, 3 commanders, 20 lieutenants, 24 sublieutenants and 6 midshipmen – and another 40 pilots, pursers, surgeons, etc.[7] The Government's first act was to recall veterans of the War of Independence, many of whom occupied posts in the port control of Buenos Aires. This provided an international nucleus of experienced men like Captain Juan Azopardo, Commanders Tomas Espora and Ceretti, and Lieutenants Rosales, Pinedo, Jorge, Mason, Robinson, Curry, Kearney, Lee, Dandreys, Francisco Segui and Richitelli. The Government then began to recruit others for the remaining posts in the officer corps and to provide the 1300 sailors and marines the squadron needed. The vacancies in the commissioned ranks were soon filled with volunteers from the foreign communities in Buenos Aires who had sea experience; and, unlike in Brazil, there were no difficulties in finding crews to man the ships. Few native Argentinians were familiar with the sea, but the city was filled with newly arrived migrants who were glad to undertake a spot of temporary paid employment afloat. In national complexion they were a mixed group, but the disciplines of naval service seemed to be more attractive to Britons and Americans who made up over half of the original 56 sea officers. More individualistic nationalities, such as French and Italians, preferred the free and easy regime of the privateer. In all of this, Brown's reputation for activity and success was a great asset. As Woodbine Parish noted in one of his despatches, 'his character for courage and activity has induced many English, Americans and other foreigners to join him as volunteers. ... It is his declared determination to endeavour to carry the Brazilian ships by boarding and there is no doubt that he will make the attempt.'[8]

The characteristics of the two navies were in many ways directly opposite as they prepared to fight it out on the River Plate. The Brazilian Navy had powerful resources in terms of ships and supplies, but it was short of sailors, lacked experienced officers, and was led by a cautious and pessimistic admiral. The Argentinians, on the other hand, had few warships, but were abundantly supplied with both seamen and experienced officers, and were led by an audacious, even rash, commander. But they shared one characteristic. Both navies had a large nucleus of British, Irish, Scottish and – in the case of Buenos Aires – American officers and men who not only brought with them the technical skills and discipline needed to handle ships of war, but an aggressive fighting spirit born of a tradition of victory at sea.

PART II: CAT AND MOUSE IN THE RIVER PLATE

CHAPTER 5

THE BATTLE OF CORALES: ACTION AND ACRIMONY

At the beginning of February 1826, the Legislative Assembly elected Bernadino Rivadavia as the President of the United Provinces of Rio de la Plata. Commodore William Brown was keen to mark the event by mounting his first large-scale sortie since being appointed as commander-in-chief of the newly formed Argentinian Navy. He was also anxious to satisfy public opinion in Buenos Aires which, inspired by patriotic fervour and his own dashing reputation, was looking forward to an easy victory.[1] At 6.30 am on 9 February, with the wind favourable and no sign of the Brazilian blockading force, Brown hoisted the signal for departure and led the ships of the squadron through the channel into the Outer Roads.[2] In the van went the flagship, the corvette *25 de Mayo* manned by a picked crew of 200 British and Americans and commanded by Captain Henry Parker, followed by the brigs *Congreso Nacional* (Lieutenant William Mason), *República Argentina* (Lieutenant Robert Beazley) and *General Belgrano* (second-in-command Captain Juan Azopardo), with the schooner *Sarandí* (Commander Martin Warnes) bringing up the rear. Behind came nine new gunboats shepherded by Commander Bartolomé Ceretti in the *General Balcarce*, accompanied, in a somewhat dramatic gesture, by a hospital ship, the *Pepa*, commanded by Lieutenant Victorio Dandreys.

Nothing has survived to show what Brown's objectives were in mounting the sortie or what plan he had in mind. Probably he wanted to give his newly recruited crews a shake-down cruise and, if it could be done safely, to test the mettle of his Brazilian opponents. The morning developed into a cloudless late summer day with a moderate breeze from the north-east. Brown steered east south-east – as close to the wind as his ships could lie – sailing at a moderate pace to enable the gunboats to keep up. After four hours, the Argentinian ships had covered some 16 miles when their lookouts spotted the sails of the Brazilian blockading squadron to the south-east. It comprised three corvettes, four brigs, two brigantines and five schooners or smaller craft, and was a formidable sight, outnumbering the Argentinians in guns and men by three to two. Both squadrons maintained course, drawing uncomfortably close to the Ensenada Spit on the southern bank of the river. But at 11 am, with the ships only nine miles apart and closing, the wind suddenly veered to the east. Both squadrons immediately turned and raced northwards[3] into deep water on parallel courses.

Just after 1 pm, with the fortress of Colonia just in sight to the north, the wind slowly veered until it blew from the north northeast. On the port tack it was now possible for the Argentinian squadron to attack the long line of Brazilian warships still dimly visible to the south-east. William Brown was keen to try his luck, but in his headlong dash northwards only the three brigs and the *Sarandí* had managed to keep up with the flagship – the *General Balcarce* and the gunboats had been left far behind. The impatient Argentinian commander reversed his course to bring his scattered flock together then, at 2.30 pm, he signalled for his five major warships to form line of battle and, with the *25 de Mayo* in the lead, steered east south-east for the enemy.[4] The three masts and greater bulk of the Argentinian flagship soon pushed it ahead of its consorts and brought it within extreme cannon shot of the *Itaparica* and *Liberal* at the head of the Brazilian line. The two

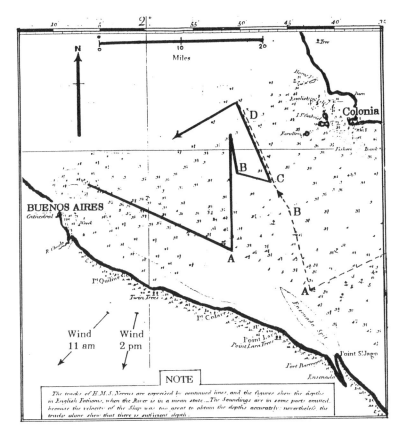

THE BATTLE OF CORALES, 9 FEBRUARY 1826

Superimposed on the British Admiralty Chart of 1819
surveyed by John Warner RN, Master of HMS Nereus, 1810-14

————— Argentinian track
– – – – – – Brazilian track

A = 11 am   B = 2.30 pm   C = 3.30 pm   D = 5-6 pm

corvettes promptly opened fire on the *25 de Mayo*, with other Imperial ships joining in as they came within range.

Sailing close-hauled with the lightest of breezes, the Argentinian approach was long and slow. For almost an hour Brown's flagship was subjected to a steady ration of long distance cannon fire with the *Congresso Nacional, Sarandí, República Argentina*, and *General Belgrano* slowly following in its wake waiting to come within range. The audacity and excitement of Brown's attack was not lost on either his commanders or his crews. Neither were the dangers inherent in an assault by six vessels with less than 100 guns against a force of 14 warships mounting more than 140 pieces of artillery. The Brazilians were unperturbed by Brown's attack, and advanced in good order, firing steadily as they came. The *25 de Mayo* began to reply, turning slightly into the wind so its guns would bear.

Then at 3.30 pm the unexpected happened. The Argentinian flagship slowly veered off course, tacked and headed north north-west directly away from the Brazilian line. Some of his captains saw Brown's limp signal to discontinue the action, others did not.[5] But all followed, each ship in the line coming under enemy fire as it tacked in turn to join the *25 de Mayo* in what appeared to be a headlong flight from the approaching Brazilians. Second-in-command Juan Azopardo in the *General Belgrano* was dismayed by the resulting Argentinian confusion and later described the squadron's manoeuvres as resembling those of a crowd of fishing boats rather than a disciplined naval force. But whatever the rights and wrongs of the affair, Brown and his ships soon managed to get out of range of the steadily advancing enemy.

For Vice Admiral Rodrigo Lobo and the crews of the Brazilian squadron the day had begun like any other. They had anchored for the night between Colonia and the end of the Ortiz Bank, and in the early morning had begun to patrol in a southerly direction. Lobo's flagship, the 22-gun *Liberal*, was in the lead, followed by the corvettes *Itaparica* and *Maceió*, the brigs *29 de Agosto, Real Pedro, Rio da Plata* and *Caboclo*, the brigantines *Dona Januária* and *Pará*, the schooners *Conceição* and *Liberdade do Sul*, and the gunboats *Leal Paulistana, No 8* and *Montevideana*. At 10 am, Lobo's lookouts had spotted sails on the north-western horizon and there was a flurry of excitement when they were identified as those of the enemy. The Brazilian squadron immediately turned and then began to close on an intersecting course. At 11 am, Lobo, like Brown, had reacted to the change in wind by turning his squadron northwards. But the more precise and cautious Brazilian commander was taking no chances. There was no headlong rush: merely a steady progress with Lobo keeping his ships together by a succession of fussy signals. Then at 1.30 pm, with Colonia in sight, it had become clear that Brown was marshalling his ships for a head-on attack. Sure that his superior numbers would be more than a match for his opponents, Lobo prepared for action and, Nelson fashion, hoisted an inspirational signal: 'The admiral reminds you of the Glory of the Nation and is confident that all will fight this day with decisive courage!' An hour later, with the Argentinian line steadily bearing down on them, the leading Brazilian ships began to exchange long-range fire with the *25 de Mayo*.

Brown's sudden turn away at 3.30 pm and the disorderly Argentinian withdrawal was as surprising to Lobo as had been his decision to attack two hours earlier. Signalling his ships to engage the enemy as best they could, Lobo set off in pursuit, his corvettes managing to maintain an intermittent long-range fire without being able to catch up with their retreating enemy. But the Brazilians could now see the slower Argentinian gunboats to the west and Lieutenant Gleddon commanding the brig *29 de Agosto* altered course to intercept them. Brown could see the peril. At 5 pm, the *25 de Mayo* and the rest of the squadron turned on the advancing Brazilians and formed a protective screen behind which the gunboats could escape[6] while the *Congresso Nacional* attempted to drive off the *29 de Agosto*. For an hour the two forces exchanged fire until the gunboats were safely out of range. Then at 6 pm, Brown broke off the engagement and retreated south-west for Buenos Aires, while Lobo – aware that he was being drawn onto the mudbanks – abandoned the chase and rallied his ships. The long-range nature of the two engagements had caused only moderate casualties and damage. On the Argentinian side, three men had been killed and 15 wounded, while the *25 de Mayo*, *General*

Belgrano and *Sarandí* all had guns dismounted and gear smashed.[7] The *Congresso Nacional* had also suffered in its rigging and spars, while the *República Argentina* had lost five guns and all its boats. The Brazilian side had also suffered damage aloft, but Lobo reported only three killed and five wounded. Tragically, one of the dead was John Rogers Gleddon of the *29 de Agosto*, while the casualty list included Commodore Diogo Jorge de Brito of the *Itaparica*.[8]

Back in his anchorage of Los Pozes, Brown was angry at his lack of success and aware that his own leadership had been far from perfect. He gave vent to his feelings in a brief despatch written before he had even spoken to his subordinates or checked their journals. Unlike his normal reports, which frequently gave details of timing, signals and manoeuvres, it was terse and damning, and began:

> With the most profound regret, I have to inform you of the events of today. At 6 am I sailed in pursuit of the enemy; and at 2.30 pm reached them in sight of Colonia, not having in my company the *General Balcarce* and the gunboats … I followed the enemy and began the attack. This corvette, the *25 de Mayo* was obliged to resist a brisk fire from three corvettes of the enemy which lasted for more then an hour, which it had to endure alone because the *Congresso Nacional*, the *República Argentina*, the *General Belgrano* and the schooner *Sarandí* placed themselves to leeward and out of the fight.[9]

It was only this desertion, he claimed, that had caused his change of course at 3.30 pm. Likewise during the second attack at 5 pm, the 'brigs and the schooner showed the same prudence as before' – only the *Congresso Nacional* had given him any support and then only after having been given direct orders. According to Brown, at the end of the action, the Brazilians had 'shied away having clearly learnt their lesson in spite of the disparity of force'. The implication was that victory had been within his grasp and had only been denied because Captains Beazley, Warnes, Mason and Azopardo had failed to do their utmost in the battle and had been guilty of grave dereliction of duty.[10]

The report on the Battle of Corales produced an instant reaction. Foreign consuls and naval officers wrote to their home governments repeating Brown's claim that his attack on a superior force had been frustrated by disaffected subordinates and that the Brazilians had finally been beaten off. The Buenos Aires public were bitterly disappointed and looked for scapegoats.[11] To their own astonishment, the four captains were removed from their commands and the clumsy process of military law was put into effect. Inquiries were instituted, written evidence was gathered from witnesses and six months later, on 16 August 1826, the court martial opened.

It did not take the defence lawyers long to put Brown's version of the battle seriously in doubt. He claimed that the *25 de Mayo* had been left alone at 3.30 pm because the other ships had deliberately hung back, and that at 5 pm the same thing had happened. Yet witnesses showed that this was not so. During the first attack, the three brigs and the schooner had all borne down on the Brazilian line in accordance with their commander's signals. The fact that they had not been engaged was due entirely to the superior speed of the *25 de Mayo*, and to Brown's inexplicable decision at 3.30 pm to turn away just at the moment when they were coming into range. Likewise, at 5 pm, all the Argentinian ships had in fact been engaged – as their damage reports and casualty figures demonstrated. The defending lawyer pointed out icily that Brown's report had only referred to the numbers of dead and wounded on the *25 de Mayo* and that he had written his letter before he had received information on what the rest of the squadron had been doing.[12]

The defence also made much of the distinguished service records of the accused in the War of Independence against Spain. Azopardo had been active in the first naval raid of the war, had been captured and had spent years in a Spanish jail before being made Port Commander of Buenos Aires in the 1820s where he was responsible for the gunboat building programme. Warnes, who had been a midshipman on the *Santissima Trinidad* at Trafalgar, had fought on both land and sea during the war in Chile and had been present at the capture of the Spanish frigate *Maria Isabel* –

which under its new name of *O'Higgins* became Lord Cochrane's flagship. Was it likely men of such proven courage and loyalty would abandon their commander-in-chief? It was a good question. The answer of the judges was given four months later in December. All four captains were acquitted, and the charges against them were shelved. Unfortunately, the proud Latin temperaments of Azopardo and Warnes had been deeply offended by the whole business, and now that their names had been cleared, both resigned from the service. Azopardo retired to his home town and remained in idleness until his death in 1848. Warnes remained in Buenos Aires for three years, than drifted to Uruguay, then to Chile where he was reappointed as an artillery officer in the Army. He died in 1842. The Englishman William Mason and the American Robert Beazley were less sensitive. Mason remained in the Navy and was present at many of the remaining actions of the war, while Beazley became a highly successful commander of privateers.

The Corales court martial had raised many questions about the conduct of the battle and, with the defence case being published in the form of a broadsheet, they were raised in public. Inevitably too, the defence of Azopardo, Warnes, Mason and Beazley implied criticism of Brown's conduct of the battle. The Ordinances required that the commander-in-chief should inform each ship of its position in the line in advance, and make clear signals before any manoeuvre. According to the defence lawyer, this had not been done. The only instructions given were for each ship to remain within pistol shot of the flagship and to follow the commander-in-chief's movements. And at 3.30 pm, it was uncertain whether Brown had made any signal at all. But a lot of water had flowed under the bridge in the ten months which had elapsed between the battle and the court martial verdict. Brown was now the hero of the hour, and his audacious and well publicized naval triumphs were the target of enthusiastic praise from both friends and enemies. No-one wanted to rock the boat or ask awkward questions about Corales. The matter was allowed to drop.

From any point of view, the Argentinians had lost the Battle of Corales. Brown had taken an enormous risk. He had rashly mounted an attack on a vastly superior force, appeared to have realized the danger at the last minute, and had only managed to escape with his squadron intact by the skin of his teeth. But unknown to the Argentinian commander, he had in fact won a minor victory in terms of undermining the already shaky morale of his Brazilian opposite number, Vice Admiral Rodrigo Lobo. Lobo was an officer of vast experience but one who had been schooled in the 'continental' tradition of maritime strategy. In other words, he regarded naval warfare as subordinate to broader political ends, and saw battles as being of minor importance in themselves. The British notion (shared by Brown and by the British commanders of the Imperial Navy) that the object of naval warfare was to secure the destruction of enemy warships wherever they could be found was alien to him. Many of his subordinates had served with Lord Cochrane during the War of Independence against Portugal and had both acquired the aggressive British way of doing things and shared in the victories which had resulted. Lobo had played no part in these triumphs. It was no wonder (as Commodore Diogo Jorge de Brito ruefully commented in a private letter to the Minister of Marine) that few of the officers of the squadron felt any confidence in an officer like Lobo whose 'school was the modern Portuguese Navy'.[13] The Vice Admiral's personality reinforced his strategic views. Whatever his administrative skills, in action he invariably chose safety rather than risk; was reluctant to make any aggressive move unless backed by overwhelming force; and, like so many cautious commanders before him, tended to exaggerate his own weaknesses while minimizing those of his opponents.

Lobo's report on the battle reflected all these attitudes:

> On 9 February we had two minor engagements with the enemy in sight of Colonia and of Buenos Aires. ... As a result, the enemy were forced to retreat but I was unable to capture any of their ships ... due to the lack of skill of some commanders who had never seen action before. ... I have also to lament the lack of skill of our gunners who hardly know how to point a cannon ... the

guntrucks are also badly constructed, as are the gunports so that
we cannot fire when we are to windward of the enemy.[14]

With the Argentinian squadron clearly unwilling to take on a
force so superior it is difficult to see what more the Brazilians
could have done on 9 February 1826. At 5 pm, a more aggressive
and confident commander might have ordered the smaller ships in
his rear to leave the line and attack the vulnerable Argentinian
gunboats while the larger Brazilian vessels kept Brown and his
brigs occupied. Indeed, Sublieutenant José Joaquim Ignacio,
second-in-command of the *Pará*, later claimed – when he was an
admiral and a viscount – that he had urged his captain to make
such a move.[15] But Lobo was unwilling to take the risk and, in his
report, typically blamed the inexperience of the junior officers
whom the hurried expansion of 1825 had put in command of
ships such as the *Caboclo*, *Rio da Plata*, *Dona Januária* and *Pará*, the
inaccuracy of the gunners and, indeed, design flaws in the guns
themselves. Only the *Itaparica* was singled out for any kind of
praise. His lack of confidence in his subordinates was so great that
although he understood the desirability of showing that he was
'master of the seas' after the battle by flaunting the Imperial flag
off Buenos Aires and instituting a tight blockade, he decided
against it. Instead he reported that further action would be impossible without reinforcements, withdrew his squadron and divided
his forces.

The strategic problem facing Lobo in the River Plate was certainly a tricky one. The Brazilian commander had two objectives
which were not easy to reconcile. The first was to neutralize
Brown's activities by bottling up the Argentine squadron in
Buenos Aires. The second was to support the Imperial effort in
the Banda Oriental by preventing any reinforcement of the rebels
across the River Uruguay and by safeguarding Colonia and
Montevideo against any sea-borne attack.

Unfortunately for Lobo, the city's geographical position presented serious problems for a blockading force. The narrow
channel which linked the Inner and Outer Roads was easily
defended and the shallows before the city prevented any large ship
of war from getting nearer than five miles. Only the smaller

Brazilian schooners and brigantines could get near, but these could easily have been outgunned by Brown's bigger ships or over-whelmed by the host of Argentinian oared gunboats during the first foggy night. Blockading Buenos Aires was no easy task. For Lobo, there was a second option – to divide his forces, keep most of his ships on blockade duty at a safe distance, and send small units to reinforce the Flotilla of the Uruguay and help the defence of Colonia and Montevideo. Conscious of the prob-lems of a close blockade, lacking confidence in the ability of his younger commanders to keep out of trouble, and hopeful that his distant blockading squadron would act as a floating reserve if Argentinian attacks were mounted, the Brazilian commander chose this course of action.[16] The brig *Real Pedro*, the brigantine *Pará* and the schooners *Conceição* and *Liberdade do Sul* were sent to reinforce Colonia. The gunboats *Leal Paulistana*, *No 8* and *Montevideana* were despatched to the island of Martim Garcia to strengthen the Flotilla of the Uruguay. The seven ships which remained were withdrawn to a new blockading position on the eastern side of the Ortiz Bank, north of the Punto del Indio, over a hundred miles from Buenos Aires, the port they were attempting to blockade.[17]

Lobo closed his eyes to the fact that his strategy ran the risk that the Argentinian Navy – whose base lay only a day's voyage from the Brazilians' western outposts – could attack each in turn and destroy the Imperial naval units piecemeal. Unfortunately for him and for the Imperial cause this is exactly what happened. The withdrawal of the Brazilian blockading line to the east of the Ortiz Bank left Buenos Aires unwatched, passed the initiative to Brown and left him free to create havoc through the length and breadth of the River Plate.

CHAPTER 6

THE ASSAULT ON COLONIA

The reaction of the Buenos Aires public to the Battle of Corales was one of uncertainty. The performance of the squadron had been puzzling to say the least. On the one hand it had bravely confronted a far more powerful Brazilian force and had skilfully extricated itself without serious loss – indeed Commodore Brown claimed that the enemy had fled. On the other, four senior captains had been abruptly dismissed for, it was said, abandoning their commander at the height of the action. But there was no sign of the Brazilian squadron, and comforting rumours from sympathizers in Montevideo were soon circulating claiming that Lobo had lost 45 dead and 75 wounded.[1] In view of the long range over which the action had been fought it must have been obvious that these figures were untrue – but it did neither public morale nor Brown's reputation any harm for these reports to be believed.

Anxious to put Corales behind him, and believing instinctively that attack was the best form of defence, Commodore Brown was already preparing his next move. The damage sustained by the squadron was rapidly repaired and the commanders of the major warships were reshuffled. Flag-Captain Parker was moved to the *Congresso Nacional* and was replaced in the *25 de Mayo* by Tomas Espora. Leonardo Rosales, Bartolomé Ceretti and José Maria Pinedo were given command respectively of the *General Belgrano*, the *General Balcarce* and the *Sarandí*; and William Clark, the American lieutenant of the *República Argentina* was promoted to be captain of the same vessel. After ten days of preparation, they were ready to go.

On 21 February 1826, Brown led his six men-of-war into the brown waters of the river while the gunboats stationed themselves in the Outer Roads, their movements noted by the watching British corvette *Jaseur*.[2] For the next two days the ships were put through a series of manoeuvres under sail to exercise their crews and familiarize the new commanders with their positions in battle. Then, on 23 February, they met a cutter returning from Montevideo where she had delivered to Vice Admiral Lobo a long-winded protest against the conduct of the blockade from the US Consul, Colonel Forbes.[3] From her captain, they learned that the Brazilians were taking on stores in their blockading position to the east of the Ortiz Bank. Commodore Brown cautiously set sail down river to establish their exact whereabouts, carefully timing his arrival to coincide with daybreak.

The Brazilian squadron sighted the sails of the Argentinians looming out of the mist as dawn broke on 24 February. The corvette *Itaparica* was being repaired in Montevideo while the *29 de Agosto* and the *Itaparica* schooner were away on detached service, so Lobo's command had been reduced to eight ships – the *Liberal*, *Maceió*, *Caboclo*, *Rio da Plata*, *Dona Januária* and schooner *Alcantara*. All were anchored close to the Ortiz Bank, with the armed ship *Jurujuba* and the heavy frigate *Imperatriz* (recently arrived from Rio) beyond. Lobo immediately signalled his ships to withdraw to the deeper water, spending hours manoeuvring them into position. But Brown did not follow. Reversing course, he crept back into the morning mist. Satisfied that his enemy was safely out of harm's way, the Argentinian commander crammed on sail and headed for his real objective, the Imperial outpost of Colonia on the north bank of the river. Behind him he left Lobo in a state of extreme anxiety. Worried at losing numerical superiority, the Brazilian Vice Admiral withdrew to the roadstead of Montevideo until the *Itaparica* was ready for service.[4]

Perched on a high promontory overlooking a shallow bay fringed by a series of rocky islands, the city and fortress of Colonia de Sacramento had been under siege by land for almost a year. Its governor, General Manuel Jorge Rodrigues, was a tough and experienced soldier of 53 years who had commanded a *caçadores* battalion under Marshal Beresford in the Peninsular War and during the invasion of France in the Napoleonic Wars. For this veteran of the Battle of Bussaco and the sieges of Cuidad Rodrigo and Badajoz, it was child's play to hold off the attacks of Lavalleja and his Uruguayan insurgents. As long as the Brazilian Navy controlled the waters of the River Plate with its vital supply routes, Colonia would remain firmly in Imperial hands. It was to cut this maritime lifeline that Commodore Brown now turned his attention.

On the morning of 25 February 1826, the Brazilian sentries on the walls of Colonia were surprised to sight a group of strange sails advancing menacingly over the western horizon. As the six Argentinian warships drew closer their identity was only too apparent: Governor Rodrigues and his men were facing a new and serious threat. Vice Admiral Lobo's redeployment had left Colonia defended by only four small Brazilian naval vessels, the brig-of-war *Real Pedro* (10 guns), the brigantine *Pará* (8) and the schooners *Liberdade do Sul* and *Conceição*. Realizing that his tiny force had no chance against Brown's squadron, the senior naval captain, Commander Frederico Mariath, a Portuguese-born officer of English extraction, decided to beach his three largest ships below the city and move their guns and crews ashore to form two new batteries commanding the mole in the harbour.[5] Only the *Conceição*, under Sublieutenant Thomas Thompson, remained afloat ready for offensive action or to summon help should it be needed.

Just before 2 pm, the Argentinians passed the island of Farallon and dropped anchor to the north of Fishers' Bank, just out of cannon shot of the city. Brown immediately sent in a boat with a flag of truce and an elegantly phrased request that the garrison surrender within 24 hours in order to avoid bloodshed and the destruction of the city. With equal courtesy, Governor Rodrigues refused the ultimatum, invited the Argentinian commander to do his worst and confided that the fate of Colonia would be determined by the fortunes of war.[6]

His ploy having failed, at 8 am on 26 February, Brown launched his first attack. It achieved nothing. His advancing ships were struck by a storm of cannon fire from the Brazilian positions and in the confusion the *General Belgrano* and the *Sarandí* ran aground. The schooner was refloated but the brig was stuck high and dry on the rocks at the foot of the island of S. Gabriel, within musket-shot from the defenders who commenced a lively fire on the stranded vessel. All that could be done was to salvage her guns and call off the attack. Brown tried to buy time with a second unsuccessful call for the garrison to surrender, but Governor Rodrigues would have none of it and sent his emissaries packing with the laconic reply, 'Tell the General that what I have said, I have said.'[7]

By nightfall, the Argentinians had completed their withdrawal and Brown began to count the cost of his first attack. Writing to Commandant-General Zapiola in Buenos Aires, he was forced to admit that in the first engagement one ship had been lost, ten men wounded and seven killed, including Captain Cerretti of the *General Balcarce* who had been cut in two by a cannon ball[8] while covering the evacuation of the stranded *General Belgrano*. But Brown was undismayed by the reverse, and was already planning another attack in conjunction with the Uruguayan land forces. In a second letter he asked for immediate reinforcements from Buenos Aires across the estuary, where the boom of distant artillery fire from Colonia could easily be heard. Brown had no sooner finished his despatches when the calm of the night was shattered by the sound of fighting around the *General Belgrano* as Sublieutenant Thompson with the crew of the *Conceição* tried to board and burn the stranded vessel. The attack was seen off by the *Sarandí*, but the disappearance of the Brazilian schooner over the horizon in the direction of Montevideo confirmed Brown's conviction that rapid action was vital before Brazilian reinforcements could arrive to disrupt his plans.

Two days later the defenders watched glumly as Brown's own reinforcements hove into view. There were eight vessels in all, the schooner *Pepa*, an armed launch and six gunboats. His force now complete, at midnight on 1 March, Brown left his anchorage and began his second attack. The plan was for the gunboat flotilla, deployed in two columns under the command of Captains Rosales and Espora and manned by 280 volunteers, each fortified by a tot of rum, to enter the bay under cover of darkness and seize the Brazilian warships beached before the citadel. The objective was simply to burn the three vessels where they lay. Unfortunately (according to Argentinian accounts), the boats were carried further by the current and the crews were forced to try a frontal attack on the mole below the city.[9] The *Real Pedro* was soon ablaze but otherwise the attack was a disaster. The Argentinians were met with a storm of deadly fire from the cannon in the batteries and the *caçadores* on the walls and were thrown back in total confusion. Three gunboats (*No 4, No 6* and *No 7*) went aground and were captured with heavy losses. A fourth (*No 8*) only just managed to escape because of the efforts of Lieutenant Turner. Captain Charles Robinson and Lieutenant John Curry (of *No 4*) and Sublieutenant Felix Echevarria (of *No 6*) were killed; while Captain Rosales, Captain James Kearney (of *No 6*) and Lieutenant Turner (of *No 7*) were wounded. Argentinian losses were heavy and amounted to two-thirds of those involved. Men who had survived the fire of the defenders drowned as they threw themselves into the water in a panic-stricken retreat. No less than 89 of the attackers were captured, 38 dead were left in Brazilian hands and many more were reported missing.[10] But it had been a hard fought action, with 22 dead and 71 wounded on the Imperial side. In their reports on the action, the Buenos Aires newspapers were lyrical in their praise of the courage of their troops and the 'paternal attitude' and 'patriotic energy' of their commander,[11] but from any point of view, the Argentinian forces had suffered a serious defeat.

But once again, Commodore Brown's resolve was stimulated rather than depressed by the rebuff. He became even more determined to bring Colonia to its knees before Lobo could arrive with help. And with a corvette, three brigs, a schooner and seven gunboats still at his disposal he seemed to have the means of doing so. On the evening of 3 March, the city suffered a new bombardment, and on the following day the garrison watched as Brown was reinforced by four more gunboats and the schooner *Rio de la Plata*.[12]

The Imperial defenders of Colonia had been cheered by their success in beating off the Argentinian attacks, but as time passed,

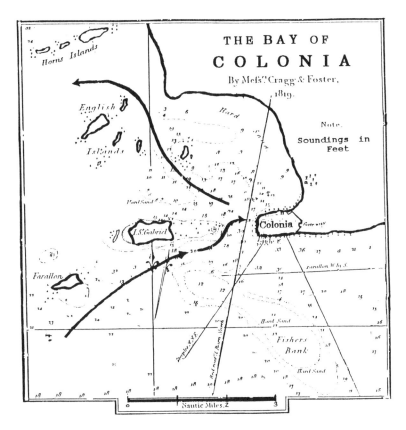

THE ATTACK ON COLONIA, FEBRUARY 1826

Brown's approach ... attack ... and retreat

the sight of new enemy preparations and the non-appearance of any Brazilian relieving force turned elation to depression. Then, on 6 March 1826, the sails of Lobo's squadron were seen on the horizon. Battling against contrary winds, it had taken him over a week to cover the short distance from Montevideo. Lobo's despatches bewailed his lack of reinforcements,[13] but the squadron he had brought with him seemed formidable enough, comprising the frigate *Imperatriz*, the corvettes *Liberal*, *Itaparica* and *Maceió*, the brigs *Caboclo* and *Rio da Plata*, the brigantine *Dona Januária*, the schooners *Alcantara* and *Conceição* and half a dozen store ships. Because of calms, it took the Brazilian ships another day and a half to come within striking distance of Colonia, but the slow approach did nothing to lessen the relief of the defenders.

Then, to the dismay of the watchers in Colonia, the Brazilian squadron turned and sailed away again, anchoring harmlessly ten miles away from the besieged city. Lobo's nerve had failed him once again. Although he could see the Imperial flag flying on the ramparts and the smoke-shrouded citadel appeared to be under attack by day and by night, the Brazilian Vice Admiral was fearful that Colonia had already fallen and that the whole thing was a trick to lure his ships under the guns of the enemy. He decided to keep well out of harm's way until he could establish the truth.[14] It was not long in coming. Within hours, two small boats carrying letters from Governor Rodrigues and Commander Mariath were making their laborious way out to the *Liberal* with reports on the situation and requests for immediate assistance. Even the etiquette observed in official correspondence could not disguise General Rodrigues' annoyance at Lobo's lack of vigour. 'People are saying that it appears incredible that an Imperial squadron made up of more than 40 sail should allow 6 ships of the enemy to attack Colonia,' he wrote on 10 March, and went on to express amazement that having reached the city, Lobo should then have decided to 'withdraw without any communication with the land and to place himself in a position where he could be of no help to the defenders, merely be a witness to any catastrophe that might occur!'[15]

Now fully aware of the strength of the enemy and the strategic situation, Vice Admiral Lobo responded in typical fashion.

Escorted by the *Conceição*, reinforcements of men and munitions were sent into the city together with letters expressing a confidence which he clearly did not feel. Although in terms of warships, his force outnumbered the enemy by two to one, the frigate *Imperatriz* could get no nearer than five miles from Colonia because of its draught and Lobo was convinced that the odds were insufficient. He therefore called for reinforcements, summoned the schooners of the Flotilla of the Uruguay to his aid and ordered that the garrison on the island of Martim Garcia be evacuated and its defences destroyed. That done and – having carefully justified himself on 13 March to the Minister of Marine[16] – Lobo advanced at last to the relief of Colonia.

In spite of the arrival of the Brazilian squadron, the Argentinians and their allies had remained determined to take the Imperial outpost. Ignoring Lobo's presence, and taking full advantage of his inaction, the Uruguayan patriots under Lavalleja's personal command launched assaults by land on 11 and 12 March, while Brown's ships entered the bay and began a vigorous bombardment of the town behind a screen of gunboats which had been thrown across the entrance should any of Lobo's ships intervene. But the sight of the Brazilian squadron advancing en masse toward Colonia on 13 March could not be ignored. Lobo's intention was to bottle up Brown's force within the bay by sealing the exit between the city and the island of S. Gabriel, place it between two fires and destroy it at leisure. To his relief, the Argentinian ships seemed to be making no attempt to escape his trap and Lobo retired for the night in the expectation the morrow would give him the victory which his careful planning deserved.

But 14 March brought a rude shock. Dawn broke to reveal the bay and port of Colonia totally empty. Aided by a change of wind during the night, Brown had executed a carefully planned withdrawal, escaping to the north-west through the tortuous channels between the English Islands and the Hornos. Assured by pilots that such a route was impossible, the Brazilian Admiral had only posted two small schooners to watch the western exit armed with signal rockets. Brown had managed to evade them with ease.[17]

While Lobo glumly surveyed the empty waters before Colonia, the enemy was well on its way to the safety of Buenos Aires. The Brazilians set off in belated pursuit but it was too late. Lobo stayed in sight of Buenos Aires for three days, wearily wrote his despatches, then withdrew once more to his chosen blockading station east of the Ortiz Bank.

Back at his base, Brown repaired his ships, reorganized his crews, transferred his wounded and buried his dead. *La Gaceta Mercantil* published a special list of the 42 English and Americans who had fallen or had been casualties in the national cause.[18] Then, to the thud of minute guns from the ships in the anchorage and accompanied by an 80-man guard of honour, the remains of Commander Cerretti and of Lieutenants Curry, Robinson and Echevarria were carried in state from Naval Headquarters to the Convent of San Francisco where they were laid to rest in the presence of senior representatives of the Argentinian state.[19] There was another senior fatality, Captain Henry Parker, who died on 27 March as a result of 'the rigours of the campaign'. The Argentinian forces had clearly suffered a serious reverse. They had lost a brig, three gunboats and over 300 men in the assault, yet Colonia de Sacramento remained firmly in Brazilian hands.

Although Brown had skilfully extricated himself from a potentially disastrous situation, there seemed to be nothing in the attack on Colonia which could bring comfort to the Argentinian commander. Indeed, the Minister of Marine was becoming distinctly nervous and had already begged him to exercise more caution and use less powder![20] But, although he did not know it, Brown had secured a major strategic gain for Buenos Aires. His audacity and fighting spirit had, once again, shaken Vice Admiral Lobo's nerve and reinforced the conviction that his only hope of defeating the Argentinian commander lay in gaining overwhelming superiority of force. The arrival of the six armed yachts built in Rio Grande do Sul for the Flotilla of the Uruguay gave him the opportunity to disarm three of its older schooners and to sink two more as blockships in the canals round Colonia.[21] But disastrously, Lobo had also ordered the evacuation of the island of Martim Garcia, the destruction of its fortifications and the removal of its guns.

Thus, without a shot being fired, the Brazilian commander had abandoned the strongpoint which commanded the mouth of the River Uruguay and provided the strategic 'hinge' which linked his naval forces in the Uruguay and the Plate. Once again, Lobo's failure of nerve had handed the Argentinians an undeserved victory which seriously weakened the Imperial defences to the west of the River. It was a weakness which Commodore Brown was later to exploit with devastating results.

CHAPTER 7

NIGHT ATTACK ON THE *IMPERATRIZ*

Unshaken by the setback at Colonia, Commodore William Brown was ready to take on the Brazilians again. His crews were paid; supplies in the form of dried meat, rice, salt, firewood, black tobacco and rum were loaded on board;[1] and his shot-damaged ships were repaired. Their numbers had also been augmented by the purchase on 23 February for 23,000 pesos (£4600) of the British brig *Harmony*, which had arrived a month before with 150 Scottish immigrants. Armed with 22 guns and renamed *Independencia*, the brig was ready for action by the beginning of April under the command of William Bathurst, the 30-year-old cousin of Captain Walter Bathurst RN of HMS *Genoa*, later killed at the Battle of Navarino.

On 9 April 1826, Brown left his anchorage to reconnoitre the Imperial positions and devise whatever mischief he could for his powerful enemy. Once off Buenos Aires, he divided his forces. The *General Balcarce* (Nicolas Jorge), *Independencia* (William Bathurst) and the schooner *Sarandí* (José M. Pinedo) were ordered north to see what they could find off Colonia, while Brown himself with the *25 de Mayo* (Flag-Captain Tomas Espora) and the brigs *Congresso Nacional* (John King) and *República Argentina* (William Clark), headed eastwards. Learning from a friendly blockade runner that the enemy's strength had been augmented by the arrival of the frigate *Niterói* under its dashing British captain James Norton, Brown decided to see for himself and set course for the main channel through the Ortiz Bank.

Brown's approach was delayed by adverse winds and currents but, near Montevideo on 10 April, the flotilla surprised and captured the five-gun schooner *Isabela Maria* and chased a smack which was only just able to escape across the mud. Then, next day, flying French colours to confuse the enemy, the *25 de Mayo* came within sight of the Brazilian base. There, as expected, lay the *Niterói*, taking in stores near the familiar profile of HMS *Doris* of the British South America Squadron anchored just over two miles to the south-west of the cathedral.[2] *Doris* had been in, or near, Montevideo since November 1825, keeping a watchful eye on British interests. Brown confidently hove-to within point-blank range of the British frigate then, getting under way again, was crossing the bay under easy sail when a coaster came out of the harbour. The *25 de Mayo* turned in pursuit and, at 12.30, the French colours were replaced by the blue and white of Buenos Aires and a commodore's broad pennant hoisted to the main. It was immediately clear who she was. The *Niterói* promptly ran up a red flag and fired two guns to attract attention from the shore. Within minutes a fleet of boats was seen pulling towards the Brazilian frigate. Not only were officers and crew rushing back to rejoin their ship, but the boats included Commander John Pascoe Grenfell and men from the *Caboclo*,[3] then undergoing repairs in the port, who were equally keen to see off the insolent Argentinian interloper.

At 1.10 pm, the *Niterói* had weighed anchor and set topsails, and by 2.30 pm was heading straight for the Argentinians with the schooners *Conceição*, (Sublieutenant Thomas Thompson), *Itaparica* (Sublieutenant J. Leal Ferreira), *Maria da Glória* (Sublieutenant J. Lamego Costa) and *Maria Theresa* (Lieutenant Martius Boldt) following boldly in her wake. Brown signalled for his scattered ships to rejoin and then, with the wind coming fresh from the north-east, headed south on the starboard tack with the Brazilians following. Brown's tactic was to head away from the enemy in the hope that the frigate and the schooners would separate so that he would be able to fall on one or other with superior force.[4] But the plan did not work, and at 2.50 pm the two squadrons were close enough to exchange long-range fire. The Argentinians were too far away for the *Niterói*'s maindeck 32-pounder carronades but they were within reach of the upper deck long guns manned by Commander Grenfell and his men, while the Brazilian frigate was just within range of the *25 de Mayo*'s long 16- and 9-pounders. For three hours the cannonade continued, but with the approach of night, Norton reluctantly called off the chase and headed back to Montevideo. He had achieved his objective and had seen the Argentinians off, although with damage to spars and rigging and the loss of five dead and five wounded. Unless Brown had decided to stand and fight – which he was determined not to do – he could do no more.

Vice Admiral Lobo was pleased with the performance which seemed to justify his continual pleas for bigger ships and more experienced officers. He reported to the Minister of Marine with satisfaction:

> The valour which Captain Norton, and Commander Grenfell of the *Caboclo* and [Acting] Captain Charles Rose of the *29 de Agosto* who both accompanied him, together with the commanders of the schooners, showed in fighting the enemy for so long; and the promptitude with which they followed did them honour. All acted courageously in an incident which was of the greatest importance since it was done in sight of the whole population of Montevideo and showed them that our ships know how to comport themselves in battle.[5]

Brown too was pleased. Although the *25 de Mayo* and the *República Argentina* had lost 9 dead and 14 wounded, and the flagship's rigging and mainmast had been damaged, he had flaunted the Argentinian flag before the principal Imperial base in the River Plate and had demonstrated the resilience and audacity of the navy he commanded. Satisfied, he sailed for Colonia to pick up the rest of the squadron, then headed back to base. On 12 April he dropped anchor off Buenos Aires, a plan for a return visit to Montevideo already forming in his mind.

While the damage was repaired and his crews reinforced, Commodore William Brown worked out the details of his plan. The aim was as simple as it was dramatic – namely to surprise and take by boarding the Brazilian frigate *Niterói*. The method was to approach the anchorage of Montevideo at night, relying on the darkness to prevent detection by Lobo's blockading force, and then for boats from the Argentinian ships to rush the *Niterói*, overwhelm the defenders and carry off the frigate before help could arrive. Brown's many admirers have always regarded this plan as a carefully calculated piece of daring which deserved success. His detractors have seen it as a rash gamble which could only succeed if blessed with enormous good fortune. Certainly, cutting-out expeditions against an anchored and unprepared enemy were common. Normally, however, the victims were merchantmen or minor ships of war while the predators were more heavily manned frigates or corvettes. For minor warships to cut out a frigate as Brown intended was unusual to say the least. Still, theoretically it was possible. The *Niterói* was a small frigate (in 1826 terms) of only 800 tons, armed principally with short-range carronades and with a crew of only 280,[6] while the ships selected for the attack – the *25 de Mayo* and the *Independencia* – although significantly smaller in tonnage, carried crews totalling 400.[7] On the debit side however, to cross a treacherous river at night and then mount an attack in an unfamiliar anchorage was a high risk enterprise. The element of surprise was vital, and success would depend on being able to mount a coordinated attack in which each commander knew exactly what was expected of him – two conditions which Brown had failed to secure in any of his previous engagements.

In the two weeks which followed, Brown continued his preparations undisturbed by any Brazilian appearance off Buenos Aires. Lobo claimed to be eager to attack the enemy base but was unable to do so until the wind was favourable, the river higher and his ships had recovered from a freak storm on 18 April.[8] But on 26 April Brown was ready. At dawn his seven ships weighed anchor and left the anchorage of Los Pozos to look for the Imperial squadron at its normal blockading station to the east of the Ortiz Bank. With weak northerly winds, progress was slow and it was not until 3 pm on the following day that the Argentinians reached their destination. There was no sign of Lobo's force, so Brown called his international group of captains together to reveal the details of his plan. Experience had already shown Brown the need to ensure that his subordinates understood his intentions and knew precisely what was expected of them. One by one they reported to the flagship; all five were lieutenants – the Englishman William Bathurst of the *Independencia*, the Greek Nicolas Jorge of the *General Balcarce*, the American William Clark of the *República Argentina*, the Irishman John King of the *Congresso Nacional* and the Argentinian José Pinedo of the *Sarandí*. The crews of the *25 de Mayo* and *Independencia* were ordered to supply the boarding parties which were to carry off the *Niterói*. The men were to carry pistols, cutlasses and axes, and to wear white shirts over their uniforms to distinguish them from the enemy. One group was to cut the frigate's cable, another to loose the sails, another to man the sheets. The password was to be 'Santa Maria'. The tone of the meeting was euphoric and, fortified with both confidence and wine, the captains returned to their ships to complete their preparations.[9]

It was night by the time the Argentinians reached their destination. At 8 pm on 27 April, they were surprised to see Lobo's squadron anchored in the gloom to the south of the port, the flagship showing a recognition signal of three horizontal lanterns, the other vessels displaying one light each. In spite of a full moon, Brown's ships managed to slip by undetected and were soon off Montevideo. Seven ships could be seen at anchor, but in the darkness it was impossible to decide which was which. As the Argentinians slowly approached the head of the line, Brown hailed the first, shouting in English, 'What ship is that?' Moments later came the unhelpful reply in the same language, 'What is that to you?' Brown consulted his officers. One was sure it was HMS *Doris*. Another identified it as the USS *Cyane*. Then came the sound of a dog barking and the crowing of a cock. Convinced that no British warship would have such a mass of livestock on board, Flag-Captain Espora and Commodore Brown decided that the ship had to be the Brazilian *Niterói*. The *25 de Mayo* promptly fired a broadside and began the attack.

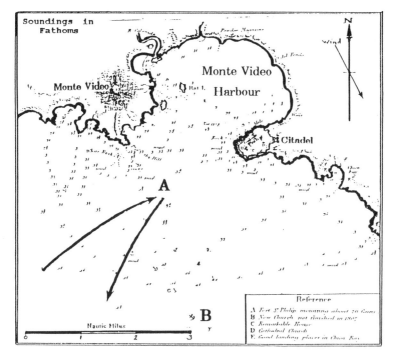

Soundings in
Fathoms

Monte Video

Monte Video
Harbour

Citadel

A

B

Nautic Miles

0   1   2   3

Reference

A *Fort St Philip mounting about 20 Guns*
B *New Church not finished in 1807*
C *Remarkable House*
D *Cathedral Church*
E *Good landing place in Chica Bay*

BROWN AT MONTEVIDEO, 27-8 APRIL 1826

Superimposed on British Admiralty chart
surveyed by Capt. F. Beaufort, RN, 1807

A = *Imperatriz* and ships at anchor   B = Position of HMS *Doris*

Brown's approach and retreat

Unfortunately for the Argentinians, the mystery vessel was not the *Cyane*, or the *Niterói*, or the *Doris*, which had moved her anchorage only the day before.[10] It was the *Imperatriz*, a big 1070-ton, 50-gun Brazilian frigate with a crew of 360 which had taken the British warship's place. By this time the element of surprise had also been totally lost. The officer of the watch had already roused Captain Luis Barroso Pereira – who had been John Taylor's second-in-command during the *Niterói*'s dramatic pursuit of the Portuguese convoy during the War of Independence – and the *Imperatriz* was ready and cleared for action. Thus, as the *25 de Mayo* and the *Independencia* bore down on the mystery ship and prepared to launch their boarding parties, they were met by a storm of musketry and cannon fire from the Brazilian frigate's big 18-pounder maindeck guns. Instead of a surprise cutting-out expedition, Brown found himself involved in an artillery exchange with a heavily armed and prepared opponent. The only relief was that the greater height of the *Imperatriz*'s gundecks above the water meant that its fire was smashing into the rigging of the Argentinian ships instead of into their crowded decks. Gamely, Brown began his approach, but was frustrated by the *Independencia* which, firing a broadside, came between the two ships, caught its jib-boom in the Brazilian frigate's main rigging and prevented the flagship from boarding.[11]

For an hour and a quarter the darkness was rent with the roar and flash of cannon and musketry, the Argentinians maintaining their fire but unable to get near enough to launch an attack by boats, the *Imperatriz* defending itself with skill and gusto and attempting to make sail. Most broadsides went deliberately high, but one smashed through the Brazilian frigate's great cabin, reducing all the fittings to shreds except the portrait of the Emperor on the bulkhead which was miraculously preserved. One of the ships in the anchorage hoisted lights and flags to identify herself as the USS *Cyane*. Another, obviously a Brazilian ship (it was the *Niterói*), began to make sail so as to render assistance. There were also signs that the main Brazilian fleet, alerted by the firing, was preparing to join the action. With his plans now shattered, Brown decided to cut his losses and call off the attack.

His ships had suffered heavy damage to their rigging from the vigour of the *Imperatriz*'s defence but casualties had been light. So, hoisting his night signal to discontinue the action, Brown and his ships slipped back into the night and, driven by the lightest of breezes, headed south-west for the safety of the Ortiz Bank. Dawn on 28 April found the *25 de Mayo, General Balcarce, República Argentina* and the schooner *Sarandí* heading south-west with the Brazilian squadron just visible on the north-eastern horizon. There was momentary concern at the non-appearance of the *Independencia*, but the brig's shredded sails were eventually spotted to leeward. Brown adjusted his course and at noon the vessel rejoined, to be given a hero's welcome by the rest of the squadron. Then, still having the wind, Brown turned east and slowly outpaced the pursuing Brazilians. The *Imperatriz* remained behind in Montevideo. She had been much battered in sails and rigging and had a casualty list of ten wounded and three dead,[12] including Captain Luis Barroso Pereira who had been killed in heroic circumstances on his quarter deck. Next morning, the officers of HMS *Doris* came aboard with their surgeon to offer medical help and the congratulations of their captain Sir John Sinclair on the skill and success of the Brazilian defence.

For three days the Argentinians cruised off Maldonado searching unsuccessfully for enemy merchantmen or supply ships, and patching up the damage the best they could. Then, on 1 May, Captain Pinedo of the *Sarandí*, which had been patrolling to the west, reported that a Brazilian squadron of 16 ships was in the offing. Brown decided that it was time to return home. Skirting to the south, he made for the main channel through the Ortiz Bank hoping for a clear run to Buenos Aires. But it was not to be. Lobo had doubled back and at dawn on 3 May the Brazilians were once again in sight. Unalarmed and confident in his knowledge of both the river and its perilous shallows, Brown retreated towards the edge of the bank with the Brazilians following. His plan worked. First the *Niterói* slithered to a halt in the mud, then the brig *29 de Agosto*, throwing the pursuing Brazilians into confusion. Suddenly the *25 de Mayo* too ran aground. Both the *Maria da Glória* and the

Liberal drew too much water to risk going on, so Lobo ordered the *Maceió* into the attack. Unfortunately, Captain Antonio José de Carvalho refused to go and held back. On the Argentinian side, the *Sarandí* was instructed to advance and bombard the *Niterói*, but finding a foot of water in the schooner's hold, Captain Pinedo dropped anchor and stayed where he was. The two forces were stalemated, rallying round their stricken vessels which were frantically trying to heave themselves off the mud while maintaining an ineffectual fire against the distant enemy. By nightfall the ships were refloated but any thought of an engagement was over. Lobo withdrew into deeper water, while Brown steered west for Buenos Aires.

On 4 May, back in Montevideo, Vice Admiral Lobo dictated a despatch to his home Government. There was nothing in the way of good news to report. Once again, Brown had launched a surprise attack – this time on the Imperial Navy's principal base on the River Plate. Once again, he had evaded the Brazilian pursuit and had escaped unscathed to fight another day. This time Lobo laid the blame for failure on the timidity of the *Maceió*'s captain, the draught of his ships and the mud.[13] His tone was resigned and justifiably gloomy.

For his part, Commodore Brown had learnt many things in his four months of command. And the most significant was the importance of Buenos Aires public opinion in sustaining the Argentinian war effort. During the return voyage he therefore penned his report on the expedition.[14] But unlike Lobo, his tone was triumphant, glossing over the failure of the assault on the *Imperatriz*, and emphasizing the skill and bravery of the Argentinian attack. On 4 May, *La Gaceta Mercantil* published a letter from one of the flagship's officers eulogizing 'the brilliant and noble audacity of the corvette *25 de Mayo* and the brig *Independencia* on the night of 27th in the port of Montevideo which should be judged as worth a victory'. Public opinion took them at their word. Newspapers enthusiastically reprinted the story and the Order of the Day of the national army for 3 May 1826[15] decreed a 15-gun salute, fanfares of trumpets, rolls of drums and 'vivas' for the nation in every military establishment 'in celebration of the triumph achieved by our squadron against the Brazilian Empire!' Brown returned to port to find himself a hero. The master of naval tactics was becoming the master of propaganda.

CHAPTER 8

THE NEW BROOM:
CHANGES IN COMMAND

The dejected tone of Vice Admiral Lobo's report on the *Imperatriz* affair reflected more than his embarrassment at yet another failure to anticipate and neutralize Brown's audacious tactics. The despatch case delivered by the *Niterói* on 2 April had included a letter which relieved him of command, ordered him to hand over to his deputy, and recalled him forthwith to Rio de Janeiro to face a court martial. Brazilian ministers had been increasingly worried by the failure of Lobo's defensive strategy and by the defeatist tone of his despatches since February 1826. In spite of his superiority of force, Lobo seemed incapable of controlling either Brown's depredations or of catching him and bringing him to decisive action. With growing alarm they read of the stalemate at Corales, the withdrawal and fragmenting of the blockading squadron, and the timidity of Lobo's relief of Colonia. His decision to abandon the key outpost of Martim Garcia had come as the last straw. On 19 March, the Minister of Marine signed a sharp letter of recall.

Rodrigo Lobo was stunned by the news. He could see nothing wrong with his strategy and was shocked to find himself abruptly dismissed after 43 years' service at a time when the requested reinforcements were beginning to arrive. His sense of propriety was equally offended by the fact that no ship large enough to reflect his rank was available to carry him back to Rio de Janeiro.[1] But Lobo was to remain at his post for another month. The wound received by Commodore Diogo de Brito at Corales prevented him from taking over, and it was not easy in the newly created Brazilian Navy to find another commander of sufficient seniority and vigour. In the event, the choice fell on no less a person than its senior naval officer, Admiral Rodrigo Pinto Guedes, who took command amid the thunder of salutes on 13 May 1826.

But another month was to pass while a ship was prepared for Lobo's transportation to Rio de Janeiro. Eventually on 19 June, the Vice Admiral boarded the suitably proportioned armed ship *Jurujuba* and sailed for Rio de Janeiro in company with two small warships, four Brazilian merchantmen and four prizes. After a slow and tedious passage the vessel sailed into the Bay of Guanabara on 26 July. Before he could land, Lobo was arrested and taken to the Fortress of Santa Cruz under the shadow of the Sugar Loaf to await the convening of a court martial.

The case against Lobo boiled down to eight charges: his failure to destroy the enemy at Corales, his hesitancy during the relief of Colonia, his inability to prevent Brown's subsequent escape, his abandonment of Martim Garcia, his absence during the sortie against Montevideo, his exposure of the *Imperatriz* to attack, and his failure to intercept Brown's ships thereafter. The real complaint was, however, summarized in the last accusation which pinpointed 'the poor disposition, use and application of the substantial forces which were entrusted to his direction against the enemies of the Empire'.[2] In reality the charges against Lobo lacked substance. It was not his actions as much as his attitudes which were on trial. He was not being accused of cowardice or of criminal negligence, but of being timid in his tactics, over-cautious in his deployments and defensive in his mentality – characteristics which should have been well known to the Imperial Government before he was even appointed to command.

The court martial was convened on 11 September 1826. Twenty-one of the Vice Admiral's despatches were presented as evidence, supplemented by other documents and by sworn statements by witnesses. But from the beginning it became clear that however hesitant Lobo may have been in deploying warships, he was completely at home when handling paper. His defence was detailed and skilful and was summarized in a letter written to the

Minister of Marine from Santa Cruz.[3] In it he stressed the navigational hazards posed by the mudbanks and currents of the River Plate, the almost impregnable position of the shallow Argentinian anchorage off Buenos Aires, the length of the lines of communication which had to be defended and the limited number of vessels available to do it. Using the blockades of Toulon and Brest during the Napoleonic Wars as examples, he demonstrated that warships, being at the mercy of the elements, were never able to wholly prevent the entry of blockade runners or the departure of privateers; and he hinted darkly that he was being made a political scapegoat for the unsatisfactory results of the naval war, comparing himself to the British Admiral Byng who had been sacrificed to satisfy public discontent at the loss of Minorca in 1757. The court martial went on intermittently for six months. Eventually, in February 1827, Lobo was acquitted of all eight charges, the prosecution being unable to show any evidence of criminal behaviour. But he was never employed again.

Rodrigo Pinto Guedes was 64 years old when he arrived to take up the Brazilian command in the River Plate – his first sea-going assignment for 20 years. The second son of a noble Portuguese family, Pinto Guedes had been originally destined for the Church, a profession for which his intellectual qualities made him ideally suited. Instead he entered the Royal Portuguese Navy in 1781 and rapidly made his mark. In ten years he was a commander, serving with the Portuguese squadron which had answered Lord Nelson's request for aid to assist in the siege of Malta in 1798. Ten years later Pinto Guedes was a commodore. By 1805 he had become a junior member of the Portuguese Admiralty Board and two years later became 'Major General da Armada', the chief of staff of the Navy. Moving to Brazil with the Royal Family in 1808, Pinto Guedes had settled in the country and, when independence had come in 1822, he had thrown in his lot with the Brazilian cause and stayed on to serve the Empire. By this time he was an admiral, a man of vast administrative experience and senior naval member of the Supreme Military Council. His appointment to the River Plate command was greeted with enthusiasm by the *Diário Fluminense* which noted that 'the well known talents of this gallant and brave officer, his courage and firmness of character have made his nomination extremely popular'. However, as the mouthpiece of the Government, the *Diário* could hardly have said less.

Sources hostile to the Imperial Government were critical of Pinto Guedes' style, complaining that instead of being in the thick of the fighting, the Admiral chose to remain aloof in the distant splendour of a well appointed frigate. This criticism – repeated, as usual, by John Armitage and thence by many Brazilian historians – is entirely without foundation and overlooks both the nature of the job of a commander-in-chief and the nature of the man. Pinto Guedes was first and foremost an administrator, and like all good administrators, knew that the secret of success was to pick skilful subordinates, give them clear guidelines, and then ensure that they had the ships and men they needed to do the job. He was, in short, a decentralizer, and it was this style which was immediately introduced into the River Plate in place of Lobo's fussy centralization. Pinto Guedes was also determined to pursue an aggressive policy against the Argentinians and to punch the Imperial Navy's very considerable weight. With 16 warships, 11 schooners and 15 gunboats and yachts now under his command, the task did not seem too difficult.

Pinto Guedes' first act was to replace five of the most timid or inexperienced captains with officers in whom he had confidence, most of them British. Captain Bartholomew Hayden, Commander William Eyre and Lieutenant Stephen Clewley, who had fought with distinction under Lord Cochrane in the War of Independence and the suppression of the 1824 rebellion in Pernambuco, were given command respectively of the corvettes *Liberal* and *Itaparica* and the brig-of-war *Pirajá*. Commander Fredrick Mariath, naval hero of Colonia, was sent to replace the timid Antonio José de Carvalho of the *Maceió*, and his comrade in the siege, Lieutenant José Regis, was made captain of the brig *Independência ou Morte*. That done, Pinto Guedes turned his attention to the deployment of his ships.

Determined to both tighten the blockade and adopt a more aggressive policy, the Brazilian commander-in-chief divided his forces into three divisions and a reserve. The First Division, under Pinto Guedes' direct command, was to provide an external line of blockade operating out of Montevideo and covering the mouth of the river. It was made up of the heaviest ships, supplemented by a handful of schooners, namely the frigates *Piranga* (50 guns), *Dona Paula* (50) and *Imperatriz* (50); the corvette *Carioca* (26); the brigs *Real João* (10) and *Rio da Plata* (10); and the schooners *Maria Theresa*, *Alcantara* and *Maria da Glória*.

The Second Division, deployed in the deeper water to the east of Buenos Aires, between Colonia and the Ensenada Spit, was to enforce a strict blockade of the Argentinian capital aimed at containing and, if possible, destroying Brown's squadron of warships. It was entrusted to the command of Captain James Norton of the *Niterói*, an experienced officer with previous service in the Royal Navy during the Napoleonic Wars and with the East India Company afterwards. Norton was a man of distinguished connections and in India had married Eliza Bland, widow of a Waterloo veteran, Colonel Esme Erskine, who was the son of a peer, Lord Erskine. He had also assumed responsibility for her three children, Thomas, Harry and Esme Erskine, the last of whom was to serve as a sublieutenant in the Brazilian Navy. Norton had been appointed as captain-of-frigate in 1823, and had been instrumental in the secret recruitment of British officers and sailors by the Brazilian Agent in London, General Felisberto Brant. Arriving in Brazil too late to play a prominent role in the War of Independence, Norton had nevertheless distinguished himself during the storming of Recife during the Pernambuco rebellion of 1824, and had already gained a reputation for daring and leadership. The couple were enthusiasts for their new home, as the names of four of their five children – Marina, Fletcher Carioca, Fredrick de la Plata, and Maria Brasilia – were to testify. Norton's main force in the River Plate consisted of 10 medium-sized warships and four schooners, namely the frigate *Niterói* (36 guns); the corvettes *Maria da Glória* (26), *Liberal* (22), *Itaparica* (22) and *Maceió* (18); the brigs and brigantines *Pirajá* (18), *29 de Agosto* (16), *Caboclo* (16), *Dona Januária* (14) and *Independência ou Morte* (14); and the schooners *Providência*, *Itaparica*, *Conceição* and *7 de Março*.

The task of the Third Division, like its predecessor, the Flotilla of the Uruguay, was to control movement on that river and to prevent any communication between the Argentinian provinces on one bank and the Banda Oriental on the other. Selected for command was Captain Jacinto Roque de Senna Pereira, a 35-year-old officer who had been serving on the Uruguay since 1818. He was the obvious choice. His knowledge of the river was unchallenged and, being married into a local family, he had useful contacts and a profound knowledge of the local scene. His force consisted of eleven smaller craft: the schooners *Oriental* (11 guns), *Bertioga* (8), *Dona Paula* (4), *Itapoão* (1) and *Liberdade do Sul* (1); the armed yachts *9 de Janeiro*, *7 de Setembro*, *12 de Outubro* and *1 de Dezembro*; and the gunboats *Montevideana* and *Leal Paulistana*.

In Buenos Aires, news of the Brazilian reorganization was received with alarm. There was ample information on what was going on from newspaper reports, talkative captains of British packets, sympathizers and – indeed – spies in Montevideo. The harbourmaster of Buenos Aires, Francisco Lynch, kept a careful record of reports on Brazilian movements brought by incoming blockade runners, privateers, and small boats illicitly trading across the estuary; and the rebel commander of the coastal region of the Banda Oriental, Colonel Raphael Hortiguera, ran an effective intelligence service in the western Plate and the Uruguay. The Imperial naval commanders had been irritated for some time by the fact that their plans seemed to be well known in Buenos Aires,[4] and heavy suspicion fell on a certain Michael Brown. Brown was a retired master in the Royal Navy who was now captain of the merchant ship *Hutton*, detained by Admiral Lobo in February. Unfortunately, he was also the brother of William Brown, commander of the Argentinian Navy. As time went on, the authorities became convinced that he was the culprit,[5] especially in July when three of his crew absconded to Buenos Aires. Michael Brown protested that he was innocent of passing information, but the Imperial Government thought otherwise and ordered his expulsion from Montevideo on 4 September. He was forced to sell his impounded cargo by auction at great loss and left hurriedly in October.[6]

Meanwhile, Argentinian merchants and shipowners were beginning to feel the pinch as the Brazilian blockade began to bite, sealing them off from the outside world and leaving them with goods and bullion which could not be moved. In 1825, 387 foreign vessels had entered the port of Buenos Aires, mostly British and American.[7] Between the imposition of the blockade at the end of January and May 1826, fewer than half a dozen ships managed to get through. But the Argentinians were not down-hearted. The land campaign in the Banda Oriental was going well and Lavalleja's wild irregulars, reinforced by troops from the United Provinces under the veteran General Martin Rodrigues, had gained control over most of the countryside. The Imperial regulars bottled up in Montevideo and Colonia seemed powerless to deal with the unorthodox fighting methods of their opponents, and Lecor and his officers seemed to prefer the social life of the garrison towns and the company of local Spanish-American ladies to the rigours of a campaign in the inhospitable pampas. Commodore William Brown too was optimistic. To increase its speed, the *Congresso Nacional* had been given an extra mast and a new captain, William Mason, so that Brown now had two corvettes, two brigs, three schooners and nine gunboats at his disposal. Even if the Imperial reorganization restricted his activities, he was confident that the defences of Buenos Aires were almost impregnable to a seaborne attack.

There was also hope of naval reinforcement from England and from Chile. In March urgent orders had been sent to Captain Robert Ramsay, now acting on behalf of Buenos Aires in London, to buy two 40-gun frigates and a 1000-ton East Indiaman capable of carrying 60 pieces of artillery. Armed and fully manned, they were to be sent without delay.[8] And in regard to Chile, Colonel Ventura Vasquez had been sent overland to Valparaiso during the same month and was already negotiating the purchase of three warships, the frigate *O'Higgins* (50 guns) and the corvettes *Independencia* (24) and *Chacabuco* (20). The *Chacabuco* was a converted merchantman, but the history of the other vessels was interesting.

The *O'Higgins* had been built in Russia. Bought with seven other warships by Ferdinand VII of Spain from the Tsar behind the backs of his ministers, it was the only one which had not proved on arrival to be totally and embarrassingly rotten. Renamed *Maria Isabel*, the frigate had been captured just in time to become Lord Cochrane's flagship during Chile's war for freedom. The *Independencia* on the other hand, was a big United States-built corvette, which before purchase had been called *Curiatii*. She was, ironically enough, the sister ship of the Brazilian corvette *Maria da Glória*, which in the same classical tradition, had originally been named *Horatii*.

By the middle of the month, Norton's division was in position before Buenos Aires. There were tentative skirmishes on 23 and 24 May, but heavy weather prevented any decisive move by either side. But 25 May was Argentina's National Day, and having marked the occasion at noon by hoisting flags and firing gun salutes, Brown felt obliged to celebrate it with some dramatic initiative. The Government welcomed the idea. A naval victory might restore its flagging popularity with the public. The day was clear and autumnal, the wind from the south south-east. At 1.15 pm the Imperial squadron was reported in sight to the east having escorted some English merchant ships to Colonia. This was Brown's opportunity. Ordering his ships to weigh anchor he rapidly led them out to meet the Brazilians. Seeing their movement, Norton immediately tacked and, with the Argentinians following, sailed east for two hours into deeper water where his ships could manoeuvre. Then, at 4 pm, he tacked again and advanced south-west to engage the enemy. Brown promptly turned away, crammed on sail and made for Buenos Aires, trying to lure the pursuing Brazilians into the shallows near the city. There was an exchange of ineffectual long-range cannon fire, but at 5 pm, the weather began to deteriorate and Norton, realizing that his ships were sailing into danger, called off the chase and began to retire. Brown attempted to follow, but it was soon too dark for any further action. At 9 pm he showed a night signal and fired a rocket to rally his ships in the darkness. As dawn broke, the Argentinian squadron returned to its base.[9]

For James Norton, the operation had been a revelation in terms of both Brown's tactics and the problems inherent in blockading Buenos Aires. In a subsequent despatch he wrote apologetically to Pinto Guedes:

> Your Excellency can continue to have confidence in the division I have the honour to command although we have lacked any chance so far to demonstrate it. The tactics of Brown have always been the same, namely to manoeuvre so as to draw us on to the banks so that our larger ships run aground or are restricted to firing at long range. This is what happened on 25/26 May. ... But if he decides to attack us outside the banks, I am sure Your Excellency will have no doubt of the outcome.[10]

James Norton had noted the narrow and easily blocked channel which was the only access to Buenos Aires, the shallows surrounding it and the ability of the Argentinians – unlike his own ships – to carry minimum stores and water so as to lessen their draught. He began to have serious doubts as to whether a frontal attack on the anchorage of Los Pozes was the best way of dealing with the Argentinian Navy.

CHAPTER 9

NORTON TIGHTENS THE SCREW: THE BATTLES OF LOS POZES AND LARA-QUILMES

Admiral Rodrigo Pinto Guedes was keen to show that his arrival in the River Plate meant a new and aggressive Brazilian strategy. The blockade of Buenos Aires received a new impetus, and what – according to Consul Hood in Montevideo – in Lobo's time had been little more than 'a temporary or casual interdiction of trade', became a tight and effective stranglehold.[1] But Pinto Guedes also wanted direct action against Buenos Aires, and the Brazilian Second Division, cruising between Colonia and Ensenada, was the obvious instrument. In numbers it was more than a match for Brown's squadron, and its British commander, James Norton, was imbued with the aggression and the qualities of leadership needed to ensure success. Captain Senna Pereira, commanding in the Uruguay, was of a similar opinion and, visiting to pay his respects to the Admiral on 1 June, he produced draft proposals for just such an attack. Surrounded by papers and charts in the great cabin of the Piranga, Pinto Guedes and his staff worked out the details. Norton's division was first to be reinforced by seven vessels from the Flotilla of the Uruguay and nine gunboats – increasing his command to a mixed force of 31 ships. It was to be deployed in three parts – a vanguard of seven heavier ships and four gunboats commanded by Norton in the Niterói; a right wing of six shallower draught warships led by John Pascoe Grenfell in the Caboclo; and a centre squadron of nine schooners, yachts and gunboats under

Senna Pereira in the *Dona Paula*. Once ready, the division would mount a frontal attack on the Argentinian anchorage of Los Pozes.

Senna Pereira delivered the Admiral's orders to Captain Norton off Colonia on 4 June 1826. The following days were devoted to assembling ships, finalizing details and issuing orders to the individual captains. Success could not be guaranteed when operating in such difficult waters against an opponent of proven skill, but all agreed that a demonstration of Brazilian naval superiority would be salutary, and any mistake by Brown would give the opportunity to inflict a severe blow on the Argentinian squadron. It was well worth the effort. On 9 June, after a delay caused by unfavourable winds from the south-west, all was ready. The Brazilian armada weighed anchor and headed for Buenos Aires.

Commodore Brown had not been idle during the interim. First, he had organized a convoy of six ships to carry reinforcements of cavalry and light infantry to the Banda Oriental. Keeping in the shallow water to the west, it had sailed on 6 June, commanded by Captain Leonardo Rosales in the *Rio de la Plata*, with the brig *General Balcarce*, two gunboats and the schooners *Sarandí* and *Pepa*. Then, the following day, Brown himself had put to sea with his remaining four ships to be near at hand should the convoy get into difficulties. Thus, Brown was cruising to the north of Buenos Aires on 10 June, when the dawn mists rose to reveal the mass of Norton's ships advancing remorselessly from the north-east. The Brazilian commander had noted the convoy's departure and had decided that this dividing of Brown's forces provided him with the opportunity he needed. Sensing an imminent attack, the Argentinian commander withdrew to Los Pozes to prepare his defence. Carefully he anchored his four ships in a line north to south across the narrow channel which linked the Inner and Outer Roads, then placed his five anchored gunboats between them. Each vessel then rigged a spring from her anchor cable and round the capstan so that she could be pivoted to present her broadside to the enemy whatever his line of approach. In defensive terms it was a masterly disposition. Bristling with guns, Brown's ships were arranged across the entire navigable width of the channel in a line which could neither be broken nor outflanked.[2]

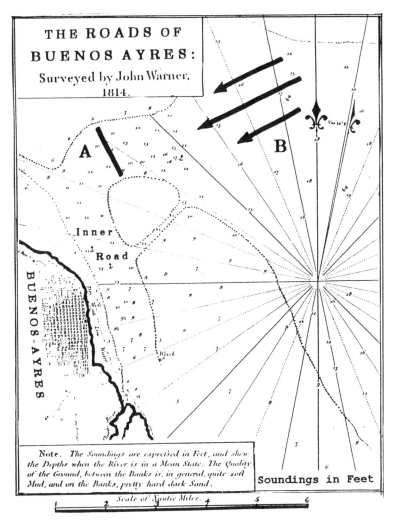

LOCATION OF THE BATTLE OF LOS POZES, 11 JUNE 1826

A = Argentinian defensive line   B = Brazilian attack

Sunday 11 June 1826 was a bright winter's day in the River Plate, with blue skies and light northerly winds. Norton's force had anchored for the night in attack formation off Quilmes, and, as the morning mists cleared, the citizens of Buenos Aires were treated to the awesome sight of a huge Brazilian fleet filling the horizon. As they watched, the enemy squadron made sail and slowly began its advance, the bigger ships towing the gunboats so they were not left behind. Brown, confident in his defensive positions and keen to enthuse his men, issued an inspiring order of the day:

> Sailors and soldiers of the Republic! Do you see that great floating mountain? It is 31 enemy ships! Do not suppose that your chief feels any fear, because he has no doubt of your valour and he is confident that you will imitate the *25 de Mayo* which would rather sink than surrender!

By 1 pm, the Brazilian advance had reached the Outer Roads, the *Niterói* in front, its launch going ahead to sound the depth of water. Almost within gunshot, the *Niterói* had to anchor over four and a half miles from the cathedral to avoid running aground. The *Maria da Glória* followed suit. Norton first moved his flag to the *Itaparica*, which drew only 14 feet of water then, as the corvette too touched bottom, to the shallower draught *Caboclo*, then to Senna Pereira's flagship, the schooner *Dona Paula*. One after another, the *Liberal, Maceió, Pirajá* and *Independência ou Morte* were forced to halt as the water shoaled. It was now 2.30 pm and Brazilian frustration was beginning to mount. The mudbanks had prevented any of their warships from getting closer than long cannon shot from their enemies.[3] Only the smaller schooners and gunboats could get within range, but in the light wind many of these had drifted to leeward and – even if they had not – none would have been able to withstand the fire-power of Brown's anchored warships. The Brazilian attack began to peter out.

Then at 3 pm, Commodore Brown took the initiative. Rosales' convoy escort could be seen returning over the northern horizon. Brown signalled it to join the action while Norton ordered Grenfell's flotilla to intercept. Then, thinking that the *Niterói* was aground, Brown led his gunboats forward to the attack. This led to a brief but inconclusive exchange of fire before the Argentinians realized their mistake and retreated to their original positions. It was now 5 pm and was already cold and dark. There was no point in continuing. The Brazilians slowly withdrew, anchored two and a half miles from their enemies and pondered on the lessons of the day.

The Brazilian captains did not give much importance to the action of 11 June 1826, later called the Battle of Los Pozes. The fact that there was only one casualty spoke for itself. Senna Pereira in his *Memoirs* dismissed it in two terse sentences. 'Nothing was done in the attack proposed for 11 June. The enemy suffered some damage to their gunboats but it was little more than a skirmish.'[4] The only gain was that three Brazilian sailors had gallantly taken advantage of the confusion to retake the schooner *Maria Isabel*, captured off Montevideo on 10 April, and had managed to escape and rejoin the Imperial squadron.

The following day, Norton wrote to his senior captains – Hayden, Eyre, Beaurepaire, Mariath, Grenfell and Senna Pereira – asking for their reflections on the day and their conclusions for the future. Opinion was unanimous.[5] Teodoro de Beaurepaire of the *Maria da Glória*, reflected the views of all when he wrote:

> Any attack we mount on the position which the enemy now occupies ... will be unfortunate, because our ships cannot get close enough without going aground – as we experienced yesterday – which reduces the attack to a fight between gunboats, a disadvantage for us in view of the fact that the enemy, in addition to being able to protect them with bigger ships, can assist them in case of damage while ours would be exposed.

It was also dawning on the Brazilians that the policy of arming their warships with heavy carronades had been a mistake. They had increased the weight of their broadsides but at the cost of a shorter range.[6] The mixture of Spanish 6-, 12- and 16-pounders carried on Brown's ships[7] fired a lighter shot but over a longer distance. The Brazilian Navy was learning what the British had learnt in the American Lakes in 1812. In relation to strategy for the future, Bartholomew Hayden argued that the answer was a reversal of roles. Instead of attacking Brown's carefully chosen positions, the Brazilians should go on the defensive and tempt the Argentinian commander to attack them. Once he had left the shelter of his anchorage for deeper water, the superior numbers and discipline of the Brazilians would quickly turn the tables. Accordingly, Hayden recommended a passive blockade, sure that if the squadron were to remain continuously in sight of Buenos Aires, public opinion would force Brown to come out and fight.

Norton and his men may not have considered 11 June an important engagement, but to the people of Buenos Aires things looked different. All day long, thousands of people had watched as a vast Brazilian armada had advanced on Brown's heavily outnumbered ships. To the spectators it seemed that they must be totally destroyed.[8] The billowing smoke, the flash and thunder of gunfire – which at times was so intense as to shatter windows – had added to the awesome nature of the spectacle. Yet the flimsy line had held. The enemy had not only been repelled but had been pursued into the smoke by the gunboats. Unaware (or forgetful) of the impregnable nature of Brown's defensive position and of the shallows which made it impossible for any Brazilian ships to approach, they saw the apparent repulse of a force so great by one so tiny as a mighty victory. William Brown came ashore to find himself a national hero. As he made his way from the Mole to the Fort to be greeted by the President of the Republic, he was greeted with cheers and 'vivas' by a public that was wild with enthusiasm and relief. Flowers were thrown from balconies as he passed and the commodore was crowned with a garland of laurel. Days later in a public ceremony at La Sala Argentina, he was presented with the national flag in silk, fringed with gold and embroidered with the date of the battle by Dona Maria de Mendaville, secretary of the local Benevolent Society. Amid speeches denouncing Brazil, lauding the freedom of Buenos Aires and comparing its deeds to those of the Roman Republic in which the American Consul Colonel Forbes enthusiastically joined, Brown entrusted the flag to Rector Manuel de Irigoyen of the Colegio de Ciencias Morales with the hope that it would serve as an inspiration to future generations of students.

The newspapers took up the theme. On 15 June, *El Mensagero Argentino* discovered that six wives had been present on the *Independencia* during the battle, handling cartridges. They were declared 'Heroines of the Republic' and a public subscription was raised for them. On 27 June, it announced that amateurs of the British community, not to be outdone in demonstrating its support, and always sympathetic to the underdog, had presented a performance of the comedy *The Mountaineers* at the Teatro Argentino to raise funds for the wounded, and that the presentation of Brown at the end of the fifth act to President Rivadavia had been the signal for such a wave of 'vivas' and applause that it had 'tested the commodore's modesty'. Not to be outdone, *El Correio Nacional* reported with satisfaction that 'we have been informed by a person who spoke to Commodore Norton, that Brown is a hero and the officers under his command incomparable!'

The truth however, was different. Rather than viewing Brown's activities with wide-eyed admiration, Norton and the officers of the Brazilian squadron were at first amazed, and then annoyed by the junketing ashore. To represent a minor cannonade from an impregnable position as a great victory seemed both absurd and insulting, and there was unease lest this version of events should be believed. They were right to be worried. Whereas in republican Buenos Aires, the importance of public support meant that information on events was made freely available and slanted to give a favourable impression, the monarchical regime in Rio de Janeiro was unconcerned about public opinion and merely printed official despatches with little comment. As a result, many – particularly foreigners – based their assessment of the situation on the fuller reports coming from Buenos Aires. John Armitage, whose contemporary *History* is filled with inaccurate and Argentinian-derived accounts was one of them. He was not alone. Writing to the Foreign Office on 29 June, Consul-General Henry Chamberlain reported that there were wild rumours in the capital that the Imperial Navy had suffered a major reverse on 11 June at which the *Niterói* and two brigs had been lost and Captain Grenfell killed![9] Mild official denials did nothing to counter the mood of pessimism.

Admiral Pinto Guedes' despatches reflected the mood of his subordinates. One contained an exasperated description of events in Buenos Aires and mocked Brown's pretensions to be the 'Hero of 11 June!'[10] Another, enclosing Norton's own account of his operations, concluded wearily, 'all this shows the type of warfare we have to put up with here.'[11] Turning to future operations, however, he supported Norton's intention to replace an attacking strategy with a close blockade of Buenos Aires in the hope that Brown would be forced to come out and fight in deeper water to safeguard his reputation. To increase the temptation, Pinto Guedes withdrew the *Maria da Glória, Independência ou Morte, Dona Januária* and the schooners *Maria da Glória* and *Providência* to make the balance of forces between the two sides more even.

The psychological pressure being applied by the Brazilians eventually achieved the result they wanted. For over six weeks, the sails of Norton's squadron, sometimes at anchor, sometimes on manoeuvres in the channel, were a familiar sight to the citizens of Buenos Aires. Brown and the Argentinian squadron stayed at its anchorage waiting for the reinforcements from Chile. Then news arrived that, although they had been purchased, the three ships had not been able to leave Valparaiso until mid-July.[12] Unable to wait any longer, Brown was goaded into action. He now had 18 vessels at his disposal – the corvettes *25 de Mayo* and *Congreso Nacional*; the brigs *Independencia, República Argentina* and *General Balcarce*; the schooners *Río de la Plata, Pepa* and *Sarandí*; and 10 gunboats, as well as the privateer brig *Oriental Argentina* commanded by a French officer, Pierre Dautant, which was about to sail on its first cruise but had volunteered to help the squadron. Commodore Brown was confident that handled correctly, this force was sufficient to challenge Norton's squadron which – following the arrival of the corvette *Maria da Glória* with extra men for the Uruguay division – now consisted of 19 vessels – eight warships, three schooners and eight small yachts and gunboats.

Commodore Brown's arrangements on 11 June 1826 had been a masterpiece of defensive tactics. But his proposals for an Argentinian attack involved enormous risk. Revealed at a council of war with his captains on 29 July 1826, his plan was for a night attack aimed at cutting off part of the Imperial squadron and carrying it off to Buenos Aires before the rest could recover and come to its aid. Brown reasoned that whether he succeeded or not, the attempt would shake the confidence of the Brazilian commanders and cause them to withdraw from their close blockade. Had Lobo still been in command, his reasoning would have been sound. But against Norton and his captains – highly experienced men who had served together for over three years in the War for Independence against the Portuguese and in the suppression of the Confederation of the Equator – Brown's plan was a gamble.

At dusk on 29 July, with a light wind from the north north-east, Brown's squadron passed through the channel into the Outer Roads, the lighter gunboats being towed by the heavier ships to where the British packet *Dove* lay quietly at anchor. Then, the whole force slipped into the darkness intent on surprising the Brazilian fleet as it lay in line parallel to Quilmes Point. But things soon began to go wrong. Suddenly, the shapes of two Imperial schooners loomed out of the darkness – Norton had posted a night watch an hour's sail from Buenos Aires to prevent such a surprise. A quick broadside dismasted the *Dona Paula*, which slowly drifted away, but the *Conceição* put up her helm and disappeared into the darkness to give the alarm, firing night signals as it went. Alerted, Norton burned three coloured lights, and within an hour the Brazilian squadron had weighed anchor and was preparing to meet the enemy.

Undeterred by losing the element of surprise, Brown pressed on. At 11.30 pm, judging herself to be near the Imperial squadron, the *25 de Mayo* went into action, her presence dramatically illuminated as she fired broadsides of cannon and batteries of Congreve rockets in the enemy's direction. Brown looked round for support before planning his next move, but was infuriated to find himself alone. Only Leonardo Rosales' schooner *Rio de la Plata* was in sight. Of the *Congresso Nacional*, *República Argentina* and *Sarandí*, which should have been giving close support, nothing could be seen. Frustrated and baffled by the darkness, Brown withdrew to find the rest of the squadron and to anchor for the night. Nothing further could be achieved. Norton did likewise, receiving reinforcements during the early morning in the shape of the lugger *Principe Imperial* and the schooner *Rio da Plata*. He now had 21 armed ships at his disposal, with a flotilla of gunboats hurrying from Colonia in the unfulfilled hope of arriving in time for the battle. As well as reinforcements, Norton had received additional moral support in the shape of his wife Eliza, who had arrived from Montevideo in the corvette *Maria da Glória*. Mrs Norton was on board the *Niterói* during the whole of the battle, and was allowed on deck to witness its final stages, climbing on top of a gun-carriage to get a better view. Her description of what she saw was later published in the *British Packet and Argentine News*.[13]

Dawn on 30 July 1826 found the opposing forces back near their original positions – the Argentinians off the Outer Roads, the Brazilians to the east between Colonia and Lara Point in two lines, one made up of Norton's corvettes and brigs, the other of Senna Pereira's schooners and armed yachts. First, Brown sent his Catalan flag-lieutenant Antonio Toll with a severe rebuke to Captains Fisher, Clark and Pinedo for their lack of energy the previous night. Then he issued an order expressing complete confidence in victory, telling his commanders to follow the manoeuvres of the flagship but adding, Nelson fashion, that no man would be failing in his duty if he were engaging an enemy ship. Then, taking advantage of the light northerly wind, Brown led his squadron eastward towards the enemy position in the *25 de Mayo* followed closely by the *Congresso Nacional* and the *Sarandí*. Norton, for his part, withdrew to get sea room and lure his enemy away from its base. Then, satisfied with the distance but anxious to keep the weather gauge, he ordered his squadron to tack and form a line heading west north-west on the starboard tack.

At 6.30 am, Brown's squadron was almost at right angles to the leading Brazilian ships as it approached their line obliquely from the south-west. Commodore Brown seemed full of confidence that he would be able to cut the enemy line and fall on some of the smaller ships in the rear before their companions could rescue them. It was nevertheless a dangerous manoeuvre. With the wind northerly, the Brazilians held the weather gauge and could turn and fall on the Argentinians any time they wished. No wonder that some of Brown's captains were highly nervous and used any excuse to leave the scene of battle. Brown, however, seemed oblivious to the danger, pacing his quarterdeck in full dress uniform, issuing tots of rum to inspire the crew and calling for repeated 'vivas' for the patria. At 6.43 am, the *25 de Mayo* began to exchange fire with the brig *29 de Agosto* which had strayed out of the main Brazilian formation. But Captain Norton was preparing a nasty surprise. Before Brown could reach the centre of the enemy line, the *Niterói* suddenly hoisted a string of signal flags causing the ships in the Brazilian van to turn in succession and head towards him. If the Argentinian squadron continued its course it would sail into a trap and be caught between two fires.

Seeing the danger, Brown turned and retreated west. But it was too late. The *25 de Mayo* was immediately assailed by fire from the leading Brazilian corvettes – Eyre's *Itaparica*, Beaurepaire's *Maria da Glória* and Hayden's black-painted *Liberal* – as, one by one, they turned and came within range. The *Congresso Nacional* was struck aloft and, losing its main topsail halyards, dropped out of the line and headed promptly for Buenos Aires and safety, accompanied by the uninjured schooner *Sarandí*. The *General Balcarce* and the *Independencia* likewise turned back to avoid Norton's trap, followed by the *República Argentina* which fired a long distance broadside which missed the enemy but, to Brown's exasperation, hit the *25 de Mayo*. The *Oriental Argentina* too ran for it. Some of the privateer's officers were so alarmed that they had deserted their posts. Soon the Argentine squadron was in headlong retreat, the flagship – in the rear – being subjected to a devastating pounding from the chasing Brazilian warships. At the end of three hours the *25 de Mayo* was almost unmanageable. Rigging and hull had been shot to pieces and the decks were heaped with wounded including Flag-Captain Tomas Espora who was hit first in the arm then in the leg.

Only the schooner *Rio de la Plata* was on hand to give assistance, engaged so fiercely that it shot away all its cartridges and was forced to make new ones out of sailors' shirts and trousers. Watching Rosales' efforts, Brown turned to Lieutenant Shannon on the *25 de Mayo* and said admiringly, 'Malcolm, that lad certainly knows how to fight!'

But the damage to the flagship was now so serious that Brown had himself rowed to the nearest large warship, the *República Argentina*. Climbing aboard the brig, he furiously berated Captain Clark, told him he was a disgrace to his uniform and put him under arrest. Then, hoisting his flag, Brown turned to confront the advancing Brazilians. By this time, both squadrons were approaching the shoaling waters near Los Pozes with the wind turning north-westerly and strengthening. Nervous of the obvious navigational hazards, the heavier Brazilian ships had already begun to haul off, leaving the shallower draught brigs *Caboclo* and the *29 de Agosto* to engage the *República Argentina* and continue the pursuit. As the shot smashed into Brown's new flagship it began to suffer as much as the old. At one stage Captain Grenfell hailed the Argentinian commander, and invited him to strike his colours and take tea in the *Caboclo*'s cabin. Brown called back that his colours were nailed to the mast, then unleashed a broadside on the Imperial brig which left one dead and five wounded, including Grenfell himself whose right arm was shattered.

By noon the leading ships of the two squadrons were near to the shallows by the Outer Roads with the wind rising to storm force. Argentinian gunboats began to pull out from Buenos Aires, some to form a defensive line, others to tow in the stricken *25 de Mayo*. In those conditions it was a difficult job. Now near to sinking, the corvette was blown into the mud where it lay beached while the hospital ship *Pepa* took off the dead and wounded. With difficulty the other ships reached the channel and anchored, Brown in the *República Argentina* – now badly damaged in the hull and leaking badly – covering the last stages of the retreat with the help of the gunboats. Further action was impossible. Eliza Norton, standing on her gun in the *Niterói* described the scene:

The first thing I saw was the flagship of the Buenos Aires admiral aground, abandoned and a complete wreck. His flag had been hoisted in one of the smaller ships which was retreating in good order. I looked round at our own vessel and found it as much of a wreck as our antagonist: her sails were filled with holes, her masts and yards full of shot, cannon balls were stuck in her sides, and the decks were covered in muck and blood.[14]

The leading Brazilian ships hauled off and, joining the rest of the squadron, began to repair their damage and care for their casualties. In all, there were six dead and twenty wounded who were carried off to the military hospital in Montevideo in the *Caboclo*. These included John Pascoe Grenfell, Captain José Raphael de Carvalho of the *29 de Agosto* – both hit in the arm – and Sublieutenant James Taylor of the *Niterói* who had been shot in the stomach.[15] In the battle, the ships had suffered much in their sails and rigging, but the only serious casualty was the *Itaparica* which had lost her foretopmast. Norton was therefore able to carry out the necessary repairs at sea. Within a week, the Imperial squadron was full restored and once more enforcing the blockade of Buenos Aires.[16]

Brown's report on what is called the Battle of Lara-Quilmes was a model of brevity. 'Provoked into leaving' his anchorage, he wrote to the Minister of War and Marine, 'we have fought but not overcome the enemy: But permit me to assure Your Excellency that the Nation is still free!' The excited citizens of Buenos Aires had once more been the witnesses of the last desperate stages of the battle, and the heroism of Brown, Rosales and their crews was soon being talked about. President Rivadavia issued a decree expressing thanks and admiration. Commenting on the battle, the newspapers reflected the mood and attempted to deflect public opinion from the fact that they had witnessed a crushing defeat by dwelling on the bravery involved in attacking an enemy so superior in numbers and fighting against such odds. And once again, they used the alleged admiration of their enemies to prove the point. In issue no 70, *El Mensagero Argentino* wrote that:

Norton assured the captain of the English packet [viz, the *Queensbury*] which anchored in this port on 1 August that Admiral Brown had fought with extraordinary valour. The result of the action ... has demonstrated once again that bravery and decision can overcome numbers. [It was] a combat in which the unbeatable Brown and the valiant men who follow him, after seeking an enemy incomparably more powerful, fought unflinchingly, shed their blood and maintained their posts.

Nevertheless, the Argentinian Government was reluctant to release casualty figures and admitted to only 18 dead and 30 wounded, although private letters to Montevideo described the ships as being like slaughterhouses and told of at least 90 in the hospitals.[17] Consul Hood and Pinto Guedes reported rumours of over 100 men killed. The hospitals and the streets themselves were full of wounded. Patriotic citizens raised public subscriptions for the officers and men of the squadron, and the enthusiastic amateurs of the British community put on two more plays to raise funds. But the sight of shattered ships, and of the Brazilian squadron chasing Argentinian vessels into the shallows had been visible to all. The battle of 30 July had been a disaster and, with the Brazilians under new and aggressive command, the omens for the future were gloomy. Valour was not enough. Woodbine Parish put things in a nutshell when he wrote to Foreign Secretary Canning: 'The action, although it has added to Brown's already well established character for gallantry, has shown that if the Brazilians chose to fight, their superior numbers and weight of metal must give them a decided superiority.'[18] Commodore Brown was under no illusions. Not only was the size of the Imperial fleet giving the blockade of both merchantmen and warships an extra bite, but the tactics being followed by James Norton were seriously restricting his freedom of manoeuvre. Norton had tightened the screw and his days of rampaging freely over the River Plate were over. Brown and the Government had to devise new ways of waging war against the Empire of Brazil.

PART III: THE WAR ON TRADE

CHAPTER 10

THE CLIMAX OF THE BRAZILIAN BLOCKADE

As the largest naval power in the Americas, it was inevitable that Brazil would use a blockade of Buenos Aires as its major weapon in the war against the Argentine Provinces. The seat of government, the heart of pro-war sentiment and the centre of a flourishing sea-borne commerce which linked the trade of the world with the produce and wealth of the interior, Buenos Aires was an obvious target. The abolition of the old Spanish restrictions had led to a dramatic expansion of trade in the western River Plate, so that by 1825, the value of foreign goods entering the region had reached £2 million carried in 387 ships.[1] In return, the United Provinces supplied the world with specie and with hides, tallow, jerked beef and other products of its booming cattle industry. Buenos Aires had become an international emporium, handling cottons, woollens, earthenware and clothing from Britain; lace, silks and cambrics from France; wine, oil and brandy from Spain; sugar, rum, coffee and tobacco from Brazil; flour and lumber from the USA; and a miscellany of goods – like glass, cordage, gin, firearms and tar – from a host of other countries. But it was Britain which dominated this international kaleidoscope. In 1825, goods worth over £1 million were imported in 95 British vessels.

In second position, £360,000-worth of American produce arrived in 107 ships; while in third place, French luxury goods to the value of £260,000 were unloaded from the holds of 29 merchant vessels.[2] With war in the offing, it was clear that Brazil would try to stifle this thriving trade and the revenue which the Argentinian Government derived from it.

On 10 December 1826, the Brazilian Government declared war on Buenos Aires. The coasts of the United Provinces were put under blockade, the licensing of privateers was authorized and the rights of the Crown were waived in respect of prizes captured by ships of the Imperial Navy. This was normal practice among maritime powers and meant that, as an incentive, the value of all prizes would now be distributed according to a set formula among the officers and crews of the vessels which captured them. During its War of Independence, Brazil had used traditional Portuguese prize laws as the legal framework for the conduct of blockades, but the unorthodox nature of both the conflict and the campaign followed by Lord Cochrane had caused enormous difficulties. On this occasion therefore, the Brazilian Government kept its options open and, instead of enacting a body of written rules on the subject, followed the British practice of leaving the prize courts free to interpret the law according to accepted international practice and relevant Portuguese and Brazilian precedents.[3]

The need to cripple the trade of the United Provinces was clear to Minister of Foreign Affairs Santo Amaro and to his colleague in the Ministry of Marine, the Marquis of Paranaguá, but so were the potential problems which might result from seizing neutral merchant vessels, many of which flew the flags of the most powerful nations on earth. On 17 December therefore, Lobo was sent secret instructions, which ordered him to impose a strict blockade on the ports of Argentina, but

> warning Your Excellency that in order to avoid disputes in the future you should proceed with the necessary circumspection in respect to the ships and vessels of friendly powers which may be attempting to enter the ports referred to; using only minimum force if they fail to comply with your warning and attempt to break the blockade in any way.

To reinforce the message that neutrals were to be treated with kid gloves, the Minister of Marine wrote again on 24 December, warning Lobo of the imminent arrival in the Plate of the British commander-in-chief, Sir George Eye, in the 74-gun *Wellesley*, and adding:

> the warnings which, in accordance with the Aviso of 17 December, you will give to the vessels of friendly powers must be official in order that they may constitute documentary evidence by which your proceedings against them may be justified.[4]

Although they did not know it, in their anxiety to avoid antagonizing neutral states, the Brazilian Government's orders had made a concession on the enforcement of the blockade which was to have disastrous long-term results.

On 21 December 1826, Vice Admiral Lobo issued the formal notification of blockade. All ports along the coast of the United Provinces and of the Banda Oriental were placed under interdiction with immediate effect, although neutral vessels already in the area were granted a period of two weeks in which to unload their cargoes and leave. Alas, it took ten days for the news to reach Buenos Aires, and its arrival produced a wave of panic. British merchants immediately petitioned Consul-General Woodbine Parish protesting that with only four days remaining before the expiry of 14 days grace, it would be impossible for their ships to unload and put to sea. In company with the other foreign consuls, Parish wrote urgently to Admiral Lobo explaining the problem and asking that the time be extended to give neutral shipping time to leave. Colonel Forbes, the pro-republican consul for the United States wrote in similar terms, demanding an extension and threatening to write again to the Brazilian Vice Admiral to expound his Government's interpretation of what was permissible under the laws of blockade.[5]

Lobo recognized the problem and acted with moderation. On 7 January 1826, he replied to the foreign consuls agreeing to delay the beginning of the 14-day period until the date on which his squadron made its appearance off Buenos Aires.[6] A week later

Lobo's ships could be seen cruising to the west of the Ortiz Bank, and on 25 January, Captain Gleddon anchored the brig-of-war *29 de Agosto* in the Buenos Aires roadstead flying a flag of truce and handed over the second notification of blockade. As an extra concession, Vice Admiral Lobo had decided to delay the beginning of the 14-day period until 31 January. This solved the difficulty, and neutral vessels were able to leave within the time allowed. The first problem of the blockade had been successfully defused.

By the beginning of the nineteenth century, naval blockades were a widely used weapon of war, but there were basic principles which had to be observed if they were to be legal and accepted. The first was that neutral governments and their ships had to be formally notified of the fact of a blockade, and that a sufficient period of time had to elapse before ships were liable to seizure. The second was that a belligerent was required to have enough warships on blockade duty to enforce it. And the third was that, to be valid, a blockade had to be continuous. In other words, if warships left their stations or returned to port voluntarily for any reason other than stress of weather, then the blockade ceased to be operative. The Brazilian commander was aware of these conditions and of the legal minefield constituted by international prize rules. Lobo was therefore typically wary about the formalities, and went out of his way to inform foreign consuls and naval officers that with over 40 vessels at his disposal his blockade would indeed be both effective and continuous.[7]

But aside from the broad principles of blockade, there was a wide range of opinion as to how belligerent states should treat neutral vessels. At one extreme, the United States was a leading exponent of 'free trade and sailors' rights' and favoured a regime which severely restricted the actions of the blockaders. Its position was that a blockading force should not only be in the vicinity of an effected port, but should actually be in sight. It also argued that it was not enough for a belligerent to inform a neutral government of the existence of a blockade; every ship had to be warned individually and could only be seized if it then attempted to defy the blockade. Even before the war had begun, the American consul in Rio de Janeiro, the ill-mannered and hot-headed Condy

Raguet, had written to the Brazilian Government explaining the view of the United States, and arguing that it was in the interests of all American countries to interpret neutral rights liberally, rather than follow the harsher view that prevailed in Europe.[8]

The American position was re-expressed on 13 February, when Colonel Forbes carried out his threat and wrote to Lobo challenging the Brazilian conduct of the blockade. In a letter which was given wide publicity in Buenos Aires and secured great popularity for the writer from his fellow republicans, Forbes accused the Brazilian Navy of conducting an 'imaginary' blockade by breaking the basic requirements of presence and of continuity. To claim that the coast of Patagonia was under legitimate blockade because of the solitary presence of the corvette *Maria da Glória* was unacceptable, he argued, and the squadron's frequent returns to Montevideo had left the Plate unguarded for long periods during which both the blockade, and any prizes taken, were invalid. Forbes claimed that many vessels had reached Buenos Aires without even sighting the Brazilian squadron and, to prove his point, named nine merchantmen which had arrived there without the slightest difficulty since the beginning of the blockade. A weary Lobo ignored the complaint and merely deflected it to Rio de Janeiro. On 4 May, however, Lobo made a major concession when, in response to a protest from Captain Elliot of the USS *Cyane*, he agreed that in future the area covered by the blockade would be limited to the estuary of the River Plate.

Unlike the United States, Great Britain supported the Brazilian position. As a naval power itself which relied on blockades in time of war, Britain was keen to ensure that the principle of strict blockade was maintained unhindered by petty restrictions designed to protect neutrals. On the question of notification, its view was that once neutral states had been officially informed of the existence of a blockade, it was their responsibility, and not that of the belligerent, to ensure that their merchant ships were informed. Thus, when news of the outbreak of war was received in February 1826, the British Government immediately recognized the legality of the Brazilian blockade, advertised its existence in the *Gazette*, and wrote to its diplomatic representatives in the region ordering them to observe it. Technical infringements, but not the principle could be challenged. And when letters and petitions from the owners of British ships seized as a result of the blockade began to arrive in the Foreign Office demanding Government intervention, they received a firm refusal. As Canning explained, blockades were legitimate, ships taken in contravention would be judged by process of law, and official British interference was only possible in cases of blatant miscarriages of justice.[9] The result of this attitude was that the number of British ships sailing for the South Atlantic fell dramatically, partly because of the obvious dangers of entering a war zone, partly because of the impossibility of securing insurance.

An experienced diplomat, Woodbine Parish in Buenos Aires had already anticipated his Government's approach. In March, he reported on the Forbes initiative with undisguised hostility. He did not agree that Brazilian forces in the Plate were inadequate and, commenting on Forbes's case that nine ships had entered Buenos Aires unmolested, demolished each example in turn.[10] On 27 May, following the arrival of the packet ship from England carrying news of the Government's recognition of the Brazilian blockade, he wrote again, confirming that 'it is generally well maintained' and pointing out that it was being enforced by more than 50 ships – although because of the size of the estuary and the uncertainty of the weather the occasional vessel would always slip through. For the first two years of the war, the British Government's view was that the Brazilian blockade was both effectively enforced and continuous.

In accordance with his interpretation of the order to be 'circumspect' with neutrals, Lobo's initial enforcement of the blockade was less than rigorous. In the period from December to February 1826, four British ships got through to Buenos Aires, while nine were intercepted and sent to Montevideo.[11] One of them was Michael Brown's ship *Hutton*. As the ships had left Britain before the news of the blockade had arrived, they were not seized as prizes but merely detained. This was not a recognized practice under international law and caused a protest by Sir George

Eyre and other commanders. In March, Lobo innocently apologized and promised to abandon the practice – but by then the blockade was in force and he had no need of it.[12] Unfortunately, once in the port of Montevideo, the ships were forced to unload and deposit their cargoes ashore. Re-exportation was only possible after the war or once a local resident had put down a substantial cash bond as a guarantee that the vessel would not enter an Argentine port. The last requirement, which amounted to a 'hidden blockade', caused a universal outcry and was eventually abandoned.

Once Admiral Lobo had agreed to extend the time limit for ships to leave Buenos Aires, the only real problem with the British concerned the monthly packets which ran from Falmouth to Buenos Aires via Rio de Janeiro and Montevideo. Carrying mails, cash and passengers, these packets were familiar features of the South American scene. Lobo recognized their usefulness to both sides and agreed that the packet service could continue unhindered subject to endorsement by the Imperial Government. This was given in April 1826. But the problem was raised again in July when Pinto Guedes complained that British packets were carrying both passengers and substantial quantities of money to and from Buenos Aires and were thus aiding the enemy war effort. The matter was referred to Rio de Janeiro, while Woodbine Parish comforted himself with a report from the captain of the packet *Queensbury* that both Admiral Pinto Guedes and Commodore Norton had said that they were unconcerned with what came out of Buenos Aires, only with preventing anything getting in.[13] The Imperial Government took a similar view and was easily persuaded by Consul-General Chamberlain to issue orders in September which banned the landing of passengers and specie in Buenos Aires but allowed packets to carry both away from the city.[14] This was a great relief for British merchants for, as Woodbine Parish explained, the packet service was 'a vital means of remittance' which shipped out £200,000-worth of coin and bullion to Britain every year.

The appointment of Pinto Guedes as Brazilian commander-in-chief brought a new rigour to the blockade. The Admiral was an expert on the subject and immediately adopted the strict interpretation favoured by the British. Aware, for example, that news of the blockade had reached Europe three months earlier, and that the British Government had accepted its legality in February, Pinto Guedes decided that any ship leaving a British port after that date for Buenos Aires was now legal prize. At the end of May therefore, the merchantmen *Monarch* and *Jessey* were seized by Brazilian cruisers. Consul Thomas Hood in Montevideo was less experienced than Woodbine Parish and was less aware of the British position on blockades. In mistaken zeal, he therefore wrote to Pinto Guedes on 28 May protesting against the seizure. Hood argued that while the principle of blockade was acceptable, it was necessary to show an intention to break it before arrests were valid. Referring to the arguments of Colonel Forbes, the consul claimed that the laxity of Lobo's enforcement of the blockade had been such that it had amounted to little more than 'a temporary or casual interdiction of trade with the city of Buenos Aires'. As a result, rumours had grown in England that the blockade had been lifted with the result that both the *Monarch* and *Jessey* had sailed for Montevideo to find out whether it remained in force before going further.[15]

Protests against the blockade were the last thing British ministers wanted from their diplomatic agents. But they need not have worried. Pinto Guedes was an expert on international prize rules. In a reply dated 29 May, he savaged Hood's arguments, explaining that the legality of a blockade did not require the proximity of a blockading force and pointing out that in the Napoleonic Wars the Royal Navy had frequently declared ports blockaded which never saw a British ship. Likewise, it had been established during the blockade of Malta in 1798 that the fact that occasional blockade runners were able to slip past did not invalidate a blockade. Turning to the point that the two ships had been innocently trying to find out if the blockade remained in force, the Brazilian Admiral merely quoted the great British Prize Court judge, Sir William Scott, who had rejected the same argument and had ruled it illegitimate 'to send a vessel to a place under blockade in order to learn the views of the blockaders'. However, Pinto Guedes was not unreasonable. The *Jessey* was released under oath that it was not bound for an Argentinian port; though the *Monarch* was detained. He was not convinced by Hood's claim about the ship's destination and claimed that it had only made for Montevideo after it had been fired on.[16] In the event the 'problem' was solved when the crew of the *Monarch* recaptured the vessel en route to Rio de Janeiro, put Sublieutenant Charles Appleton and his Brazilian prize crew into an open boat and sailed back to Liverpool!

The beginning of war in the River Plate caused immediate concern to the powers whose merchant shipping was most likely to suffer disruption and interference. Warships were sent south to protect national interests. The British South America Squadron took the problem in its stride. Sir John Sinclair's frigate, HMS *Doris*, was posted to Montevideo on almost permanent watch from 24 November 1825, reinforced temporarily by the 74-gun *Wellesley*, flagship of commander-in-chief Sir George Eyre, and the corvette *Jaseur* and the frigate *Briton*. A year later, the same duty fell to HMS *Ganges* flying the flag of his successor, Rear Admiral Sir Robert Otway, supported occasionally by the *Forte*, *Heron* and *Cadmus*. Other nations had to take special steps. The USS *Cyane* was the only American ship on the South America station. Commanded by Captain Jesse Elliot – whose controversial career had included ambiguous service against the British on the Great Lakes and acting as a second in the duel which had resulted in the death of Commodore Stephen Decatur – the *Cyane* remained on lonely vigil off Montevideo and Rio de Janeiro until Congress authorized the deployment of two more warships in April. The USS *Boston* arrived in June and Commodore Biddle's USS *Macedonian* in August. The French Government of Louis XVIII, always keen to fish in troubled waters, sent the brig *Faune* to watch over its interests in February, reinforced in May by Rear Admiral Rosamel with the frigates *Marie-Thérèse* and *L'Arethuse*, the corvette *Moselle*, the brig *Cygne* and the schooner *Provençale*.

The purpose of these moves was to prevent abuses of the blockade and to defend national shipping from privateers. In the event, few of the watching warships found themselves interfering with either privateers or the operations of the blockading squadron during 1826, but their presence prevented excesses and ensured that infringements of the blockade by the Brazilian Navy were immediately followed by protests backed by force. In the months which followed the appointment of Admiral Pinto Guedes, the bag of detained merchant vessels sharply increased. His captains had orders to seize every vessel found in the area.[17] Doubts as to the legality of any arrest, they were told, would be settled in the Prize Court in Montevideo – an unfortunate ruling in view of the inexperience of the presiding judge, Oliveira. Thus between May and July, six British, one American, two French and one Danish merchantmen were seized valued in total at £395,000.[18] Foreign protests immediately followed. Consul Hood complained over the *Monarch* and *Jessey*. Admiral Rosamel protested in similar terms and for similar reasons about the detention of the *Junon* and *Le Courier*. And Commodore Biddell demanded the release of the *Leonidas*, on the grounds that she had sailed from Canton long before news of the blockade could have arrived. On the instructions of their home governments, the Rio legations of Britain, France and the USA protested to the Ministry of Foreign Affairs, which found itself attempting simultaneously to satisfy three maritime powers, each of which had a widely differing interpretation of the law of blockade.

Meanwhile the Imperial Navy had to deal with the Argentinian privateers which began to fan out into the Atlantic in search of the vulnerable Brazilian coasting trade. During the first six months of 1826, the priority given to the arming of Brown's squadron in Buenos Aires meant that only five privateers managed to put to sea, four of which had no luck at all. The new tactics and strength of the Brazilian Navy convinced the Argentinian Government that commerce raiding rather than naval action was now the best weapon. But it was a slow business, and the Brazilian Navy were constantly on the alert. Only 14 Argentinian privateers were active during the 1826, and of these, no less than eight were eventually captured or destroyed.[19] As most were commanded and manned by foreigners thirsty for loot, there were inevitable examples of rapacious and brutal behaviour. The Brazilians reciprocated, and there were complaints of violence and looting by boarding parties from the brigs *Empreendador* and *Independência ou Morte*. Cruisers of the Imperial Navy began to seize any ship which was manned by foreigners, had no obvious cargo and was in possession of artillery as a potential privateer, removing its crew and sending it into port under arrest. In many cases they were right, but it provoked more trouble with neutrals.

The impressment of foreign seamen to satisfy the Imperial Navy's desperate manpower shortage, and the treatment of crews which had been taken to Brazilian men-of-war from captured prizes also caused angry protests. There were claims that men from the *Atlantic*, *Leonidas*, *Le Junon*, *Fortuna* and other ships[20] had either been forced to enlist in the Brazilian service, or been punished and starved if they refused to work their passages. The worst offenders were said to be Captains James Shepherd of the *Piranga*, a strict disciplinarian, and John Charles Pritz of the *Dona Paula* – a Danish officer who was said to have such a grudge against the British because of Nelson's victory at Copenhagen that he placed the whole of the crew of the prize *Atlantic* in irons.

In Rio de Janeiro, US Consul Condy Raguet had spent two years unsuccessfully demanding compensation for seizures of American ships and seamen during the Brazilian War of Independence and the subsequent rebellion in Pernambuco. News of the capture of American ships and men in the Plate now reduced him to unreasoning fury. Recommending to Congress that he should be instructed to 'demand the immediate surrender with damages of all vessels which have been, or may be captured in opposition to the laws respecting blockade ... the suspension of taking American seamen from American ships, and to demand satisfaction for any aggressions committed',[21] Raguet bombarded the Ministry of Foreign Affairs with rudely worded demands for action, passing on grossly exaggerated claims for compensation.

The atmosphere was made worst by two incidents which had taken place far from the River Plate. One was the arrest and looting of the schooner *Pilar* off the African Coast by the Brazilian cruiser *Empreendador* commanded by the French lieutenant Clemente Poutier. In fact, the *Pilar* had already been taken by HMS *Redwing* as a suspected slaver and was on its way to the nearest port with a British prize crew under the command of the master's assistant, Mr Fawconer. Although the schooner's papers were not in order, the truth of the matter must have been obvious to all. Nevertheless, on arrival in Rio in July, the *Pilar* was charged with piracy while Mr Fawconer and his men were imprisoned for six months before the combined protests of Consul-General Chamberlain, Rear Admiral Sir George Eyre and newly arrived Ambassador Robert Gordon got them out.[22] Lieutenant Poutier was later court martialled, dismissed the service and – in spite of his bravery during the Patagonia expedition – was briefly imprisoned. At the same time, US Consul Condy Raguet was reaching the climax of another series of complaints following the seizure of the American brig *Ruth* in June in mid-Atlantic while on her way from Gibraltar to the Plate by the *Independência ou Morte* on the justified suspicion that she was heading for Buenos Aires to obtain a privateering commission.

Confident of a quick victory in the war, the authorities in Rio at first ignored the wave of international protest about the seizure of neutral ships and the treatment of their crews. Arguing ingenuously that individual prize questions were *sub judice*, ministers attempted to side-step the problem by saying they could not intervene politically in a legal matter. But the complexity of the procedures, the absence of clear Brazilian prize laws, and the inexperience of the judges who effectively had to make them, removed all confidence in the legal process. By the end of 1826 no single prize had even reached the appeals stage and international patience was wearing thin. There were also bitter complaints that both the inexperienced Judge Oliveira of the Prize Court in Montevideo, and the military officers who comprised the Superior Admiralty Court in Rio, had accepted and were enforcing Pinto Guedes' own interpretation of the law of blockade.[23] As a result, protests were proving to be futile. Meanwhile, to the dismay of the diplomats, the blockading squadron seized 16 more neutral ships – the Swedish *Anders*, the French *Salvador*, *Jules*, *Le Jenny* and *La Belle Gabrielle*, the American *Flora*, *Matilda* and *Pioneer* and the British *Caroline*, *Dickens*, *Cocquito*, *Henry* and *Isabella*, *Agenoria*, *George*, *Utopia* and *John*. The case of the *Cocquito* caused an immediate furore. A well built schooner intended originally for the slave trade, she would have made an ideal warship and Pinto Guedes began the conversion even before condemnation by the prize court. Only diplomatic protests and an order from the Emperor stopped him.

The enforcement of the blockade by the Brazilian Navy reached its highest point of effectiveness during 1826. Indeed, during the six months which followed the Battle of Lara-Quilmes in July, the Argentinians mounted no serious challenge in the River Plate. The National Squadron was laid up while Commodore Brown went off to search for the frigates expected from Chile and to raid enemy commerce in the Atlantic. As a result, the Brazilian Navy dominated the estuary, strangling enemy commerce and seizing all but a handful of the neutral merchantmen which risked the voyage to the Plate. From February to June, only 18 ships managed to avoid Norton's squadron and enter Buenos Aires. Between July and December two ships got through.[24] As a result, the price of foreign commodities went up by 250 per cent and customs revenue plummeted from £429,300 in 1825 to £81,900 in 1826.[25] The naval blockade of the River Plate was proving to be Brazil's most successful weapon in its struggle with the United Provinces.

CHAPTER 11

'BLACKGUARDS OF THE MOST CUT THROAT DESCRIPTION': THE ARGENTINIAN WAR ON TRADE

Just as a blockade of the River Plate was the obvious tactic for the Brazilians with their powerful Navy, so the disruption of Brazil's extensive maritime trade through the use of privately owned corsairs was an obvious strategy for the Argentinians with their tiny naval forces. Indeed, attacks on Spanish commerce had been common during the War of Independence, and there were still plenty of national and foreign residents in Buenos Aires who had experience of owning or commanding privateers. Likewise, the war had given the Government of the United Provinces experience of the organizational aspects of licensed commerce raiding, and the necessary legislation already existed. This was the 'Reglamento de Corso Provisional' of 15 May 1817.

The Argentinian Government declared war on 1 January 1826, and it was no surprise that only the following day it authorized privateering against the Brazilian flag and reactivated the 'Reglamento' of 1817. Based on Spanish prize legislation, this awarded the value of enemy ships and property taken at sea to the captors and laid down detailed procedures for the inspection and licensing of privateers. For its part, the Government undertook to assist in manning and arming these vessels. As was the practice with other seafaring nations, the 'Reglamento' established a detailed code of conduct to regulate the behaviour of privateers, and owners were required to pay a bond of 10,000 pesos (£2000) to guarantee that it would be observed. For example, privateers had to fly the national flag; could attack enemy ships at will but were forbidden to use violence in the case of neutrals; had to retain ships' papers and logs as evidence; and were required to leave all cargoes untouched and sealed until judged by an official prize tribunal. Significantly also, for a nation about to go to war with the largest slave-owning state in the world, there were rules for the disposal of captured slaves. All were regarded as free once they reached Argentinian territory – although adult males were required to serve as soldiers for four years – and to ensure that privateersmen were sufficiently motivated, the Government offered 50 pesos (later increased to 200 pesos) 'head-money' for every slave released. To complete the picture, on 10 April, the Government issued an 'Ordenanza' which set up a network of prize courts and established the rules for their operation.

The possibility of waging war against Brazilian commerce through the use of privately owned ships was a cheap and attractive one to the hard pressed Government of the United Provinces and, in the enthusiasm of the first year of the war, 118 privateering licences – internationally described as Letters of Marque – were distributed. Of this number, batches of 34 and 58 were sent respectively to agents in the United States, Chile and Colombia bearing the names of obviously fictitious ships which could be changed when the real names were known. A third batch of 14 was reserved for the use of Commodore Brown and the Navy.[1] Unfortunately for the Argentinians, this mass distribution proved to be little more than a paper exercise and only a small number of these licences were actually taken up. In the event, the war against Brazilian commerce during 1826 was restricted to the activities of the 13 privateers which sailed from ports in the River Plate.

To Argentinian merchants and shipowners, the return on investment in a commerce raider in terms of captured ships and merchandise could be substantial. A typical privateering contract laid down that 50 per cent of prize money would be the property of the owner, while 16 per cent was divided among the officers and 33 per cent among the crew. The 'armadores' – that is, those who owned and fitted-out the privateers – were generally well established and respectable Argentinian or Spanish merchants, diversifying into commerce raiding either as a gamble or to make up for the loss of their normal business as a result of the blockade. Of the 30 or so active *armadores*, six were particularly successful – the Basque-born Vicente Casares (owner of the *Lavalleja*, *República Argentina*, *Vengadora Argentina* and *General Brandzen*); the Spaniard José Julio Arriola (of the *Hijo de Mayo*, *Hijo de Julio* and *Cometa*); and the Argentinians Severiano Prudente, Juan Aguirre, Martin Bonorino and Francisco Ugarte (who between them owned individually or jointly such ships as *El Gaucho*, *Oriental Argentina*, *Vencedor de Ituzaingú*, *Sin Par* and *Presidente*). For these and other lucky ones, the value of captured ships and cargoes was the foundation of private fortunes which made them into powerful political and commercial figures in the early days of the Argentinian Republic.

In the early years of the war, the 30 or so *armadores* who received the Letters of Marque tended to be merchants or shipowners, but as the war went on, owner-captains appeared on the scene as successful commanders invested their prize money in vessels of their own – men like the Londoner James Harris of the *Hijo de Mayo*, the Catalan Antonio Cuyas of the *Rayo Argentino*, the Italian José Clavelli of the *Estrella del Sur* and the American William Wright of the *Constante*. The size of these ships also varied widely. At one extreme, the *Cometa* and *República Argentina* were little more than row-boats of less than nine tons, capable of little more than dashing out to seize unarmed merchantmen in sheltered waters; while at the other, the *General Brandzen* and *Presidenta* were powerful sea-going vessels of 200 tons well able to take on the smaller warships of the Imperial Navy.

But even if fortunes were made, it was a risky business. Of the 57 commerce raiders who are recorded as being active on the High Seas or in the Plate during the war, 27 were captured and 18 wrecked. Many made no captures at all, and of the 405 prizes taken, 139 reached an Argentinian port only to be condemned by the prize courts.[2] To prosper in the privateer business, both luck and skilful commanders were needed. Fortunately for Buenos Aires, there was no shortage of either. The rewards to be gained by legalized commerce raiding attracted captains of audacity and skill, and the chances of growing rich at the expense of the Brazilian coastal trade brought seafarers flocking to Buenos Aires from the four corners of the globe in search of loot and excitement. In a private letter to his father, Consul-General Woodbine Parish described them as 'blackguards of the most-cut throat description and the most proper fellows for the purpose'.[3] And whereas officers and men of British and American origin tended to predominate in the official naval forces, the senior ranks of the privateering service attracted members of more individualistic nationalities. Of the 50 most audacious and successful privateer commanders, for example, 10 were from North America, 9 from Italy, 7 from France, 5 from Britain, and 3 from Spain and Argentina. Among the crews, the proportion of men from Italy, France and Latin America was greater, although the predominant group in any particular ship tended to have the same nationality as its commander.[4]

The threat of large scale commerce raiding under the blue and white flag of Buenos Aires at first caused consternation among foreign naval commanders on the South America station. Rear Admiral Sir George Eyre had little experience of such things, and writing to London on 26 January he asked for guidance on how to deal with the 'swarm of privateers (many of a piratical nature) which were likely to appear'. What was the legal definition of a privateer? What proportion of the crew should be from the state which licensed it? To which British Vice-Admiralty Court should captures be sent?[5] In the event he need not have worried. The operations of Buenos Aires privateers in 1826 were modest in scale and there were no incidents involving neutral merchantmen. During this early period of the war, the attentions of both foreign consuls and commanding admirals were focused exclusively on the Brazilian blockade.

The Buenos Aires Government had passed all the legislation necessary for the inspection and registration of privateers by the end of January, but for much of 1826 priority was given to the manning and arming of Commodore Brown's squadron. As a result only five privateers were active between January and June. Of these, four had no luck at all. The first, *Liberdad del Sur*, was captured immediately by Bartholomew Hayden of the *Pirajá* in January; the *Escudero* was taken by the *Empreendador* as soon as it reached its cruising station off the coast of Africa in June; *El Gaucho* only took one prize which was judged to be illegal; and the commerce raiding career of the fourth, the *Oriental Argentina* was delayed for months after it had become unprofitably involved in the Battle of Lara-Quilmes in July.

The fifth and largest privateer, the 182-ton *Lavalleja*, was already at sea when war was declared under the command of the audacious François Fourmantine – the latest representative of a long-established family of French corsairs. Fitting-out in Buenos Aires during 1825, the *Lavalleja* had dodged the Argentinian patrols in November and, hoisting the rebel Uruguayan colours, had begun a successful two-month cruise off Rio Grande. During this period, Fourmantine claimed 21 Brazilian prizes, five of which (*Emilia*, *Andorinha*, *Flor do Brasil*, *Felicidade* and *São José Diligente* with 384 slaves on board) successfully reached the tiny port of Carmen in Patagonia. The Imperial Navy began the hunt. The *Independência ou Morte* scoured the waters off Rio de Janeiro, the *Maria da Glória* cruised between Rio Grande and the Rio Negro, while the brig *Rio da Plata* patrolled the coast of Patagonia. Between them the Imperial ships re-took four of the prizes and drove one ashore while two more were recaptured by their crews. The only casualties were Captain Alexander William Anderson and a boat's crew from the *Rio da Plata* who, ignorant of the declaration of war, landed innocently near Carmen in January and were seized by the Argentinian authorities who had just received news overland of the declaration of war. But the first voyage of the *Lavalleja* was also its last. Attempting to sneak back along the coast to Buenos Aires from its temporary base in Patagonia, the privateer was intercepted by an Imperial detachment and was driven ashore near Salado.

After the Battle of Lara-Quilmes, the Argentinian emphasis moved to commerce raiding. Many national ships were laid up, their crews and officers free to join the privateers whose manning was now a priority. As a result, 19 more corsairs were commissioned and active in the next 12 months although, like their predecessors, they had mixed fortunes. Eight privateers – of which five were taken or wrecked – captured nothing. But the other 11 more than compensated their owners in terms of prize ships and property. Managing to evade the tight Brazilian blockade, they suddenly appeared in the waters of the Paraná or in the shipping lanes in the Atlantic snapping up unsuspecting prizes.

A popular cruising ground for Argentina's smaller privateers were the waters off Rio Grande and the mouth of the Plate itself, where defined shipping lanes made the coasters easy prey. The first alarm was in June 1826, with the appearance of the 17-ton lugger *Hijo de Mayo*, commanded by the Englishman James Harris and manned by a crew of 36 English and Americans. Venturing no further than the mouth of the estuary, Harris intercepted the Imperial transports *Murmurador* and *Bella Flor* loaded with stores and munitions, and seized both. In October, her sister ship, *Hijo de Julio*, appeared off Rio Grande under the command of Fourmantine. There, in just over a month, six prizes were taken, four of which – the *Penha*, *Anna Maria*, *Lilia* and *Amelia* – safely reached port loaded with rum, sugar, flour, wine and coffee. These four ships and their cargoes secured the fortunes of both their commanders and of owner José Arriola. Arriola's bank balance continued to increase the following year when in February, his tiny *Cometa* appeared in the same waters under the command of an Englishman, John Thomas, and took two prizes. One was recaptured, but the *Ines Maria* reached Patagonia safely to be sold for a useful 5000 pesos – or £1000. A month later, the *Sin Par* was in the area under Swedish captain Tidblon. In six weeks, he captured an impressive bag of nine vessels, five of which reached home to raise around 20,000 pesos for the *armadores* Francisco Ugarte and the ubiquitous Arriola.

For the bigger sea-going privateers a more popular haunt was the waters round Cape Frio, the landfall for all vessels from the north heading for Rio de Janeiro. The first 18 months of the war saw 5 Argentinian vessels cruising in this area capturing, between them an astonishing total of 42 prizes. The first and financially most successful was the brig *Oriental Argentina* under its dashing Dutch captain (of French origin), Pierre Dautant. Eventually managing to evade the blockade of Buenos Aires in November 1826, he headed for Cape Frio and captured three merchantmen, one of which was the 700-ton *Condessa de Ponte*, richly laden and inward bound from the Indies. Once condemned, this ship alone brought a small fortune to its *armadores*, Aguirre and Prudente. Then, in February 1827, came the *Union Argentina* under Captain Thomas Prouting and the *General Mancilla* commanded by the American Thomas Beazley, recently exonerated by the Corales court martial. Prouting took *Flor de la Puerta* and the *Santa Rita*; while Beazley took the *Ninfa Veloz* and the *Alejandro*. Then, finding that the *General Mancilla* was in need of repairs, Beazley transferred his crew to the latter and went on to capture four more merchantmen. This time it was Medrano and Casares who, as *armadores*, benefitted. The last two commerce raiders – the schooners *Vengadora Argentina* belonging to Casares, and the *General Brown*, originally the captured Brazilian warship *Maria Isabel* – appeared off Cape Frio in April 1827. Between them the ships made 19 captures, of which 9 reached Salado or Patagonia in safely. For good measure, Captain Cuyas of the *Vengadora Argentina* mounted a raid on the Brazilian village of Buzias to the north of Cape Frio and sacked the place.

At the other extreme, Argentina's tiny oared corsairs were also active in the upper reaches of the Plate Estuary. Four weeks after returning in the *Hijo de Julio*, Fourmantine was afloat again, this time patrolling the waters of the Uruguay and the Paraná in command of 17 men in the tiny four-ton *República Argentina*. Once more his luck held and he immediately snapped up two Brazilian oared privateers with four small prizes. A few months later, the three-ton *Republicana* was doing the same.

But in addition to attacks on unarmed merchantships, there were some remarkable feats of daring. In September, the *Profeta Bandara* commanded by Cesar Fournier, an audacious Italian-born 38-year-old of French *emigré* origin, was driven ashore and wrecked in the Banda Oriental. Unperturbed, Fournier transported his crew overland to Maldonado and overwhelmed the eight-gun *Leal Paulistana* in a fierce night attack by boats. The gunboat was promptly bought by the authorities to sail under Argentinian colours as the *Maldonado*. But the incident made Fournier overconfident. When his *21 de Septiembre* ran aground off Colonia two months later, he attempted to repeat the performance. But this time his prey was the 12-gun Imperial brig *Rio da Plata*, now commanded by 24-year-old Sublieutenant José Lamego Costa with a crew of 75 which included his younger brothers Jesuino and Fermino serving as volunteers. Assailed on all sides by 200 privateersmen, the defenders beat most of them off with gunfire, then, fighting hand to hand, repelled with heavy losses the ones who managed to reach their decks. The grateful merchants of Montevideo raised a public subscription to celebrate the *Rio da Plata*'s victory. Her commander was promoted, and young Jesuino commissioned as the first step in a career which would lead to his becoming an admiral and a baron.

A threatening cloud had however appeared on the horizon for neutral ship owners. At first there had been no unpleasant incidents between Argentinian privateers and foreign vessels, but in January 1827, the British cutter *Dove* was detained by an Imperial cruiser for illegal sealing. Sent in to Montevideo with a Brazilian crew – but alas without papers – she was seized in turn as a prize of war by the privateer *Cometa*. It took months of diplomatic activity to sort that one out.[6] But a more audacious event took place on 28 March, when Fournier seized the British brig *Florida* for illegal fishing off the Castillos Rocks at the north-eastern extremity of the Plate. The captain and the crew were put ashore, the brig was converted into the privateer *Venganza* and, under Buenos Aires colours sailed to the Brazilian coast on a commerce raiding expedition. In two months she took 14 prizes. Meanwhile, back in Buenos Aires, Woodbine Parish and Lord Ponsonby launched a vigorous diplomatic offensive,[7] demanding the return of the ship and the court martial of Fournier. Captain Lord Thynne of HMS *Ranger* was sent off to find and recapture the brig. In Buenos Aires, the problem was passed from department to department, becoming an increasing embarrassment. Eventually, on her return in July, the *Florida/Venganza* was handed over to the British Legation and restored to its owners. Fournier was tried and, predictably, acquitted.[8]

In the first 18 months of the war, Argentinian privateers seized 160 Brazilian merchantmen and coasters. Not all managed to reach the safe havens of Carmen in Patagonia or Salado at the southeastern tip of the Plate, but the value of the 50 ships and cargoes which successfully made it brought instant wealth to the privateersmen and their owners.[9] The triumphs of these commerce raiders were also good news, and to raise public morale in Buenos Aires, *La Gaceta Mercantil* published a complete list in its edition of 22 June 1827. In Brazil, the loss of so many vessels large and small – mostly very small – may have caused momentary panic but, scattered as the losses were over an 18-month period, they were not important enough to seriously disrupt the Empire's enormous coasting trade. They were, nevertheless, an unpleasant foretaste of what was to come.

CHAPTER 12

BROWN'S RAID ON THE
SOUTH ATLANTIC

The lessons of the Battle of Lara-Quilmes and the increased efficiency of Norton's blockading squadron caused the Government of Buenos Aires to change its maritime policy. In place of confrontation, it decided to give priority to commerce raiding and even to use the squadron daily expected from Chile in this role. It was known that Colonel Vasquez had succeeded in his mission and had purchased (through the device of a public auction to maintain Chilean neutrality) the frigate *O'Higgins* and the corvettes *Independencia* and *Chacabuco* for a modest 168,000 pesos. On 23 May, Argentinian flags had been hoisted, the *O'Higgins* and *Independencia* had been renamed respectively *Buenos Aires* and *Montevideo*, and the ships had switched allegiance, together with their officers and crews. All were British, American or Chilean, and two of the captains were British officers who had fought in the independence wars with Lord Cochrane – Henry Cobbett, a Royal Navy veteran who was also the nephew of Henry Cobbett the radical pamphleteer, and James (Santiago) George Bynon, originally of the East India Company's Service and later destined to be the Rear Admiral commanding the Chilean Navy.

There was general relief when news arrived that the three warships had sailed from Valparaiso on 15 July[1] and were already heading south to Cape Horn and their rendezvous off Cape Corrientes. On 3 August 1826, General Alvear, now Minister for War and Marine sent Commodore Brown his orders. There were 13 separate instructions, but the message was clear and aggressive – he was to proceed to Cape Corrientes, take command of the

squadron from Chile, and then sail northwards so as to 'make the
Emperor of Brazil feel the full weight of War' by vigorous action
on sea and land. The only qualification was yet another reminder
to avoid attacking superior forces. Alvear knew William Brown's
temperament only too well.

The news was received with concern by the Brazilians in Montevideo. On 20 August, Admiral Pinto Guedes reported it to Rio
de Janeiro then put to sea with the frigates *Piranga*, *Dona Paula*,
Paraguassú and *Imperatriz* and a handful of scouting vessels. The
Brazilian commander cruised off Patagonia for a fortnight then,
fearing that his quarry had eluded him, headed northwards to
waters near the capital. On 22 September, the *Maria da Glória*
unexpectedly arrived in Rio de Janeiro to announce that Pinto
Guedes and his squadron were off Cape Frio. The Imperial Government took a dim view of this initiative and – fortunately for
Commodore Brown – promptly ordered the Admiral back to the
Plate.[2] .

On receiving his orders, William Brown set off on the long
overland journey to the rendezvous at Cape Corrientes, a rocky
promontory standing against the ocean some 160 miles south-east
of the capital. Travelling by carriage and with an escort of 40
lancers, the Commodore spun over the green pampas of Buenos
Aires Province, crossed the Rio Salado, then lurched over the low
barren hills which led to his destination. Arriving in early September, he set about his task. With the help of the escort and of 40
slaves freed from a Brazilian prize, Brown erected a signalling
station on the headland – marked by flags by day and lanterns by
night – established coastal patrols, and settled down to wait.

Unfortunately for the Argentinian Government and for Commodore Brown, the news that the Chile squadron had sailed on 15
July was premature. It was not until 8 August that preparations
were finally completed and the captains summoned to the *Buenos
Aires* to receive their orders from Colonel Vasquez, now commanding the squadron. The plan was for the three ships to head
south-east until they reached 77°W, then south as far as 59°S and
then, turning east, to sail past Cape Horn to the rendezvous. In the

likely event of a separation, they were to meet off the Falklands/Malvinas and then sail together to Cape Corrientes.

Heading south, the ships almost immediately lost contact, although they sighted each other intermittently during the voyage. But the *Montevideo* was already in trouble. The North American woods with which she was built were too soft, and when the strain became too great, the corvette had no choice but to turn back. She managed to reach Talcahuana but went immediately aground and eventually had to be sold for scrap. Her consorts persevered, sighting each other three times on the voyage south and sailing together for days at a time. On 23 August, the *Chacabuco* caught a glimpse of the *Buenos Aires* at 56°68'W before she turned east to fight her way through gales and snowstorms past Cape Horn and into the South Atlantic. It was the last time the frigate was ever seen. After that sighting, the *Buenos Aires*, together with Colonel Vasquez, Captain Cobbett and its British-American-Chilean crew disappeared without trace.

For three long weeks, Commodore Brown scanned the seas off Cape Corrientes for the missing ships. Then, on 30 September he gave up and returned to Buenos Aires to learn of the delay in their departure date. A fortnight later, news reached the capital that the *Chacabuco* had reached Cape Corrientes – alone. Plans were changed. It was decided that the National vessels *Congresso*, *República Argentina* and *Sarandí* – commanded respectively by William Mason, William Granville and John Halstead Coe, a young American who had served with distinction as a volunteer at Lara-Quilmes – would join the Chilean corvette and participate in the raid against Brazil. The ships were hastily prepared for sea and the other vessels in the anchorage stripped of sailors to ensure they were fully manned.

On 26 October 1826, all was ready. Brown hoisted his flag in the schooner *Sarandí* and the ships moved into the Outer Roads accompanied by Dautant's privateer *Oriental Argentina* which had been given permission to join the flotilla in its attempt to break through the Brazilian blockade. As night fell and the wind freshened from the south-east, they weighed anchor and headed for

Colonia. The shallower northern channel seemed the most promising exit route. But the attempted break-out was a failure. Brazilian cruisers were patrolling the whole width of the river to windward and it was impossible for the square-rigged ships to find their way round them. The fast, American-built *Sarandí*, with its fore and aft sails and shallower draught, managed to slip by – almost engaging an Imperial schooner in the process – but the *Congresso, República Argentina* and even the *Oriental Argentina* were forced back to Buenos Aires. There was some sharp questioning on their return, but they had clearly had no choice.[3]

Unaware of the fate of her consorts, the *Sarandí* navigated its way down the channel north of the Ortiz bank, slipped past Montevideo and Maldonado and, at 3 pm the following day, found itself at the eastern extremity of the River Plate. Here Brown turned and headed south for Cape Corrientes. Three days later, on 30 October, the *Chacabuco* came in sight. But the strain of the voyage round the Horn had taken its toll. The corvette had lost copper and, even with its pumps regularly manned, was taking in 36 inches of water an hour. Brown had himself rowed over to take a look. Then, grim faced, he addressed the ship's company, asking them bluntly whether they preferred to stay for repairs or sail immediately to the Brazilian coast. The unanimous reply was to head for Brazil, leak or no leak. Preparations were completed – bread and rum were ferried over to the *Chacabuco*, charts of the enemy coastline were provided, and Brown agreed to reinforce the crew with 20 liberated negroes from the shore. High seas prevented any reinforcement, but ten hours after Brown's arrival, they were ready. At 10 pm the signal for departure was hoisted; the ships made sail, then, leaning close hauled on the port tack, they disappeared eastwards over the horizon.

With blustery winds, Brown took his ships in a broad sweep into the Atlantic, heading north-east as far as 40°W, before standing northwards towards Cape Frio, the landfall for all vessels bound for Rio de Janeiro. Then, after 11 days at sea and a remarkable piece of navigation, they came in sight of the rugged promontory that was their destination. Last minute changes were made as Lieutenant John Gard and an extra pilot were rowed over to the

Chacubuco. Then, on 10 November, under full sail and clear blue skies, they sighted their first ship. Disappointingly it proved to be an American brig inward bound from Virginia. But the following morning off the tiny island of Porcos to the north of Cape Frio, they spotted topsails on the horizon. The *Chacabuco* set off in pursuit flying the green and yellow flag of Brazil, and by nightfall had taken the *Perpetuo Defensor,* arriving in ballast from Sierra Leone. Next day the corvette added two more ships to the bag – the *Urania,* en route from Pernambuco with a cargo of salt, and the Portuguese merchantman *Nova Piedade* bound for Rio from Lisbon. The Portuguese ship was allowed to proceed, but only after its captain had been fed with false information about a combined Argentinian-Chilean force which was now blockading Pernambuco, Bahia and Rio de Janeiro.

In view of the different sizes and sailing qualities of his ships, Commodore Brown now decided to divide his force. The *Chacabuco* was ordered to convoy the two prizes to their first rendezvous off the island of São Sebastião and then to patrol the sea routes to the south, while the smaller, handier *Sarandí* harried the traffic along the coast. Accordingly on 12 November, the two ships went their separate ways. The schooner, heading eastwards with the purple smear of land just in sight to starboard, soon caught up with the *Nova Piedade.* At midnight the two ships found themselves off the entrance to the Bay of Guanabara and the harbour of Rio de Janeiro. In the darkness the loom of the Sugar Loaf could be clearly seen to the left and the lights of the Fort of Santa Cruz to the right. The Portuguese ship was left to enter with news that 'Commodore Brown was off Cape Frio with a corvette in company, two brigs and a schooner',[4] while the *Sarandí,* in a final act of deception, ostentatiously headed south, only to change course again when out of sight.

Just after noon the next day, Brown and his men passed the rocky headland on the island of Maranbaya and sighted the green hills and sandy beaches of Ilha Grande. There, sheltering in the glittering waters of Palmas Bay at the eastern end were three

THE RAID OF THE SARANDÍ AND THE CHACABUCO
NOVEMBER–DECEMBER 1826

x = ships taken or destroyed

Brazilian smacks. *Sarandí* promptly dropped anchor while its boats sped over to take possession. They proved to be the *Nossa Senhora de Cabo*, *Santa Rita* and *Bomfim Santa Ana* with cargoes of rum, coffee and farinha flour. The schooner then headed south-west for the rendezvous, the captive smacks straining, and frequently failing, to keep up. On the 16 November, they passed the Isla dos Porcos and sighted the *Perpetuo Defensor* at anchor. The prize master reported that the *Chacabuco* had parted company the previous day to chase a schooner and had taken the *Urania* with him. There was nothing to do but wait. Meanwhile, Commodore Brown sorted out the prizes. The *Perpetuo Defensor* was fitted with artillery and then loaded with all the valuable cargo from the other vessels, while the prisoners were put on the *Nossa Senhora de Cabo*. The other smacks were then burnt.

There was still no sign of the *Chacabuco*, so on 18 November Brown released the *Nossa Senhora de Cabo* and entered the channel which separated the island of São Sebastião from the mainland. Amid grey skies and with an easterly wind, the Argentinian ships were surprised by an eruption of gunfire and powder-smoke. A concealed shore battery had suddenly opened fire on them with alarming accuracy. The *Sarandí* was struck in the hull and aloft while the *Perpetuo Defensor* ran aground while taking evasive action. There was a lull in the firing when the prisoners reached the shore, but it was under a renewed storm of artillery fire that the Argentinians refloated the brig and retreated the way they had come. Relieved at their escape, Brown took the seaward route round the island and headed south-westerly for Santos, just missing the *Chacabuco* by two days. On 20 November, the corvette too reached São Sebastião and, like the *Sarandí*, headed for the channel. However, when he was fired on, Captain Bynon promptly landed a shore party and attacked the battery and the nearby town of Villa Bella. Then, successfully getting through, he headed south into the Atlantic.

Meanwhile, the *Sarandí* was on its way towards Santos with a strong following wind when her lookouts sighted a Brazilian warship (which they identified as a frigate) ahead on their starboard bow. The schooner changed course, and was soon within long cannon shot of the vessel which, being directly to leeward, could clearly do nothing but wait. Then a sudden squall intervened and *Sarandí* either lost contact (the explanation given in her log) or, mindful of the orders to avoid unequal contests, made off. In the week that followed the Argentinians headed south-west, first for Santos, then for the island of Santa Catarina – the major landfall for vessels sailing for the southern ports. The voyage was enlivened by two incidents – the capture on 23 November of the *São Manoel Brasileiro* with a cargo of salt and rum, and an encounter two days later with the American brig *Gustavo*. Claiming to be from a Brazilian warship, the *Sarandí's* boarding party spread further rumours of the blockade of Rio de Janeiro by the terrible Commodore Brown and the Chile squadron, then sailed on.

The Brazilian Government was annoyed but not alarmed by the false news of Brown's activities off their coasts. They had unwisely ordered Pinto Guedes' force of heavy frigates back to the Plate at the end of September, but were actively preparing a powerful squadron to convey the Emperor on the morale-building voyage to the south – at exactly the moment when Brown's activities were reaching their climax. The Imperial Government had been worried for some time by the Brazilian Army's apparently lethargic attitude to the war in the Banda Oriental. General Lecor and his officers seemed happy to be besieged comfortably in Montevideo while the *gaucho* rebels controlled the interior of the province and the Argentinian regulars made menacing moves in the direction of the Brazilian province of Rio Grande do Sul. Troops were sent to the south but fresh recruitment proved difficult. Brazilians were uninterested in the war, and found military life so uncongenial that the Government fell back on the use of mercenaries. Agents in Europe were ordered to raise regiments of German troops and, in September, a shady officer called Colonel Cotter was sent to Ireland to recruit whole units of soldier-colonists. Reporting the news to London, Consul-General Chamberlain urged his Government to discourage anyone from offering themselves in view of the 'trickery' practised in the past.[5]

In October, the Emperor decided to put additional bite into the Brazilian effort by replacing Lecor as commander-in-chief of the Army. The new general was Felisberto Brant, Marquis of Barbacena, whose diplomatic skills had been amply demonstrated in London during the War of Independence and in the negotiations that had followed, but whose military experience was small and talents for generalship unknown. To inspire his troops to greater exertions, a personal visit to Rio Grande do Sul by the Emperor had been planned for the following month. Thus, at the same moment that Brown was nearing the island of Santa Catarina, an escorting squadron under the command of Vice Admiral the Count of Souzel was ready for sea. It comprised the 74-gun *Pedro I*, the frigate *Isabela* (Captain Teodoro de Beaurepaire), the corvette *Duqueza de Goias* (Lieutenant Charles Watson), the schooner *1 de Dezembro* and seven transports with reinforcements of 1500 troops.

On 24 November, the Imperial squadron exchanged salutes with the Fort of Santa Cruz at the entrance to the harbour and headed south into the blue rollers of the Atlantic. The voyage proceeded without incident until, at dawn on the sixth day, the Brazilians sighted a corvette flying French colours on the horizon to windward. The *Isabela* clawed her way upwind to investigate, but the ship quickly spun round and made off. As it disappeared, the tricolour of France was replaced by the flag of Buenos Aires. The corvette was the *Chacabuco*. Cheated, the Imperial expedition ploughed on in the direction of Rio Grande.

Like all sea commanders on long cruises, Brown and Coe had been continually worried by the water situation. Attempts to fill their casks had been frustrated twice already by the heavy swell. Now, off Santa Catarina they tried again. Anchoring under French colours within pistol shot of a small estuary, a boat and an officer were sent ashore to fill the schooner's four great water barrels. Over 50 Brazilians soon gathered on foot and horseback to watch, uncertain as to what to do. Discreetly covering the beach with his traversing 18-pounder, Brown sent a prisoner ashore to reveal the schooner's identity and distribute leaflets denouncing the tyranny of the 'Europeanized' Emperor and inviting his subjects to revolt. Their attention then further deflected by 'news' of the proximity of the Argentinian frigate *Buenos Aires* and a corvette, the Brazilians agreed to an exchange. The remaining captives were landed and the *Sarandí* got its water.

Brown then headed for his final rendezvous point, the Bar of Rio Grande, capturing the *Pilar* and *Brasileiro*, carrying dried meat, hides and tallow, on the way. He reached his destination on 29 November, and dropped anchor flying United States colours. Next day, a small two-masted vessel was sighted to the south. Mistaking it for a warship, Brown gave chase and for hours the two ships manoeuvred for position, finally racing each other hell for leather towards the shoreline. At the last minute, the *Sarandí* turned aside and dropped anchor, but the Brazilian plunged on, ran aground and became a total wreck. She proved to be the *Estrella do Sul*, built in Bahia only the year before.

For four days the *Sarandí* cruised off the bar, surprising and capturing one more vessel, the tiny smack *Ezequiel*, while dozens of terrified Brazilian coasters remained huddled under the guns of the shore batteries. On 3 December, Brown decided that he had done all he could and that it was time to return home. His stores were running low, his beef and salt pork had proved to be bad[6] and he had no more men or officers to spare as prize crews. So, releasing the smack with the final group of prisoners, he stood out to sea and made course for home, meeting as he did so a prize brig taken by the *Chacabuco*. But there was still no sign of the missing corvette on the voyage south and, trusting to the schooner's speed and manouvrability, Brown decided to make a dash for Buenos Aires. Leaving the South Atlantic behind him, he entered the River Plate on 24 December, managed to evade the scouts of the Brazilian blockading squadron and dropped anchor in the Inner Roads next day at midnight. On Christmas Day 1826, Brown fired a 21-gun salute and went ashore to receive a hero's welcome after a cruise of two months in which he had captured or destroyed eight enemy vessels.[7] When the leaking *Chacabuco* eventually returned to Patagonia on 1 January 1827, the recorded total for the two ships went up to fourteen, of which six had been sent back to Argentina as prizes.[8]

The cruise of the *Sarandí* and the *Chacabuco* was seen as another personal triumph for William Brown. But strategically it was a desperate second best – an improvisation following the non-appearance of the much vaunted Chile squadron and the failure of the *República Argentina*, *Congresso* and *Oriental Argentina* to escape from Buenos Aires. Neither of Brown's remaining ships was suitable for an extended cruise – the *Chacabuco* was too damaged to be truly effective and the *Sarandí* was too small to be able to provide sufficient prize crews or cope with large numbers of prisoners. Nevertheless, the rumours which Brown so carefully spread about a powerful enemy force of commerce raiders being in Brazilian waters caused the intended panic and pushed marine insurance rates up by 15 per cent. *La Gaceta Mercantil* of 22 June tried to raise morale by claiming a total of 45 captures, although the real number was much less.

The reaction of the Imperial Navy to the news of Brown's raid was correct. Looking for two small ships in the midst of the Atlantic was like looking for a needle in a haystack, and Pinto Guedes' decision to lead a squadron of heavy frigates first to Patagonia and then to Cape Frio was sound. He made the right assumptions as to what Brown intended to do and acted on them. His problem – like Brown's – was that he did not know the Chile squadron had been delayed by a month. If the Brazilian Admiral had known the true timing – and had arrived in the waters around Rio de Janeiro in late October instead of late September – the consequences for Commodore Brown might have been disastrous.

The adventure also demonstrated the efficiency of the Brazilian blockade of the River Plate. Only the fast, shallow draught *Sarandí* managed to escape their vigilance. Not only did the Imperial Navy prevent the heavier warships of Buenos Aires joining with Brown, but their watchfulness ensured that none of the prizes sent back to the Plate reached their destination – all were either recaptured or driven ashore. In the event, *Sarandí* and *Chacabuco* had only one prize to show for their efforts, and that had been sent to Carmen de Patagones.[9] The early months of the war had seen many daring initiatives by the Argentinian Navy and its commander, Commodore William Brown, but as the year went on, the superior numbers and experience of their opponents inevitably began to tell.

However poor the Empire's performance on land, and however inconvenient the losses of the coasting trade, it was clear by the end of 1826, that the military conflict at sea was steadily being won by the Brazilian Navy.

PART IV: 'SPLENDID DISPLAYS OF COURAGE MADE BY BRITONS'

CHAPTER 13

THE STRUGGLE FOR THE URUGUAY

The meeting of the Paraná and the Uruguay at the western end of the Plate Estuary marks the end of one of the great internal river systems which reach deep into South America. Geographically, the Paraná is the more significant of the two. Rising in the interior of Brazil, the river flows for 2700 miles to the Plate, and forms successively the borders of Brazil and of Paraguay before it heads south through the northern provinces of Argentina. For its last few hundred miles, the river turns south-east – Entre Rios on its left bank and Buenos Aires Province on its right – then slows and cuts its way over a red alluvial plain until it reaches its confluence with the River Uruguay near the island of Juncal. Also rising in Brazil, but only 1000 miles in length, the Uruguay is shorter than its partner but in 1826, forming as it did the border between the northern Argentinian Province of Entre Rios and the rebel Banda Oriental – it was more important in strategic terms. It was here in the Uruguay that the ships of the Brazilian Navy's Third Division were concentrated, operating out of Colonia, and patrolling the lower 100 miles of the river from Arroyo de la China to the channel between Juncal and Martim Garcia where the waters of Paraná-

Uruguay system widen to eight miles just before they reach the Plate Estuary. Only a token force was kept in the Paraná to control the oared privateers for whom the numerous islands and tributaries of the river were ideal hiding places.

Since May 1826, the old Flotilla of the Uruguay had been transformed into the Third Brazilian Division under the command of Captain Jacinto ('Jackie') Senna Pereira – universally referred to at the time by his first name. His main job was to prevent Argentinian reinforcements reaching the Banda Oriental, and to demonstrate Brazilian control of the river by sweeping it clean of enemy cargo carriers. But he had another task as well. It was well known that the *caudillos* in the Argentinian provinces were increasingly hostile to both Rivadavia's manners and his centralist policies and the resulting political tension offered the Brazilians ample opportunity to make mischief. Captain Jacinto was therefore ordered to stir up as much internal trouble as possible, particularly in Entre Rios. It was an assignment for which his knowledge of the area and family connections made him ideally suited.

The arrival of the Marquis of Barbacena as new commander-in-chief of the Brazilian Army in the south in October introduced a new strategic dimension. Barbacena's aim was simple and ambitious – to expel the enemy from Brazilian territory, drive them across the Uruguay and occupy Entre Rios. The presence of an Imperial naval squadron in the Uruguay in the enemy's rear was therefore an important part of the plan and although Admiral Pinto Guedes was senior in rank, it was made clear to him in a despatch dated 22 October 1826, that he was to cooperate to the full.[1] Pinto Guedes's own priority was to reoccupy the island of Martim Garcia, commanding the mouth of the Uruguay, which Lobo had so foolishly evacuated in March, but his recommendation had not been accepted by the Imperial Army which regarded it as being of lesser importance.[2] The best he could do was to get the Minister of War to agree on 5 February 1827 to re-garrison the island as soon as an opportunity presented itself.[3] But by that time it was too late. The Argentinians had beaten him to it.

Admiral Pinto Guedes put his own preferences aside and quickly responded to Barbacena's requests to strengthen the Third

Division. By December 1826, the size of Captain Jacinto's force had gone up to 22 vessels. They comprised the brigantine *Dona Januária*, the schooners *Oriental, Bertioga, 7 de Março, Dona Paula, Liberdade do Sul, Camões* and *Itapoão*, four armed yachts, seven gunboats, two launches and a hospital ship. The Argentinian intelligence network ensured that they knew exactly what the Brazilians were up to. They were also deeply disturbed. In December 1826 therefore, the Government began to prepare a naval force of 15 schooners and gunboats to enter the Uruguay and remove the thorn of the Third Division from their side. In Brown's absence in the South Atlantic, the expedition was to be commanded by Captain Tomas Espora, now recovered from wounds received on 30 July. The preparations were given additional urgency when, on 20 December, the schooner *Rio de la Plata* (which as the *Araçatuba* had been the first Imperial warship captured during the war) carrying 50 engineers to the army in the Banda Oriental accidentally ran into Jacinto's force near Martim Garcia. Captain Richitelli managed to land 40 of his passengers and crew in open boats but the ship had then been retaken by the Brazilians after a fierce action which left over 30 Argentinian casualties and prisoners.

By Christmas Day 1826, preparations in Buenos Aires were almost complete when the sudden appearance of a fast schooner firing a 21-gun salute announced the return of the *Sarandí* carrying Commodore William Brown from his commerce raiding voyage off the Brazilian Coast. Immediately and enthusiastically, Brown took command of the expedition which, at last, would give him an opportunity to meet the Brazilians on equal terms. A brief visit ashore was his only chance to greet his long-suffering wife Elizabeth and to attend to his mail. Among the papers was a letter and a large package from Commodore Robert Ramsay. Against all advice, Ramsay had sailed on the September packet from Falmouth to discuss his problems in buying ships for the Argentinian Navy directly with the authorities in Buenos Aires. Unfortunately for him, the British had yielded to a protest from the Brazilians and refused to allow him to land. Ramsay was therefore forced to remain on board the *Goldfinch* for the whole of November, his only contact with the land being through letters.[4] Nevertheless, his problems were settled through the allocation of £200,000, and Ramsay had taken the opportunity to write to Brown – whom he had never met – expressing his admiration and presenting him with his own sword as a token of esteem.[5] This weapon, a typical curved British naval sword of the period with a lion's head pommel and engraved with Ramsay's name, can be seen today in the Museo Histórico Naval in Buenos Aires.

The following afternoon, 26 December, Brown received his instructions. Stressing that the defeat of Jacinto's division and control of the Uruguay was a matter of national honour, the Minister of War and Marine ordered him to ensure 'the persecution and destruction of the said enemy force so as to ensure free navigation on the river and restore our communications with all parts of the coast'.[6] It was a simple objective which was entirely suited to the Commodore's active and aggressive temperament. By 4 pm, Brown had briefed his commanders on his intentions and, brushing aside an attempt by ships of the Brazilian blockading squadron to stop him, led his squadron into the brown waters of the estuary and headed north-west. The following day, off Martim Garcia, he paused to be joined by four gunboats whose departure from Buenos Aires had been delayed.[7] He now had 17 vessels – one ship of force in the shape of the 14-gun brig *General Balcarce*, the six schooners *Sarandí, Pepa, Uruguay, Union, Maldonado* and *Guanco*, nine gunboats and one armed launch. With his force complete, Brown entered the Uruguay in search of the Imperial Third Division.

By this time, Senna Pereira's ships were far up river. On Christmas Day, they had passed Martim Garcia and had reached the little port of Las Vacas, where they had bombarded the town and harassed the supply ships huddling for protection in the harbour. Captain Jacinto had then detached the schooner *Camões* with three gunboats to watch the Paraná River, and led his remaining 17 ships northwards up the Uruguay. On 28 December, he reached the swampy, mosquito-infested island of Vizcaino, 30 miles from the mouth of the river at its junction with the Rio

Negro where the Brazilians maintained herds of cattle and sheep for supply purposes. It was there that he learnt from a passing cargo carrier that he was being pursued by a strong Argentinian force which, he assumed, in the absence of Brown was commanded by Tomas Espora.

The report indicated – correctly – that the two squadrons were evenly balanced, each with 17 ships, 69 guns and around 740 men.[8] But Captain Jacinto was all too aware of the differences in quality. The Argentinian ships were well manned and were commanded by officers who had all gained experience in the engagements which had marked the first year of the war. His own situation was different. In numbers his force was adequate to the task, but there were grave deficiencies in the quality of personnel. The rapid expansion of the Imperial Navy had far outstripped the Empire's supply of trained officers. Junior lieutenants had been found for the larger vessels, but the smaller ones were commanded by a motley collection of marine artillery officers and sergeants.[9] In such circumstances, Captain Jacinto decided to fight a strictly defensive battle with the minimum of manoeuvre.

Commodore Brown caught up with his Brazilian opponents on 29 December 1826. Rounding the bend at the western end of Vizcaino, the Argentinians sighted Jacinto's ships in the distance at the point where the Rio Negro meets a smaller tributary called the Jaguary. The Brazilian squadron was waiting for them, sails furled and anchored in line across the river at its narrowest point. Not only did they fill its 350 metre width, but the Brazilian schooners and gunboats had rigged springs on their cables so that the heavy 18- and 24-pounder cannon mounted in their bows could be trained on any approaching vessel irrespective of wind or tide. It was an ideal defensive arrangement – indeed it was exactly the position that Brown himself had adopted to defend the anchorage at Los Pozes on 11 June!

Nevertheless the Brazilian defence had to be tested, and Espora was immediately ordered to advance at the head of nine gunboats. It was typical summer weather – insufferably hot, humid and with little wind. The Argentinian approach was long and laboured and was beaten off with ease. Brown then resorted to bluff, sending the young captain of his flagship *Sarandí*, John Halstead Coe, with a note demanding the Brazilian surrender. This ploy was equally unsuccessful. Senna Pereira rejected the proposal and detained Coe, claiming irregularities in the truce procedure and suspecting that the claim that Brown was in command of the enemy force was a trick. The heat, the clear cloudless skies and the light variable winds were typical *pampeiro* weather, and sure enough, that afternoon the anchorage was suddenly struck by the full force of a storm. With ships straining and pitching at their cables further action was impossible, but the following morning, with calm restored, the Argentinians tried again. Once more Espora and his gunboats advanced laboriously towards the anchored Brazilians to be repulsed by steady fire from their big guns. Commodore Brown needed no more evidence of the strength of the enemy position and decided on a new strategy. If he could not destroy Senna Pereira's force he would fortify the mouth of the river and bottle up his opponents within it. Accordingly, having rounded up the livestock on the island of Vizcaino and called on the local militia to cause the Brazilian maximum inconvenience, he led his ships southward.

Reaching Punta Gorda where the Uruguay narrows before joining the lower reaches of the Paraná, Brown paused to raise a small battery, then sailed on to Martim Garcia. The strategic importance of the island was obvious, and he decided to fortify it as a major element in his control of the Uruguay. Cannon and men were landed from the *General Balcarce* – now commanded by Captain Francisco Segui – who began work digging gun emplacements and building barracks. Command of the island was given to Tomas Espora who was succeeded as captain of the *Maldonado* schooner by a 24-year-old Scot, Francis Drummond. Drummond was a heroic but controversial figure. Recruited originally in London for the Brazilian Navy by General Brant, he had already played a useful role in the War of Independence as a sublieutenant on the *Niterói* during John Taylor's pursuit of the Portuguese in 1823, and as the commander of a shore party during Lord Cochrane's restoration of order in Maranhão the following year.

Unfortunately, Drummond had fallen foul of the Brazilian Navy's clumsy disciplinary regulations and after a period of uneasy detention awaiting court martial had fled to Buenos Aires where he had volunteered his services to the United Provinces. Commodore Brown had been so impressed with his record – and with the romantic impact made on his daughter Eliza – that he had appointed the young man to the *Maldonado*.

Leaving Espora in charge, on 2 January 1827, Brown set sail for Buenos Aires in the *Sarandí* to convince the authorities of the need to bottle up the Uruguay and fortify Martim Garcia. Minister of War and Marine de la Cruz was aware of the political damage Senna Pereira could still do in the riverine provinces and was unenthusiastic. He wanted to see the Brazilian Third Division annihilated and not just neutralized. There was a sharp exchange of correspondence between the two men, but the advantages of each course of action were clear and it was eventually agreed to go for both. The island of Martim Garcia would indeed be fortified, but as a springboard for an attack on Senna Pereira's division rather than as a defensive reaction. The compromise more than suited Brown's pugnacious spirit and two days later he sailed in the *Sarandí* once more, leaving de la Cruz to order the transportation of munitions, heavy artillery and a garrison to the island.

Brown arrived at Martim Garcia later that day. The schooner had been unable to avoid the Brazilian blockading force – now commanded by the English-hating Danish Captain Pritz in the *Imperatriz* – and the Argentinian commander had to complete the journey by boat over the shallows. The job of fortification received a new stimulus using gear and timber from the Brazilian schooner *S. José Americana*, captured on 24 January with 69 barrels of powder and a chest of silver and copper coins on board. By the end of the month a powerful battery had been completed made up of pairs of 24- and 12-pounder guns, five 8-pounders, an array of Congreve rockets and a garrison of 100 men of the Buenos Aires militia. With a range of up to 2000 yards, this ordnance could dominate both the Grand Channel to the west and Hell's Channel to the east. Argentina was now effectively in control of both entry and exit from the Uruguay-Paraná system. Meanwhile, the Brazilians were not idle. Senna Pereira sailed up river looking for supplies and political mischief while, in Montevideo, Admiral Pinto Guedes planned the next move. He was fully aware from Captain Jacinto's despatches of the rebuff which the Argentinians had suffered at Jaguary and of Brown's plan to seal off the Uruguay by fortifying its mouth and concentrating his squadron in the vicinity. His answer was to turn the tables on Commodore Brown by ordering the Third Division down river while sending an additional force into the western Plate to put him between two fires. In the first week of January 1827, Pinto Guedes and his staff completed their plans. The corvette *Maceió*, the brigs *Caboclo*, *Real João* and *Rio da Plata* and the schooners *Maria Theresa*, *Providência*, *2 de Dezembro*, *Conceição* and *Itaparica* were detached from the squadron blockading Buenos Aires and formed into an auxiliary division to cut off Brown's force from the east. The defender of Colonia, the tall, stocky Captain Frederico Mariath was moved to the *Maceió* and put in command of the whole expedition. As usual, nothing remained secret, and within days details of the Brazilian plan were known in Buenos Aires.[10] On 11 January Pinto Guedes sent out his final written orders.[11] Unfortunately, the Spanish captain charged with their delivery had been bribed by sympathetic ladies in Montevideo to hand them over to Commodore Brown when he arrived off Martim Garcia. The Argentinian commander studied the details of the Brazilian plans with satisfaction, then sent the orders on to Senna Pereira in the full knowledge that they would soon bring him and his ships down river to where he was waiting.

Mariath too received his instructions and sailed from Colonia for the rendezvous with the Third Division. On 17 January, his ships were negotiating the shallow channel leading to Martim Garcia, the *Providência* going ahead to take soundings, while the *Maceió* and the others followed at a safe distance. Mariath's caution was justified but proved futile, for at nightfall and on a falling tide, the corvette slid onto the mud and juddered to a halt. Her crew made desperate attempts to refloat her, but all was in vain and

Maceió remained firmly aground for eight long hours while the other ships of the division fell back down river to avoid a similar fate.

Meanwhile Brown was approaching Martim Garcia from the north looking for his opponents. It was a clear, bright night and in the early hours he sighted the Brazilians. Seeing Mariath aground, Brown decided on immediate action. William Granville was ordered forward to capture the corvette at the head of six gunboats with the *Sarandí* standing by to give support. Aided by a light following wind Granville was soon within range and began a fierce exchange of fire with the *Maceió* and with the *2 de Dezembro* which had taken up a defensive position on the corvette's bow. The remaining Brazilian ships remained stranded to leeward and could do nothing but watch. With only a brief pause at dawn, the contest went on for four hours, the guns of the *Maceió* being fired with such precision and effect as to astonish its opponents.[12] The Argentinians were unable to get near enough to do any serious damage and when the *Sarandí* attempted an approach she was driven back with five balls in her hull and the wreckage of her topmast trailing alongside. By 10 am, both sides were exhausted. Brown called off the attack and the *Maceió*, now refloated, was able to make sail and rejoin its consorts to leeward.

Brazilian naval history rightly regards the defence of the *Maceió* as a significant victory. Brown's report, on the other hand, belittled the importance of the engagement, and merely gave a factual report with the usual exaggeration of Brazilian casualties.[13] The engagement was certainly a failure for the Argentinians. An isolated ship in near windless conditions was an ideal target for a group of gunboats with auxiliary oars and a single heavy cannon – indeed they were designed for exactly this situation. Yet damage and casualties on the Brazilian corvette were light and there was only one fatality, Midshipman Thomé Gonçalves. Whatever the rights and wrongs of the engagement, the fact remains that by the end of January 1827, the Brazilian Navy was still in control of the Uruguay. And with Jacinto's division to the north and Mariath's to the south, the Argentinian hunters seemed likely to be the hunted.

CHAPTER 14

THE BRAZILIAN
DEFEAT AT JUNCAL

Confident in the battle-worthiness of his squadron and fully aware of Brazilian plans to rendezvous in the lower reaches of the Uruguay, Commodore William Brown anchored his 15 ships near Martim Garcia. On 5 February, the fortifications on the island were completed, the outpost was named 'the Fortress of the Constitution' and in a brief ceremony the white and blue flag of Buenos Aires was formally raised and saluted. Then Brown settled down to wait. Every day, intelligence reports told him of the progress of Senna Pereira's forces. On 3 February they left Paysandú. On 6 February they were reported as approaching Higuerita. On 7 February, Brown made his final dispositions. All captains were summoned to the flagship to be briefed on his tactics in the coming engagement then, relying on the garrison of Martim Garcia to obstruct the passage of Mariath's division – now expected daily – the Argentinian commander led his squadron northwards in search of Senna Pereira. He anchored for the night between the island of Juncal and the western bank. At dawn on 8 February, the sails of Brazilian ships could be seen heading down river with a light northerly wind. Brown immediately weighed anchor, and formed his ships into a line of battle pointing obliquely south-east off the island of Juncal. The van was headed by Captain Francisco Segui in the *General Balcarce*, the rear by Drummond in the *Maldonado*, and the centre by Brown himself on the *Sarandí*. While the Argentinians watched, the 17 Brazilian men-of-war and the hospital ship continued their approach until, at 11.30 am with the wind dying, they dropped anchor parallel to

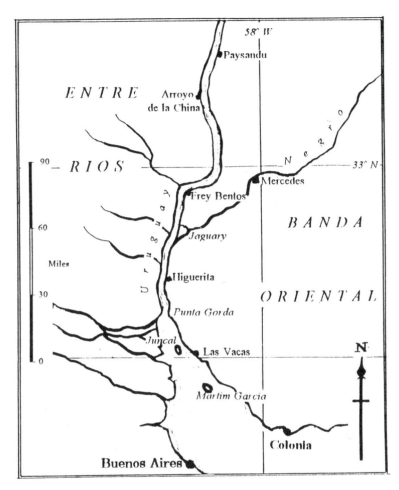

JUNCAL AND THE LOWER URUGUAY
1826

their opponents 1000 yards away, the flagship *Oriental* in the centre.

The weather was typical of the summer *pampeiro* season – stifling heat and humidity, with light variable winds which would swing unpredictably from north to south until cleared by a violent electrical storm. It was this weather pattern as much as the skill of the two commanders which was to dominate the course of the next two days. At noon the action began. In the heavy calm, six of Brown's gunboats crept forward, their crews straining at their oars, and began a long-range exchange of fire with the Brazilian line with their 18-pounder cannon. At 2 pm, a light breeze freshened from the south south-east then veered to the north. Both squadrons made sail, the Brazilians in the dominant position to windward. Senna Pereira tried to form his ships into a line of attack, but the inexperience of his captains frustrated the manoeuvre. The *Liberdade do Sul* went aground. The brigantine *Dona Januária* swung out of formation, drifted within range of the Argentinians and found itself fired on simultaneously by the *General Balcarce*, the *Sarandí* and three gunboats. Senna Pereira sent in a fireship to divert attention. It exploded short of its target but enabled the brigantine to escape. Then, at 3 pm, the wind faltered and dropped again. Movement became impossible but the two squadrons continued firing energetically at each other, the eddying grey cannon smoke obscuring visibility, the boom of heavy guns being clearly audible as far away as Buenos Aires and Colonia.[1]

Then the expected *pampeiro* broke in a storm of thunder, lightning and pouring rain. Ships struggled to maintain their positions against the violence of the wind. The *General Balcarce* was laid over on her beam ends but survived. Then, just as suddenly, the storm subsided, being replaced by a north-easterly breeze. Senna Pereira began to withdraw northwards to take up a better position. But his problems were not over. The *12 de Outubro* got into trouble and was only saved after assistance from her consorts. Then the hospital ship *Fortuna* dragged her anchor and drifted helplessly down on the Argentinian line where she was promptly captured and Captain Coe, a prisoner on board since Jaguary, released. Nevertheless, by midnight, the Imperial squadron had extricated itself and had managed to anchor in irregular formation near the island of Solis. Concealed by the darkness of the night, the Brazilians waited for the morrow, too exhausted to do much in the way of preparation or planning.[2]

As the first streaks of daylight crept over the river, Senna Pereira's captains were rowed over to the *Oriental* to agree tactics for the coming encounter. The major question was whether they should fight under sail or at anchor. The success of the latter tactic in confined waters at Jaguary spoke volumes in its favour. But the variability of the wind and the possibility of being outflanked argued for the opposite. Eventually the question was left undecided: Captain Jacinto would let his tactics be determined by the actual conditions.

At 8 am on 9 February, with a fresh breeze from the southeast, both squadrons made sail. A string of bunting rose to the mast of the *Sarandí* and the Argentinians, now occupying the windward position, turned and advanced in line against the Brazilians. Senna Pereira promptly signalled his ships to form a line across their path and drop anchor. Alas, once again, there was confusion in carrying out his orders. Some of the smaller gunboats drifted out of formation to leeward. Yelling through his speaking trumpet, Captain Jacinto tried to get his ships into order, but with the Argentinians drawing ever closer he gave up the attempt and signalled to 'receive the enemy under sail'. The *Dona Januária*, *Bertioga* and *Oriental* promptly bore up and advanced with the rest of the ships scattered behind them, many out of range. What was to have been a regular engagement in line became a melée with their three leading ships coming under devastating fire from the *General Balcarce* and the Argentinian van as they came within cannon shot. One broadside smashed the *Dona Januária*'s bowsprit, the next brought down her fore topmast in a heap of wreckage. The little *Victoria de Colonia* was sent in to tow the brigantine to safety but was driven off by the *Uruguay* arriving to take possession. Lieutenant Pedro Antonio Carvalho ordered his guns to be spiked and tried to sink his ship where she lay, then took to the boats and headed for the eastern shore. Francis Drummond's

Maldonado was now locked in a fierce struggle with the *Bertioga*, commanded by his former Brazilian comrade-in-arms, Dorset-born Lieutenant George Broom. A former Royal Navy midshipman, Broom had been prominent during the storming of Recife in the Pernambuco rebellion of 1824 and had already distinguished himself in the present war. But on this occasion he was out of luck. A stray 24-pounder shot from an Argentinian gunboat suddenly brought down the *Bertioga*'s mainmast and in half an hour the helpless vessel was pounded into surrender. Meanwhile, the brig-of-war *General Balcarce*, like a giant among pygmies, was leading a combined attack on the schooner *Oriental*. After a bombardment which left her traversing 18-pounder dismounted, half of her carronades destroyed and 37 casualties, including Senna Pereira himself, the Brazilian flagship was taken by boarding and Captain Segui accepted the Brazilian commander's sword in token of surrender.

With the loss of their three major warships, the battle was as good as lost for the Brazilians. The smaller schooners and gunboats ceased firing, abandoned the action and fled. Brown immediately ordered the *Sarandí* and the gunboats to continue the chase and switched his flag to the *General Balcarce*. Reaching the brig's shot-torn deck, the exultant Argentinian commander promptly embraced Francisco Segui and insisted that he retain Senna Pereira's sword as a token of his outstanding service during the battle. He then retired with his bigger ships and the four prizes to the safety of Martim Garcia to carry out repairs, write his despatches[3] and prepare for any challenge from Mariath's Auxiliary Division, which was clearly visible to the south of the island.[4]

In accordance with his orders, Captain Frederico Mariath at the head of his squadron of ten ships was approaching Martim Garcia at the same time as Senna Pereira's division went into action with the Argentinians. Knowing the navigational hazards, and remembering the earlier grounding of the *Maceió*, his progress was inevitably slow and cautious. Once again a schooner was sent ahead, this time to test the waters of Hell's Channel to the east of the island. The sight of a substantial Brazilian force advancing from the south-east caused instant alarm among the defenders of

Martim Garcia, who were convinced that a landing on the island was imminent. Its heavier guns had been sited facing the Grand Channel to the west, so a mobile battery of light nine-pounders had to be moved to cover the Brazilian line of approach. Alas for the Brazilians, the schooner soon grounded on the mud and defied all attempts to refloat her, demonstrating the unsuitability of the inland channel. Frustrated by the set-back and baffled by the light and variable winds, Mariath made no further attempt to join Senna Pereira and his ships fighting for their lives a few miles to the north. Instead he restricted himself to a lengthy and indecisive artillery duel with the batteries on Martim Garcia until the whole day's action was cut short by the storm.

Next day, while Senna Pereira's force was isolated and systematically destroyed, the Auxiliary Division, which had been created to prevent exactly such an eventuality, remained a distant spectator. Mariath was clearly convinced that the combination of shallow water, uncertain weather and the threat from the batteries on Martim Garcia made it too risky to attempt to pass the island. The pilot was convinced that a passage via Hell's Channel was possible, but Mariath refused to take the risk. Instead, he stayed where he was until 10 February, then withdrew, sending the *Conceição* to Colonia to report. Mariath's inaction during the Battle of Juncal caused a wave of criticism from Pinto Guedes and from public opinion in Montevideo.[5] And when he returned to Colonia a week later, notwithstanding his portly build, florid complexion and appearance of good health, he immediately took sick leave.[6] Emilio Senna Pereira in a biography of his father was also highly critical of Mariath, as have been many Brazilian naval historians. William Brown or James Norton would certainly have behaved differently and would have attempted to relieve Captain Jacinto's ships whatever the risk. But Mariath's caution did not seem unreasonable to the authorities in Rio, or incur their displeasure. Indeed, on 1 August, the Minister of Marine wrote to Pinto Guedes to make sure that Mariath was still being employed.[7] Neither did the incident affect his naval career which continued smoothly until he became an admiral in 1857.

Back in Colonia, the Imperial authorities slowly became aware of the extent of the disaster. At 4 am on 12 February, eight survivors from the *Oriental* arrived with news of the capture of the three largest ships. At noon, an open boat containing Lieutenant Pedro Antonio Carvalho and men from the *Dona Januária* brought confirmation.[8] Two days later the *Dona Paula*, *Victoria de Colonia* and *Atrevido*, the only Brazilian vessels to escape, sailed into the bay with more bad news. The schooners *Liberdade do Sul*, *7 de Março* and *Itapoão* had been burned to avoid capture and their crews transferred; while the gunboats *Brocaio*, *Paraty* and *Iguapé* had been overtaken and captured after a fight in which artillery lieutenant Luis Cipriano Gonçalves had been killed. The remaining five ships – three small yachts and two gunboats – were in full retreat up the Uruguay.[9]

By this time, Commodore Brown had completed his reorganization and Mariath's division had disappeared. On 14 February, he therefore hoisted his flag in the *Maldonado* and led seven ships northwards in pursuit of the survivors of Juncal. Arriving opposite Fray Bentos the following day, Brown was surprised to learn that the remaining Brazilian ships were already in Argentinian hands. Hours before, the senior surviving Imperial officer, Lieutenant Germano de Souza Aranha, having thrown his guns overboard, had surrendered the ships to the Governor of Entre Rios complete with gear, munitions and supplies. He, together with 351 other officers and men had become prisoners of war. There was a brief and courteous exchange of letters in which Brown demanded that the enemy vessels were handed over to him, while the Entre Rios authorities flatly refused to do so.[10] Then, seeing that he was getting nowhere, Brown filled his boats with armed men, boarded the Brazilian vessels and seized them where they lay. By 20 February he was back off Martim Garcia with the five new prizes.

Brown's reports on the battle of Juncal, written on 9 and 10 February 1827, were received in Buenos Aires with relief and delight. The Commodore had carried out his orders to the letter and had eliminated the Third Division of the Imperial Navy. Brown and his men had shown daring and courage in numerous actions during the previous 12 months, but none of them had done much to dent the overwhelming superiority of the Imperial Navy. Now, at last, he had met them on equal terms and had won a victory so spectacular that there was no need to exaggerate the result or 'manage' the news! The Brazilians had been soundly defeated and ten new ships had been added to the Argentinian Navy.[11]

Then, three weeks later, came news of another victory, this time on land. In February, General Alvear had led a combined force of 10,000 Argentinian troops and Uruguayan irregulars on an invasion of southern Brazil through the Pass of Rosario. The new Imperial commander, the Marquis of Barbacena, had confidently marched out to meet him at the head of a smaller, ill-equipped force of 7000 men and the two armies had clashed on 20 February at a place called Ituzaingú. There, the Brazilians had been defeated, and with his army pouring back in disorganized retreat, Barbacena's great dream of reconquering the Banda Oriental was shattered. So was his brief military career, for a month later he was transferred back to more suitable diplomatic duties. The Argentinian victory was not, however, followed by a triumphant march into Brazilian territory. Alvear chose the path of caution and stayed where he was, preferring to issue a succession of bombastic bulletins publicizing his achievement.

In Buenos Aires, the Government was delighted at the double victory. President Rivadavia published the reports of Juncal and Ituzaingú widely in newspapers, rejoicing at this double triumph for the Republic and hoping that the resulting enthusiasm would defuse the provincial opposition to his centralization of power.

Meanwhile, it was time for William Brown to return from the Uruguay. On 23 February, he left Martim Garcia intending to make a final dash for Buenos Aires. Senna Pereira's division may have been eliminated, but there was still the threat posed by the Brazilian squadron blockading the capital under the command of the veteran captain John Charles Pritz. At dawn on 24 February, Brown weighed anchor for the last time and headed for home with a convoy of 27 ships – the *Maldonado*, *General Balcarce*, *Union*, *Sarandí*, *Guanco*, 9 gunboats and 13 prizes. Sure enough, the sails of the Imperial blockading squadron were soon sighted off Quilmes Point, guarding the southern channel between Buenos Aires and the mouth of the estuary. Pritz had ten ships in all, the 1000-ton 50-gun frigate *Imperatriz*, the 22-gun corvette *Liberal*, the brigs *Pirajá*, *29 de Agosto*, *Real João* and *Rio da Plata* and four schooners. It was a formidable force which in numbers of guns and weight of broadside heavily outnumbered its more numerous but smaller opponents.

Well handled in the open sea, Pritz's powerful squadron could have made mincemeat of the Argentinian schooners, but here in the shallow waters of the Plate their weight and size was a disadvantage. The draught of the *Imperatriz*, for example, was 17 feet, and those of the *Liberal* and *Pirajá* were 14 feet. By comparison, Brown's largest vessel, the 200-ton brig *General Balcarce* could operate in only 11 feet of water and his schooners needed even less. The wily Brown took full advantage of this fact by keeping to the shallower water to the west of the channel. Thus, when the Brazilians attempted to approach, the *Imperatriz* went immediately grounded and the attack faltered. And when Pritz inevitably withdrew to deeper water, Brown followed with his schooners giving the impression to the anxious crowds thronging the Buenos Aires waterfront that a superior Imperial squadron was actually being chased away by their intrepid commander.[12] Behind this screen, the Argentinian gunboats and their prizes managed to reach the anchorage of Los Pozes in safety. The long-range bombardment caused few casualties and little damage to either side, but there was one appalling tragedy. The Imperial schooner *2 de Dezembro*, arriving from Colonia with 30 barrels of powder, was struck by a 24-pounder ball from Sublieutenant Wildblood's gunboat *No 12* and blew up in a thunderous explosion and a cloud of smoke. Of the 120 men on board, only three survived.

News of the victory at Juncal and the sight of Brown's fighting return to Buenos Aires produced a frenzy of joy and enthusiasm. An excited public read the reports on the battle in the *British Packet* and other newspapers and watched with satisfaction as prisoners began to arrive – including Lieutenant Broom and Captain Jacinto himself, both bearing letters from Brown praising their bravery and recommending that they be treated with consideration and generosity in captivity.[13] Even foreign diplomats were infected by the mood. Writing to London, Lord Ponsonby was lyrical in praise of Brown's 'prudence and courage' which, he felt, had now received their just reward; and the despatches of the American Consul, Colonel Forbes, were enthusiastic in praise of 'this brave and extraordinary man who has doubled his own strength by his daring and well executed operations.'[14] The public felt the same. When Commodore Brown landed, he was greeted by bands playing the National Anthem, by the assembled crews of the squadron who gave him three cheers and by enthusiastic crowds who carried him to the Presidential Palace in a litter, then insisted on pulling him to his residence in triumph in a carriage from which the horses had been removed.[15] Newspapers were read avidly for news and comment and soon prints of the hero's portrait were being snapped up by an eager public.

The Government of Bernadino Rivadavia had already decided on the most appropriate way to commemorate the victory. On 21 February it was decreed that all who had fought in the battle should be presented with an oval shield of honour – gold for Brown, silver for the officers and brass for the men – to be worn on the left arm and inscribed 'Glory to the Victors of the River Uruguay' with the date. A week later, every participant was awarded a bonus of two months' pay. And, as a more substantial reward, the value of the prize money to be divided among Brown's officers and men for the Brazilian ships taken in the action was assessed at 196,000 pesos, or £24,500.

The Battle of Juncal was undoubtedly a triumph for the Argentinian Navy. Historians have offered numerous explanations for the victory, but the reason is not difficult to see. In terms of the size and number of ships involved, the two sides were equally balanced. Likewise, there was little difference in artillery, apart from the preponderance of lighter weight long guns on the Argentinian ships as opposed to the Brazilian preference for heavier short-range carronades. The crucial difference lay in the comparative experience and skill of the officers. The Argentinian squadron was operating within hours of its base and was manned by the pick of their small navy. All of Brown's 15 captains were capable seamen. Five (Segui of the *General Balcarce*, Mason of the *Uruguay*, Granville of the *Guanco*, Lee of gunboat *No 7* and Drummond of the *Maldonado*) had had substantial previous experience – in the case of the first four dating back to the War of Independence. And another six (Coe, Maximin, Silva, Shannon, Wildblood and Zupitch) had fought as lieutenants in most of the battles and raids of the last twelve months. The Brazilians on the other hand, were fighting in a remote theatre for a navy which was cursed by severe shortages of officers and men. Only four of Senna Pereira's captains had more than three years' experience (Broom of the *Bertioga*, Wenceslau da Silva Lisboa of the *Liberdade do Sul*, Antonio de Carvalho of the *Dona Januária* and Souza Aranha of the *9 de Janeiro*). Seven were young men with little previous service, and five were not seamen at all but were artillery lieutenants or sergeants appointed to fill the gaps. These men were capable of performing their normal duties of inspecting cargo carriers and hunting small privateers, but they lacked the skills and experience to handle their ships with the precision needed by a fleet action. Indeed the Third Division had never been expected to perform such a role. By refusing to fight a purely defensive battle, Senna Pereira had made a mistake. As the course of the action demonstrated, his ships had little chance when faced with such experienced and aggressive opponents as Brown and the British, Irish and American officers who dominated his squadron.

The Brazilian authorities played down the importance of Juncal. To a navy which consisted of 69 warships and 22 packets and transports, manned by 10,600 officers and men,[16] the loss of 13 of its smallest armed vessels made little difference to the ultimate balance of naval power. Likewise, although Buenos Aires now controlled the Uruguay it was not a matter of major strategic importance. Argentina's new freedom to trade and communicate unhindered with the rebels at the western end of the Banda Oriental was inconvenient for the Brazilians, but it was unlikely to seriously influence the course of the war – especially in the stalemate which followed Ituzaingú. Nevertheless, the defeat had been a blow to the Empire's prestige and morale and represented the first serious challenge to Brazilian naval supremacy in the Plate. It was not the last.

CHAPTER 15

DISASTER IN PATAGONIA

At the beginning, the success of the Argentinian war against Brazilian commerce was hampered by the country's lack of natural harbours. Apart from the haven of Buenos Aires, the southern shore of the Plate comprised a flat and featureless estuary where it was difficult to distinguish where the water ended and the land began; while the Atlantic coast consisted of long and dreary stretches of sand or rocks, open to southerly winds and exposed to a dangerous swell. There were few river mouths to provide protection and deep water anchorages for distressed shipping. With Buenos Aires ruled out as a privateer base by the efficiency of the Imperial blockade, there were only two places on the Atlantic side that could be used – Salado on the Plate and Carmen in Patagonia – and neither was ideal.

Salado is located on the river of that name some 30 miles south-east of Punto Indio on a great curve of flat coastline extending to Cape S. Antonio at the eastern extremity of the estuary. In 1826 it formed the frontier between 'settled' Buenos Aires and Indian territory, and was a distant and desolate location. There was little to Salado except a small settlement and a four-gun battery protecting a tiny harbour and an open roadstead exposed to north-easterly winds. To call it a 'base' would be to exaggerate: but it was a useful temporary haven for privateers, prizes and blockade runners and provided them with their last protected anchorage before making a final dash to Buenos Aires.

Of far greater significance was Carmen de Patagones, located 250 miles further south where the Rio Negro cut its way through a flat sandstone plain to join the Atlantic in a system of treacherous channels and sandbanks. The old colonial town and fort of

Carmen had been built 16 miles upstream, at the limit of navigation where the river narrowed to 300 yards. It had a population of 470, a civil administration, a prize court, facilities for provisioning, repair and relaxation, and was protected by a small battery of 18- and 24-pounder cannon. With care it was possible for small craft to navigate the shoals at the entrance and the shifting sandbanks on the lower stretches of the river to reach the protection of Carmen but, as the *Sailing Directory* for the area made clear, it was a hazardous undertaking for any vessel drawing more than 11 feet of water.[1] The town's main disadvantage, however, was its isolation. Buenos Aires was inaccessible by land because of difficult terrain and hostile Indians, so that privateers, prize goods and booty still had to complete the journey by sea – as the *Lavalleja* learned to its cost. As the town developed into an important privateering base, Colonel Martin Lacarra, the local commander, strengthened his defences, building a small battery at the mouth of the river and raising his military forces to 210 men – 50 mounted militia, 20 scouts, 40 artillerymen and 100 infantry made up of freed negroes from one of the *Lavalleja*'s prizes, the slaver *São José Diligente*.

Admiral Pinto Guedes had for some time been considering a raid on Carmen, but it was only in early 1827, when he learnt that George Bynon's 'Chile' corvette *Chacabuco* had been disarmed for repair and that a number of small privateers and their prizes were sheltering in the town, that he turned his plan into reality. Four ships were selected for the task. These were the corvettes *Duqueza de Goias* and *Itaparica* – each armed with 20 guns and 160 men, the brigantine *Escudeira* with a traversing 24-pounder, 4 carronades and a crew of 80 and the schooner *Constança* carrying a traversing 18-pounder, 2 carronades and 50 men. Overall command was given to Captain James Shepherd, a Scots veteran who had fought with Cochrane (and George Bynon) in Chile and had travelled with him in 1823 to join the service of Brazil. Though lacking in imagination and a strict disciplinarian, Shepherd had nevertheless fought throughout the independence campaign in the 74-gun *Pedro I* and had sailed with Cochrane to Portsmouth in the frigate *Piranga*, where he had assumed command when her captain had resigned to follow the Admiral to Greece. Returning to Brazil in early 1826, Shepherd and his ship had been part of the River Plate Squadron since May. The *Piranga* was too large for the Patagonia expedition, so Shepherd was transferred to the *Duqueza de Goias* with 200 of the *Piranga*'s British seamen who were distributed among the ships of the flotilla to provide an additional landing force. This brought the total manpower to 650 officers and men – more than enough to deal with the 200 semi-trained troops that were thought to be in Patagonia.

Like the *Piranga*, the *Itaparica* was a ship which was largely officered and manned by British seamen. Its captain was William Eyre, formerly of the Royal Navy and a veteran of both the Brazilian War of Independence and of the rebellion known as the Confederation of the Equator. He had taken command of the corvette as a result of Pinto Guedes' 'shake up' in May and had played a creditable part in the battles of Los Pozes and Lara-Quilmes. The *Escudeira* and *Constança* on the other hand were manned by Brazilian crews and were commanded respectively by Lieutenant Clemente Poutier – the French officer who had caused the diplomatic storm by seizing the British prize *Pilar* when in command of the *Empreendador* – and a brilliant Brazilian sublieutenant, Joaquim Marques Lisboa, destined to become Admiral Marquis Tamandaré and the hero of the Paraguayan War. Although only 19 years old, Joaquim had already seen action with John Taylor on the *Niterói* during the frigate's dramatic chase of the Portuguese convoy across the Atlantic during the Independence War and with Lord Cochrane against the Confederation of the Equator.

The Brazilian force assembled off Maldonado, then sailed south on 16 February 1827. Shepherd's orders were to destroy the batteries protecting Carmen, to burn the *Chacabuco* and to seize or destroy any merchant shipping found in the town.[2] By 25 February the expedition was within striking distance of the Rio Negro and Shepherd, with exemplary caution, sent the *Escudeira* ahead flying American colours to reconnoitre the mouth of the river. The intruder was spotted and the false flag fooled no-one. The alarm was raised and the battery at the mouth of the river was reinforced. Then, two days later, the Argentinian sentries sighted the sails of all four enemy warships lifting menacingly over the horizon.

On 28 February 1827, the Brazilian flotilla crossed the bar and began the tortuous four-mile approach through the sandbanks to the entrance to the river, the *Escudeira* going in the lead with a pilot flying a blue flag to signify that there was enough water for the corvettes. Behind, in order, came the *Itaparica*, the *Duqueza de Goias* and the *Constança*. As they came within range, the *Escudeira* and *Itaparica* began to exchange fire with the battery. Then, suddenly, the *Duqueza de Goias* slid to a halt on a sandbank. The *Constança* moved in to assist but the corvette was securely grounded. For two days, the Brazilians tried in vain to refloat her, but on the third day, with the wind rising to gale force, they abandoned the attempt and began to transfer her crew and military stores. It was said that many of the British sailors took advantage of the confusion to break into the spirit store.[3] But before the evacuation had been completed, the storm struck the estuary, threw the *Duqueza de Goias* on her beam ends and smashed her to pieces. Of the men on board, 280 had been saved but 39 were lost in the crashing seas, many the worse for drink.

Meanwhile, according to plan, Commander William Eyre had arrived at the mouth of the river with the *Itaparica* and *Escudeira* and had stormed the Argentinian battery with the ships' boats. After a brisk action, the battery was taken, the emplacements and their guns were destroyed and the defenders fled inland. With his rear now secure and the men and stores from the *Duqueza de Goias* redistributed, Shepherd was ready to begin the advance on Carmen. On 4 May, the three remaining Brazilian ships weighed anchor and made their way up river. But bad luck continued to dog their efforts. After only a few miles, the *Itaparica* too ran aground. As predicted in the *Sailing Directory*, the corvette's draught was too deep to pass the changing sandbanks with safety. Anxious to get on with the job, Shepherd transferred the landing party to the brigantine and the schooner and, leaving the *Itaparica* with 107 men under the command of wounded Lieutenant Joaquim Pecuario, pressed on. On the evening of 6 March – still six miles short of their destination – the Brazilian ships anchored and the landing party, consisting of some 320 officers and men under Shepherd's direct command was rowed ashore. To make up for the losses on the *Duqueza de Goias*, their numbers included Sublieutenant Marques Lisboa and 35 men from the *Constança* which – in spite of his protests – was left with a skeleton crew in the charge of another future admiral, Sublieutenant Joaquim Ignacio. Without reconnaissance, and with the haziest of plans, Shepherd led his men northwards into the darkness. In his pocket was a confident proclamation to the civilian population stressing the limited objectives of the expedition and assuring all of good treatment.[4]

If the Brazilian commander had been fully aware of what was to confront him in Carmen de Patagones he would have been less confident. His information that the corvette *Chacabuco* had been disarmed and that three prizes – the *Bella Flor*, *Emperador* and *Chiquinha* – were anchored off the town was correct. What he did not know was that three of Argentina's boldest privateer captains were also in town with their crews – Dautant of the *Oriental Argentina*, Harris of the *Hijo de Mayo* and Fourmantine of the *Hijo de Julio*. Thus, instead of being confronted by only 200 poorly trained local militia and black troops, Shepherd's Anglo-Brazilian force was actually facing an additional 330 tough privateersmen, of whom 180 were British and American, 70 French and 70 Latin Americans.[5] In early March, Colonel Lacarra had called his military commanders, including Bynon and the privateer captains, to councils of war to decide whether they should await the arrival of the Brazilian invaders in Carmen or fight them where they landed. The decision was unanimously in favour of attack: but there were delays when the senior pilot reported that the current state of the river made a water-borne expedition impractical. But before Bynon could check the information for himself, news arrived that Shepherd and his men had already landed and were on their way. There was nothing more to do but man the defences of the town and train the guns of the ships in the harbour on the point where the assault was likely to fall. Whether deliberately or accidentally, the guide led the Brazilian invaders on a long and circuitous route

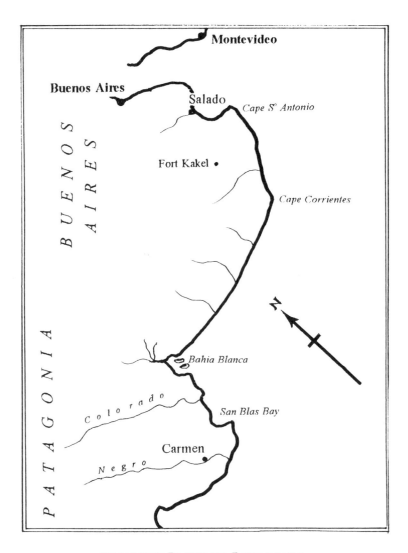

FROM THE PLATE TO PATAGONIA

through soft sand, and it was not until dawn that the now exhausted landing party arrived in sight of their destination, a low hill
overlooking the port of Carmen. It had been Shepherd's intention
to seize the hill, then to turn the guns which were said to be on its
summit on the anchorage to destroy the shipping before withdrawing in good order. But as dawn broke on 7 March, it became
clear that he had made a miscalculation. Instead of outnumbering
the defenders, it was the Brazilians who were outnumbered. And
in place of a token resistance, they found the hill and the town
defended by well manned trenches supported by guns on both
land and water. Nevertheless, the Imperial force advanced and was
immediately assailed by a splutter of long-range musketry and
cannon fire. Almost the first man to fall was Captain Shepherd,
killed by a bullet in the neck. William Eyre immediately took
command but, seeing the hopelessness of his position, abandoned
the attack. The Brazilian force turned on its heel and began to
retreat back across the desolate plain which lay between them and
their ships.

Captain Bynon and the Argentinian sea commanders realized
that the key to victory lay not in pursuing the Brazilians by land,
but in removing their exit route by seizing their ships. Leaving 90
irregular cavalrymen to harass the retreating enemy, Bynon filled
the *Oriental Argentina* and the three prizes with men and slipped
down river in search of the Imperial squadron. The first victim
was the *Escudeira*. The brigantine was attacked head-on in a burst
of fire which disabled her 24-pounder and left 13 casualties
including her commander, Lieutenant Poutier. The *Escudeira* was
then boarded and captured by privateersmen from the *Bella Flor*
led by Bynon himself. Meanwhile, a mile further on, the *Constança*
cut her cable and, in accordance with her orders, attempted to
rejoin the *Itaparica* further down river. The attempt failed. The
schooner ran aground and the remnants of the crew were overwhelmed by hordes of men from the *Emperador* under Harris and
the *Chiquito* led by Fourmantine's second-in-command, Jean
Seaber. The Argentinians then ran down to where the *Itaparica* still
lay stranded, boarded the corvette on all sides and forced her to
surrender. There was little resistance. Lieutenant Pecuario stayed in

his cabin claiming to be incapacitated by his wound, while Lieutenants David Carter and Gore Whitlock Ousley were too drunk (not for the first time) to organize any effective defence.[6]

Meanwhile, Eyre's landing party was struggling across the flat desert plain south of Carmen. Already tired and short of supplies and water, the men marched all day in the blazing sun, plagued by thirst and by the cavalrymen who harried their flanks. It was a wretched place, 'a sterile landscape which supports nothing but tufts of withered grass and low scattered bushes armed with thorns' – as Charles Darwin was to describe it only five years later.[7] The expedition was growing increasingly desperate. Then, the Argentinians raised a flag of truce, revealed that all the Imperial ships had been captured and that the escape route had been cut off, and demanded surrender.[8] At nightfall Eyre capitulated, surrendered his flags and weapons and led his 316 surviving officers and men into captivity.

Patagonia was a stunning victory for the Government of Buenos Aires. Another major Brazilian threat had been thwarted and a military force annihilated. No fewer than 660 prisoners, three fully equipped warships and large quantities of muskets, cartridges, bayonets, cutlasses, powder, slow match, boarding hooks and other munitions had been captured.[9] The magnitude of the victory at first caused problems as the prisoners-of-war outnumbered the troops available to guard them. But the situation was eased when 184 captured British seamen volunteered for service with Argentina in place of unpaid imprisonment.[10] Ironically, it improved even further when, with typical daring, Eyre and the young Marques Lisboa at the head of 93 prisoners seized control of the brig *Ana* carrying them to Salado and returned in triumph to Montevideo.

From the Brazilian point of view, Patagonia represented an embarrassing defeat. The fundamental cause had been poor planning and intelligence and, for the first time, Pinto Guedes had made a serious mistake. Justifying his actions later to the Minister of Marine, he wrote:

Shepherd was chosen to go with this expedition as an excellent officer ... taking with him the best pilots we have. ... I gave him two powerful corvettes and schooners and picked men to land, take and destroy the battery at the entrance and then to burn the *Chacabuco* and take or burn the merchant vessels. Eyre disembarked, took the battery, spiked the guns and destroyed their carriages; however Shepherd, instead of going all the way with the three ships remaining ... landed at such a distance that when they wanted to re-embark they were caught between the beach and the bush and were obliged to surrender. If Shepherd had obeyed his instructions and had restricted himself to waterborne operations all would have been well in spite of the loss of the corvette.[11]

Pinto Guedes' remarks were ingenuous to say the least. The navigational hazards of the Rio Negro for big ships were well known, and the selection of two corvettes was unwise – particularly if the expedition was expected to sail up river as far as Carmen to accomplish its mission of destruction. Likewise, even if the men were hand-picked the officers were not. No attempt was made to change the officers of the chosen ships for seasoned and able men – as was Brown's habit. No fault can be found in the selection of Shepherd and Eyre, but many of their juniors were either too young and inexperienced or – like Ousley – were well known for their excessive drinking and poor performance. But Shepherd must carry much of the blame for the debacle. Like other British officers, Shepherd was a brave man, but he seemed to have felt that audacity and fighting spirit were more important than careful planning and intelligence. To land 300 men on a hostile shore in ignorance of both the terrain and the strength of the enemy was to court disaster – especially when his opponents were either British with the same aggressive instincts or priva-teersmen fighting for their livelihoods.

But James Shepherd was dead, and it was Pinto Guedes who took the blame for Juncal and Patagonia. Opposition politicians used the defeats as rods for the backs of the Government, and ministers themselves, instead of defending their Admiral, cynically tried to protect themselves by making him the scapegoat. Ignoring the undoubted success of the commercial blockade of Buenos Aires and the energy of his subordinate commanders such as

Norton, in April the Minister of Marine wrote to Pinto Guedes blaming the defeats on the fact that he had not personally taken command and ordering him in future to be present during any major attack.[12] Such advice was clearly mistaken, but it was within the Government's rights to give it. What was reprehensible was that on 23 April 1827, the Government newspaper *Spectador* carried a personal attack on Pinto Guedes and on his style of command. He was accused of a lack of leadership, of remaining 'hermetically sealed in his cabin', of never appearing on deck and of giving all his orders through his adjutant. Unfortunately for Pinto Guedes, the resident English merchant John Armitage picked up the accusation and repeated it in his 1831 classic *History of Brazil from the arrival of the Braganza family in 1808 to the abdication of D Pedro I in 1831*, writing:

> During the whole of the war the untiring activity of Brown offered a great contrast to the apparent apathy of Admiral Rodrigo Pinto Guedes who locked himself up in a splendid cabin in his frigate of the line [sic], being seen only rarely by the men under his command. With a reputation for skill acquired in the days of absolute government when all was decided secretly by intrigue, he was more adept at making plans than putting them into execution. Cool and calculating, he showed greater energy in seizing prizes from which he gathered an immense fortune than in attacking and defeating the enemy.[13]

It is this travesty of the truth that has been repeated ever since by British, Argentinian and, indeed, most Brazilian historians. It is a tragedy for Pinto Guedes that his reputation is not based on a careful assessment of his achievements in the light of the formidable difficulties he faced in the Plate, but on rumours spread by politicians concerned principally with saving their own skins.

In Argentina, however, the reaction was different. Once again, for President Rivadavia the victory was a god-send. Faced with increased hostility from his federalist opponents in the provinces and with the disenchantment of his unitarian allies in the cities who were bearing the brunt of the disastrous economic consequences of the war, he was able to use the news of this fresh triumph to shore up his tottering regime. The victory despatches of Lacarra and Bynon were published widely in the newspapers and made the subject of a special broadsheet called 'Triumph in Patagonia'. To rub in its successes further, the Government purchased the *Itaparica*, *Constança* and *Escudeira* and added them to the National Squadron under the names of Argentina's latest victories – as *Ituzaingú*, *Juncal* and *Patagonia*. There was little doubt that Patagonia was, in the words of Lord Ponsonby's report to London, 'the most important success so far gained by the Republic'.[14]

But that was not the end. Pinto Guedes was determined to wipe out the memory of the defeat in Patagonia with a victory and in September 1827 – with the war once more in full swing – he tried again. The objective was a simple one – to recapture the Indiaman *Condessa de Ponte*, captured by the privateer *Oriental Argentina* ten months earlier and lying in the Bay of San Blas, 65 miles north of Carmen. The task was to be carried out by a small powerful and experienced flotilla led by Captain William Eyre and comprising three ships commanded and substantially manned by British seamen – the corvette *Maceió* (Commander Alexander Reid) and the brigs *Independência ou Morte* (Captain Francis Clare) and *Caboclo* (Commander William James Inglis). Pinto Guedes believed that with 20 feet of water over the bar and twice as much within the bay,[15] there would be few navigational problems, but Eyre was less certain. Other navigators agreed, and the *Sailing Directory* published subsequently in 1845 was to warn 'San Blas Bay is no place for a ship to enter unless under favourable circumstances of weather, wind and tide. It is decidedly dangerous with a south-easter because there is then a sea on the banks outside which confuses the pilot's eye and prevents him distinguishing the proper channel.'[16] Nevertheless, Eyre's ships carried the best pilots to ensure safety.

The flotilla had its first taste of trouble when the ships touched bottom on the Colorado Bank seven miles from their destination. The incident increased Eyre's misgivings, and when the expedition arrived off the bay on 21 September, he ordered the ships to heave to for a conference before making the approach. The weather was

1. View of the city and Bay of Rio de Janeiro 1830, by J M Rugendas.

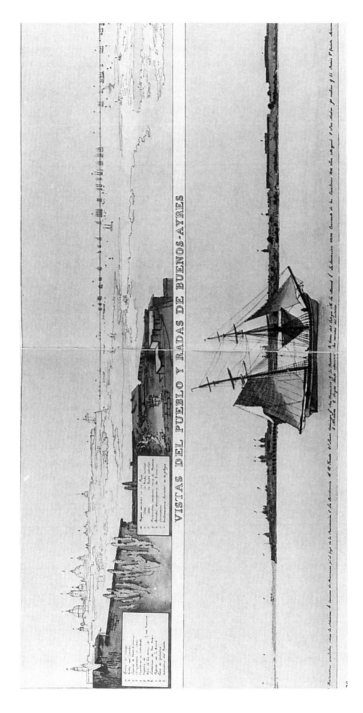

VISTAS DEL PUEBLO Y RADAS DE BUENOS-AYRES

2. Views of the city and Roadstead of Buenos Aires 1830, by C E Pellegrino.

3. The Emperor Pedro I.

4. Bernadino Rivadavia.

5. The night attack on the frigate *Imperatriz* (centre by the *25 de Mayo* (right) in Montevideo. Eduardo de Martino in the Dept de Estudios Historicos Navales, Buenos Aires.

6. James Norton

7. The *8 de Febreiro* (Capt Tomas Espora) intercepted by the Brazilian corvette *Carioca* (Cmdr George Clarence), April 1828. Emilio de Biggeri in the Dept de Estudios Historicos Navales, Buenos Aires.

8. The State Privateer *Gobernador Dorrego* (left) captured by a Brazilian Squadron, August 1828. The *Bertioga* (Cmdr George Broom) on the right, with the *Caboclo* (Cmdr William J Inglis) in the centre behind the *Rio da Plata* (Lieut J Marques Lisboa). Eduardo De Martino, Museuo Historico Nacional, Buenos Aires.

good and the pilots were unanimous that there was little danger, one claiming that he 'would lose his head if he could not take us in'.[17] The captains supported them and Eyre withdrew his objection. Slowly, the flotilla crept into the bay with a boat going ahead to take soundings when, suddenly, the water shallowed to nine feet and the *Independência ou Morte*, followed rapidly by the *Maceió* slid to a halt on the mud. Anchors were dropped to kedge the ships off, but before the manoeuvre had even begun, the weather deteriorated and the freshening wind pushed the stranded vessels even more firmly onto the banks. Eyre had done his best to prevent just such an occurrence, but his luck was out. With night falling, there was no alternative but to abandon ship. Reid of the *Maceió* seemed helpless to deal with the situation and Eyre was forced to supervise the evacuation himself. Amid darkness, confusion and crashing seas, some 40 men were drowned, but 83 others managed to save themselves by rowing ashore where they were promptly captured by the waiting Argentinians – Eyre for the second time in six months. The rest reached the safety of the *Caboclo* which had hauled off to escape the fate of her consorts and was waiting in the deeper water off shore. Captain Clare stayed on to watch as, within hours, the *Independência ou Morte* was smashed to pieces by wind and waves, while the following night the *Maceió* broke in two and sank. Then, sure that there were no further survivors, he laid the *Caboclo* on the starboard tack and headed back to Montevideo with news of yet another Patagonian disaster.

CHAPTER 16

THE EMPIRE STRIKES BACK: THE BATTLE OF MONTE SANTIAGO

The news of the victories at Ituzaingú and Juncal did much to restore the self-confidence of the Argentinian Government. Speaking to foreign envoys, President Rivadavia continued to stress his desire for peace and his concern that the strains of the conflict might destroy the stability of the Brazilian Empire,[1] but his ministers continued to plan for war. The ten warships captured at Juncal were added to the National Squadron, but most were small schooners which did nothing to increase its ability to take on the big sea-going vessels of the Brazilian Navy. To do this, ships of force were needed. Robert Ramsay had been ordered to make up for this deficiency by purchasing warships and steam vessels as early as March 1826,[2] and his visit to Buenos Aires on the *Goldfinch* in November had secured a promise of £200,000 to finish the job.[3] By March 1827 he had already begun the refit of the frigates *Chapman* and *Asia*, bought respectively in the United States and London, and now was looking for a suitable ship-of-the-line.[4] But in the interim, the momentum of the war had to be maintained and – in the view of the Government – the best method was to attack once more the vulnerable sea-borne trade of the Brazilian Empire.

On 26 March 1827, therefore, Commodore Brown received secret orders from the Minister of War and Marine. 'The Government is convinced', they began, 'that one of the most effective ways of making the Emperor of Brazil listen to the voice of Justice and Reason and be ready to make Peace, is to expose his coasts and commerce to a strong and energetic maritime war which will disrupt communications and destroy great fortunes.' Brown was ordered to select his best four ships and to lead them on an immediate raid against the sea lanes of Brazil in imitation of the cruise of the *Sarandí* and the *Chacabuco* five months earlier. He was to carry out hostilities on land and sea; to observe the laws of nations; and – as usual – to avoid engagements with superior forces.[5]

Brown responded with alacrity. His best ships and best men were picked for the task – the *República Argentina* (Captain William Granville), *Independencia* (Commander Francis Drummond), *Congreso Nacional* (Captain William Mason) and *Sarandí* (Lieutenant John Halstead Coe). Manning and preparations for the cruise began immediately. With the additional stimulus of news of the victory in Patagonia, which had just arrived overland from Salado, the ships were ready for action on 5 April. That night, taking advantage of a northerly wind, Brown and his ships left the anchorage of Los Pozes and slipped silently down river heading for the channel between the Chico Bank and the southern shore, their lookouts anxiously scanning the darkness for signs of the Imperial blockading squadron.

As usual, the Brazilians were guarding the exits from Buenos Aires in force. Patrolling the channel to the west of the Ortiz Bank was an advanced guard of four ships – the corvette *Maceió*, the brig *Pirajá*, the lugger *Principe Imperial* and the schooner *Providência*. Behind them lay the main blockading force, anchored at the western end of the Ortiz Bank. It consisted of ten warships: the corvette *Liberal* (Captain Bartholomew Hayden); the brigs *Caboclo* (Lieutenant William James Inglis), *Independência ou Morte* (Commander Francis Clare), *29 de Agosto* (Lieutenant Raphael de Carvalho) and *Rio da Plata* (Lieutenant J. Lamego Costa); the schooners *Dona Paula* (Sublieutenant Manuel da Costa Pereira), *Conceição* (Sublieutenant Bourville J. Wilson), *Itaparica* (Lieutenant Angelo Bittencourt) and *Maria Theresa* (Sublieutenant Eduardo Wandenvolk).

Also present was a familiar figure – Commodore James Norton, restored to command of the blockade in March and flying his broad pennant in the tenth ship, the 50-gun frigate *Dona Paula*. Originally the 1200-ton East Indiaman *Surat Castle*, the frigate had been purchased in 1825, refitted in Blackwall and armed with 28 medium 18-pounder guns and 22 32-pounder carronades.[6] Theoretically, the *Dona Paula*'s size and draught made her unsuitable for the shallow waters of the Plate Estuary, but the Brazilian commanders had decided that although numerical superiority could contain Brown, it would never defeat him – he was far too skilful a tactician. Their only chance of decisive victory lay in overwhelming him with superior firepower. The truth of this judgement was to be proved in the battle which was to follow.

The Argentinian squadron got no further than ten miles from Buenos Aires before it was spotted by the *Maceió* and her consorts. The corvette fired a gun and let off signal rockets to alert the Brazilian main force, then withdrew to watch the enemy's movements. Norton's ships promptly weighed anchor and deployed to block the channel leading through the banks. Brown responded by leading his ships closer to the perilous southern shore, hoping to slip round the Brazilian line in the darkness. At the best of times it would have been a difficult manoeuvre; but at night, and with a northerly wind pushing the ships to leeward, it proved to be disastrous. At 2.30 am, the *República Argentina* and the *Independencia* both ran aground on the mud off the Ensenada Spit. Frantic efforts were made to refloat them but the onshore wind and tide frustrated every move. As daylight approached Brown gave up the attempt and prepared for the inevitable attack. The *Sarandí* was ordered into a defensive position between the stranded brigs, while the *Congresso* was sent to Buenos Aires to bring help. Alas, she was promptly intercepted by the *Maceió* and her consorts and forced back. Brown cut his losses and ordered her to anchor in clear water behind the spit near the higher ground called Monte Santiago.

As dawn crept over the estuary, Brown's predicament was immediately apparent to the Brazilian blockading squadron. Huddled on a lee shore and incapable of manoeuvre, the Argentinian warships seemed entirely at their mercy. Commodore Norton's task was, however, difficult. The strength of the wind and the turbulence of the water in the shallows made an attack by boats problematic, while the draught of his ships prevented them approaching nearer than a mile without running into danger. The best he could do was to bear down on the Argentinians and try his luck with a long-range cannonade. And so it was. At 9 am, Norton transferred his flag to the *Liberal* and cautiously led the four brigs and four schooners down within range of the Argentinians and opened fire. The engagement went on all day, but the range was too great to be effective. At midday, Brown signalled his ships to discontinue the action and save ammunition. At 6 pm, Admiral Pinto Guedes, who had arrived to watch with the frigates *Piranga* and *Imperatriz* and the schooners *Rios, Bela Maria and Atlanta*, likewise ordered his ships to cease fire and to watch the movements of the enemy.

As night fell, Brown had the Articles of War read on his ships to remind the crews that there was to be no abandonment of the position until he gave the order, then made another attempt to refloat the stranded brigs. But with no change in either the direction of the wind or the depth of water, the effort proved futile. Argentinian nerves were additionally frayed by the flash of broadsides in the darkness from the *Caboclo* and the *Maria Theresa* which had recommenced firing with exactly this purpose in mind.

At dawn on 8 April, the weather moderated and the second phase of Norton's plan was put into effect. His shallower draught ships – the *Caboclo, Independência ou Morte, 29 de Agosto, Rio da Plata* and the four schooners with their traversing 18-pounders – were formed into two lines and ordered to close the range with the stranded Argentinians. They were to disable the enemy warships with cannon fire and then be prepared to take them by boarding when the order was given. Meanwhile the frigate *Dona Paula*, under Acting-Captain William Parker, was being cautiously towed within range. At 11 am, the smaller ships were in position and began the action with a burst of artillery. The firing was fast and furious. There were casualties on all sides. Granville, one of 14 wounded on the *República Argentina*, lost an arm. The *Sarandí* was struck 20 times and suffered 17 casualties. Raphael de Carvalho of the *29 de Agosto* was killed. The *Independência ou Morte*, engaged with the *Independencia*, ran aground and could only be saved by jettisoning her guns. At midday, the *Rio da Plata* and the *Liberal* – firing at a distance – ran out of shot and cartridges. Many other ships were in the same position. Drummond of the *Independencia* had to be re-supplied from his companions.

For the Argentinians there was neither relief nor succour even though a desperate Espora was waiting in Buenos Aires with a fleet of gunboats for a favourable wind. But for the Brazilians, the tide of battle was about to turn. At 2 pm, the *Dona Paula* reached its position and began to fire in a storm of thunder and smoke. As Consul Hood subsequently reported, the frigate's huge 18-pounders were turned successively on the two stranded brigs, smashing them to pieces.[7] The *Independencia* had 14 wounded and 43 killed. One of the dead was its young captain Francis Drummond whose dying thoughts were of Scotland and whose last act was to send his watch to his mother and his ring to Eliza Brown. Brown ordered Lieutenant John King of the *República Argentina* to evacuate the brig and burn it, but the boats of the *Caboclo* got there first and captured both the brig and 43 prisoners. Then it was the turn of the *República Argentina*. Recognizing the inevitable, Commodore Brown, himself slightly wounded, decided to cut his losses and retreat. Abandoning the stranded brig to the triumphant Brazilians, he moved with the survivors to the battered *Sarandí* then, taking advantage of a change of wind to the south-east, sped back to the safety of Buenos Aires with the *Congresso Nacional* in company. There was no pursuit. The victorious Brazilians were busy sorting out the wreckage of battle, gathering the dead and rounding up prisoners. Soon the haze of cannon smoke was thickened by the burning hulls of the *Independencia* and *República Argentina*.[8]

The victory of Monte Santiago was a useful corrective to the run of Argentinian successes, but in Rio de Janeiro there was no exaggerated enthusiasm. There was relief that the daring Brown had at last come a cropper, but no surprise that the superior strength of the Brazilian Navy had made itself felt. But in Buenos Aires, the mood of the public and the foreign resident communities was euphoric. They saw it as a glorious encounter in which the actual result mattered less than the bravery shown by the National Squadron in fighting against such odds. The battle had been witnessed by Colonel MacDonald of the Royal Horse Artillery whose description reflected both the mood and the inevitable British sympathy for the underdog. His account began, 'At 2 pm, I saw the Brazilian Squadron giving a heavy and destructive fire on Brown's ships – he having 3, the Brazilians 17,' and ended 'during the action Brown and his officers behaved with bravery and devotion. I have not the language to express my admiration of the conduct of Admiral Brown – never did a man in a similar situation acquit himself with more zeal and gallantry!' Lord Ponsonby's despatch to London took the same line, beginning, 'It will be hard to find even in our own brilliant naval history an action more daring', and concluding portentously, 'You will observe that all these splendid displays of courage have been made by Britons!'[9]

Lord Ponsonby was exaggerating – but only slightly. The Argentinian marines were made up entirely of Latin Americans, but the majority of the seamen and gunners were from the United States, Britain, France and Italy, the exact proportion depending on the ship. Thus, at least half of the lower deck, and the majority of both the sea officers and warrant officers, were English, Scots and Irish. They included Commodore Brown himself; three out of four captains (William Mason, William Granville and Francis Drummond); all four first lieutenants (John King, Malcolm Shannon, George Love and Innes Johnson); and half of the 15 remaining lieutenants and midshipmen.[10] At Monte Santiago, a solid nucleus of the Argentinian crews were Britons. To that extent, Ponsonby was right.

The public in Buenos Aires may have been enthusiastic, but the official mood was sober. The victory in Patagonia had frustrated a Brazilian attempt to strike a blow at the Argentinian war on commerce, but – like Juncal – had done little to push the Empire in the direction of peace. Now at Monte Santiago, two of

Argentina's precious brigs-of-war had been destroyed and the cream of its Navy had been roundly defeated. The Brazilian Navy's overwhelming superiority at sea had been reasserted in a way which neither William Brown's audacity nor Ramsay's newly purchased frigates could seriously challenge. Ambassador Gordon in Rio shrewdly summarized the situation in a private letter to Lord Ponsonby:

> The resources of this Empire seem immense and believing as I do that Brown – *great* as he is – cannot with his schooners annihilate the Brazilian Navy, you will merely have the blockade restored with increased vigour. With the same ships and the same means which the Emperor now has in his possession … it is within his power to sink Brown and his small craft and blow the town of Buenos Aires into the water. Is it possible to believe that the Government of Buenos Aires possesses the power to raise the blockade? Its mere continuance will complete her ruin.[11]

There were many in the Argentinian capital who agreed.

PART V: WAR AND PEACE

CHAPTER 17

INTERNATIONAL OUTCRY AND THE CRACKING OF THE BLOCKADE

The Brazilian Navy's efficiency in blockading the River Plate following the arrival of Admiral Pinto Guedes rapidly strangled the trade of Buenos Aires. In a normal six-monthly period over 180 foreign merchantmen would have been discharging their cargoes in the Inner Roads: in the second half of 1826, only two vessels managed to get through. The rest had either been deterred from entering a war zone or had been intercepted and seized as prizes by the Imperial Navy. The result had been a wave of international protest. Only the British supported the Brazilian position, but even they were complaining about individual cases. Then, in November 1826, US Consul Condy Raguet announced publicly that his Government refused to accept the legality of the blockade and would not allow its ships to be captured and its commerce disrupted.[1] Captain Hoffman in the USS *Boston* was sent to Montevideo with the news and to demand the unconditional release of the *Pioneer*, recently taken off Cape S. Mary 160 miles east of Montevideo.[2] At the same time, His Catholic Majesty's frigate *Alacrity* was on its way across the Atlantic with instructions from Paris which authorized Ambassador de Gestas to reject the blockade and to threaten naval reprisals unless all French prizes were released and indemnification paid.

Faced with the flat refusal of the Americans and French to recognize the blockade, the resolve of the Brazilian Government began to crumble. The Emperor also found himself distracted by a range of more immediate problems. At home his autocratic temperament was disturbed by the way things were going. The new Legislative Assembly, which had begun its sessions in Rio at the beginning of May, had reflected the public mood by denouncing the 'secret' clauses of the 1825 treaty recognizing Brazilian independence – especially that by which the Empire agreed to pay £2 million to Portugal in compensation. Deputies had also asked awkward questions about the commercial treaty which had rewarded British diplomatic support by allowing the continued importation of British goods at the derisory low tariff of 15 per cent, and at what was rumoured to be a similar but quite unnecessary arrangement with France. How, they asked, could this be squared with the need for revenue to fight the war, the costs of which were increasingly being met by debasing the currency and flooding the country with paper money and copper coins?

Abroad Pedro was also confronted by a succession crisis caused by the sudden death of his father the King of Portugal, D. João VI, in March 1826. Pedro, the heir, was clearly unacceptable to Portugal because of his Brazilian associations, while his devious and reactionary brother, Miguel, was still in exile in Vienna following a failed attempt to overthrow his father in 1825. But there was an ingenious solution. The idea was that Pedro would renounce his right to the Portuguese throne in favour of his daughter, the eight-year-old Princess Maria da Glória, who would then marry her uncle Miguel to safeguard his dynastic position. To bring about this happy solution and try to prevent Miguel resorting to his instinctive treachery, Pedro needed the support of the governments of Britain and France.

From Pedro's perspective, these problems were of far greater importance than the blockade of Buenos Aires, and concessions to international protest were a small price to pay if they gained him the support he needed. The military situation in the Banda

Oriental also needed attention. In October 1826, he had appointed the Marquis of Barbacena as his new commander-in-chief, and in November he planned to pay a personal morale-building visit to the war zone. But before his departure, the tensions of the blockade had to be defused. The Council of State met to devise a strategy. That done, on 24 November 1826, the Emperor set sail for Rio Grande do Sul in the 74-gun *Pedro I* accompanied by the frigate *Isabela*, the corvette *Duqueza de Goias*, the schooner *2 de Dezembro* and seven troopships. The *Isabela* was the Imperial Navy's newest acquisition and was one of the most modern ships afloat. Launched in the United States in April 1826, she had been built to the lines of the *Brandywine*: 1768 tons, 177 feet in length[3] and with 62 guns, including a main-deck armament of 32-pounders – the sort of guns which during the Napoleonic Wars had formed the principal battery of first-rate ships-of-the-line like HMS *Victory*. Ironically enough, one of the foreign warships in Rio de Janeiro observing the Imperial preparations was her sister-ship the USS *Brandywine*! Reporting to London, Rear Admiral Otway was highly impressed with the design of the *Isabela*, but noted that, like the other ships in the squadron, she had been 'wretchedly manned by impressment'.[4]

But before the Emperor put to sea, action to defuse foreign protests had already been taken. On 18 November, the Minister of Marine had issued a decree banning all forced recruitment of foreign seamen into the Brazilian Navy and ordering that those already in the service be handed over to their local naval authorities – the British were to be sent to the *Ganges*, the Americans to the *Macedonian* and the Frenchmen to the *Zelée*.[5] As a result, over 70 British sailors were released from the Brazilian Plate Squadron between February and May 1827. Unfortunately, Rear Admiral Sir Robert Otway was so unimpressed by the poor condition of the men that he refused to accept them on board his gleaming flagship and insisted that they be sent to Rio for repatriation.[6]

Then, on 29 November, came a concession on the blockade, designed explicitly to avoid repetitions of the *Ruth* incident. Orders were sent to Pinto Guedes which prohibited him from detaining vessels 'which are encountered on the High Seas or in the act of entering Montevideo even if their passports show that they are destined for ports under blockade', and allowed him only to seize neutral merchant ships in the vicinity of blockaded ports. But as another – and far greater – concession, the Admiral was instructed to follow the confidential orders sent to Lobo on 17 and 24 December 1825.[7] In other words, the blockading squadron was now only allowed to seize neutral vessels heading for Argentinian ports *after* they had been individually informed of the existence of the blockade. Thus, at a stroke, the Brazilian Government abandoned the British-style doctrine which Pinto Guedes had enforced with such success and openly accepted the American interpretation of the law of blockade.

In the middle of January 1827, the Emperor Pedro suddenly returned to the capital having received news of the unexpected death a month earlier of his lonely and popular wife, the Empress Leopoldina. His first act was to dismiss the Government. Court gossip said that this was because of a complaint by Pedro's openly flaunted mistress, the Marquesa de Santos, that ministers had stopped her paying a particularly tactless visit to the Empress on her sickbed. But whatever the reason, a new government was appointed. Unfortunately in view of the increasingly difficult relationship with the Assembly, every member was a nobleman. The new Minister of Foreign Affairs was the Marquis of Queluz (whose grave and confident exterior, according to the French Ambassador, concealed a weak and indecisive personality) while as Minister of Marine, the wily and experienced Paranaguá was replaced by a light-weight courtier and captain-of-frigate, Francisco de Souza Coutinho, Marquis of Maceió. Foreign diplomats reported the news to their governments with the hope that the new ministers would be more responsive to their complaints on the prize issue. They were not disappointed. One of their first acts was to speed-up the process by ordering the immediate transfer of all prize cases to the Superior Admiralty Court and the appointment of additional judges.

The steady and intemperate pressure exerted for so long by Condy Raguet seemed to have had its effect. Unfortunately, he did not have long to enjoy his success. In February 1827, the American brig *Spark* sailed into Rio de Janeiro with guns hidden in the hold. The captain attempted unsuccessfully to sell the vessel to the Brazilian authorities, then, announcing openly in the Rio taverns that he was on his way to Buenos Aires to obtain a privateering commission, he increased his crew from 14 to 27 and sailed. He did not get far. Outside the bay, the *Spark* was arrested as a suspected privateer by a waiting armed Brazilian steamship.[8] Once again, Raguet was furious. His protest to the Brazilian Government crossed with a request for information on the vessel's character and purpose which he refused to provide. In March he demanded his passports, and on 7 April, bowed coldly to the Emperor and left in the USS *Cyane*. President Adams disapproved strongly of his envoy's action and refused to employ him again. Raguet has, he explained to a friendly senator, 'such a temper and want of judgement, takes blustering for bravery and insolence for energy' and is 'too dangerous.'[9] It was a fair assessment.

Admiral Pinto Guedes was dismayed by his new orders. Even his recent elevation to the Brazilian nobility as the Barão do Rio da Plata was of little compensation. In Buenos Aires, British Consul-General Woodbine Parish understood fully their significance, and wrote to London predicting that the new rules would seriously handicap the Imperial Navy's activities in crippling Argentinian trade.[10] He was right. By abandoning Pinto Guedes' policy of strict blockade, the Brazilian Government was giving up its most successful weapon – in fact its only successful weapon – in the war against the United Provinces. With the Imperial Navy's hands now tied, enemy commerce began to revive. During 1826, the certainty that neutral merchantmen would be seized on sight made attempts to run the blockade too dangerous. In 1827 and 1828, the fact that being stopped by a Brazilian warship would lead to nothing more serious than a warning made the risk worth taking – particularly for smaller vessels which could use the weather or the mudbanks to escape detection altogether. The result was that in 1827, 42 ocean-going merchantmen managed to reach Buenos Aires.[11] Unfortunately, only two were British. The merchants of London and Liverpool were still handicapped by their Government's recognition of the Brazilian blockade and the consequent absence of insurance. It was the Americans who took advantage of the new situation to revive their trade with Buenos Aires. From the beginning of 1827, the number of American ships either sailing from the United States or freighted locally by Argentinian merchants, steadily increased. Many were intercepted and warned off by the Brazilians; some – like the *President Adams*, *Sarah*, *Shilliloh* and *Tell Tale* – were captured; others – like the *Brutus* and *Hussar* – were burnt; but 59 got through to reap their reward in terms of a handsome profit.[12]

The French and the Americans were pleased with the Brazilian Government's concessions on the blockade. The question of what to do with ships already detained remained an issue, but the effect of the new rules was soon evident. More and more ships got through to Buenos Aires, the number of neutral merchantmen seized by the Brazilian Navy fell drastically, and the Prize Court in Montevideo began handing down more moderate judgements – promptly releasing, for example, the American *Pioneer*, the French *Geneviève* and the British vessels *Dickens* and *Agenoria*.[13] But the dissatisfaction felt by Pinto Guedes can be clearly seen in his reply to a complaint by Consul Hood over the *Enterprise*, the first British vessel to enter the Plate for 18 months which was promptly captured within sight of Buenos Aires. Ordering the release of the vessel, the Admiral wearily added:

> I feel not the least repugnance to act fairly to the subjects of His Britannic Majesty, but no-one is ignorant of the mischief which citizens of the United States have done by taking advantage of the obstructions placed in the way of this squadron – obstructions which now render the blockade ineffectual.[14]

And there was another aspect to this. The Argentinian Government remained convinced that a privateering war on commerce was the way to inflict maximum damage on Brazil. Ships' owners were happy to oblige, encouraged rather than deterred by the prospects of peace promised by the visit of Manuel Garcia to Rio de Janeiro in April and May. In the first quarter of 1827, ten privateers had been operational; in the second quarter the number went up to 17. But not only were Argentinian privateers becoming more numerous, they were increasing dramatically in size. The *armadores* of Buenos Aires had learnt that the greatest profits lay in attacking the sea routes of the South Atlantic, and that to do this effectively they needed larger, better-armed and more heavily manned ships which could not only overwhelm merchantmen but could take on the smaller cruisers of the Imperial Navy. And in providing these, the American blockade runners, now entering Buenos Aires as a result of the weakening of the Brazilian blockade, were playing a major role. Of the first 11 ships to enter Buenos Aires in 1827,[15] for example, six (the 120-ton *Beauty*, the 151-ton *General Lafayette*, the 210-ton *Midas*, the 224-ton *Sylph*, the 142-ton *Montezuma* and the 97-ton *Amelia Fauden*) were immediately purchased and armed to become respectively the *Sin Par*, *Presidente*, *La Presidenta*, *General Brandzen*, *Triunfo Argentino* and *Bonaerense* – probably Buenos Aires' most formidable and successful deep water privateers.[16] By August, all had sneaked out to sea and were beginning to cause havoc in the Brazilian trade routes.

The revised rules which weakened the Imperial Navy's strict enforcement of the blockade did not of course apply to Argentinian shipping. There, the time honoured instructions remained in force – 'to take, burn and otherwise destroy'. But unfortunately for the Brazilians, Buenos Aires had no merchant marine and, instead of picking up soft targets such as well loaded traders, the Imperial Navy found itself hunting a swarm of well armed privateers, mostly manned by foreigners thirsty for loot. The job of intercepting them was far from easy. During 1827, the 27 operational privateers took or destroyed 248 merchantmen, of which only half were captured or liberated.[17] There was little the Brazilian Navy could do to prevent it except throw more ships into the ring. So, in June, Pinto Guedes' three blockading divisions were augmented by a fourth, a force of brigs and schooners watching Salado which had now become a major privateer base. Its commander was Captain João de Oliveira Bottas, a tough old veteran of the War of Independence, which had plucked him from obscurity as an artisan in Salvador Dockyard to fame as a naval sublieutenant leading a flotilla of small boats which had played a major part in the defeat of the Portuguese in Bahia.

But the Brazilian Navy had more to cope with than navigational hazards and swarms of privateers and prizes. It took time for the battered Argentinian squadron to recover from the disaster of Monte Santiago, but two months later, Commodore Brown had prepared a select group of ships which he deliberately used to test the alertness of the blockaders and to provide distractions which could cover the departure of Argentina's new, big privateers. The first foray took place at the beginning of June when he headed for Martim Garcia in the schooner *8 de Febrero* (previously the Imperial brigantine *Dona Januária*) accompanied by the *General Balcarce*, the schooners *Sarandí, Maldonado, 9 de Febrero, 30 de Julio* and *18 de Enero* and three gunboats. As a gesture of defiance, five of the six schooners were prizes of war which had previously flown the Brazilian flag!

The departure of the expedition was spotted by the *Pirajá* which had been left on watch off Buenos Aires. The brig called for assistance from João de Bottas (Norton was on leave at the time) and, on 5 June, she was joined by the corvettes *Carioca* and *Liberal* and two schooners. For the next five days, the two squadrons played cat and mouse off Ensenada but, in spite of the claim made in Brown's memoirs,[18] nothing decisive occurred. As in similar engagements the previous year, the attacks of the heavier Brazilian ships were frustrated by the shallows and the mud – the deep-draughted *Carioca* repeatedly grounding – while the smaller, more nimble Argentinians were kept at a distance by the guns of their bigger opponents.

On 14 June, Commodore Brown got tired of the game and headed east for Montevideo looking for easier prey. He was in luck. At dawn the following day, he overwhelmed the 14-gun Imperial schooner *Maria Theresa*. Heavily outnumbered, the crew ignored the orders of her young Danish captain, Martius Boldt, and just refused to fight. With a prize to justify his cruise, Brown now headed for Buenos Aires. But this time he was disappointed. That night, the prize master, Lieutenant Johnson, reported (inaccurately as it turned out) that the schooner was leaking badly.

Brown promptly evacuated the *Maria Theresa*, abandoned her and headed home empty-handed. Then he watched with growing annoyance as João de Bottas' squadron, arriving hurriedly from Salado, retook the vessel and successfully repaired the damage before chasing the Argentinians back to their base.

CHAPTER 18

THE PALADINS, PEACE AND
THE FALL OF RIVADAVIA

The declaration of war between Brazil and the United Provinces was unwelcome to the British Government but it was hardly a surprise. Britain had been an observer of the rivalry between Spain and Portugal in the River Plate for centuries, and had watched closely – but without comment or approval – when in 1816 the Portuguese had occupied the northern bank of the river. Britain had also played a major role in the recognition of Brazilian independence, although in the negotiations the subject of the Banda Oriental had been left unmentioned. Once war had been declared Britain had likewise remained strictly neutral, though disapproving of the situation and looking forward to a speedy settlement.

The British Government's motivation was largely economic. Trade with the United Provinces had reached £1 million annually, and the country was seen as a promising area for the settlement of surplus population which would increase even more the demand for British goods. This hopeful prospect was immediately undermined by the war and the Brazilian blockade. Trade with Brazil was also substantial, running at £2.6 million annually, and although there was little chance that this would be ruined by the war, there were likely to be unpleasant consequences if the strain of the conflict disrupted the Brazilian economy. But there were political concerns as well. Foreign Secretary George Canning was particularly worried lest the forces unleashed by the war upset the delicate internal stability of the participants. The monarchical regime in Brazil – the only example in the Americas and one which established a link between the Old World and the New – was one which had his unstinting support. In his view, only a monarchy could actually hold that vast country together. His fear was of a combined attack by the other South American republics which would destabilize both the monarchy and Brazil. Canning also feared that the strains of war would increase the malign influence of the South American *caudillos* at the expense of the promising liberal democracy which seemed to be developing so well in the River Plate.

As the clouds of war began to gather, Britain was represented diplomatically in the region at the humble level of consul-general by Henry Chamberlain in Rio de Janeiro and Woodbine Parish in Buenos Aires. Both were competent and experienced officials who were already well known to their host governments and to local British residents. But however good they were, it was felt in Whitehall that in matters of peace and war they were too lowly in rank to exert much influence. To reflect appropriately the power and glory of His Majesty's Government more senior and well connected personages were needed. The grandees who were finally selected were Lord Ponsonby for Buenos Aires and the Honourable Robert Gordon for Rio de Janeiro.

John, Viscount Ponsonby in the peerage of Ireland was an aristocrat to his fingertips. Polished, ironical and opinionated, the 50-year-old diplomat was an habitué of palaces and royalty and, with blue-blooded self-confidence, was overawed by neither. Regarded as the handsomest man in the three kingdoms, he had even challenged George IV for the affections of the royal favourite, Lady Conyngham, a circumstance which – it was said – had helped to ensure his selection for this distant posting. Certainly it was the first major assignment in a diplomatic career which was to take him to Brussels, Naples, Constantinople and Vienna. Ponsonby had no great love for Buenos Aires, which he described as 'the vilest place I ever saw', or for the 'republican conceit' of its inhabitants.[1] Not even the well reported charms of the local ladies won him over. Nevertheless, he had a clear view of Britain's objectives and was forceful and blunt in persuading others to support them. One of his weaknesses was to overestimate the extent to which his eloquence had won others to his opinions.

Another was to make snap and sometimes superficial judgements about personalities. Thus President Rivadavia was written off as being of little more worth than 'the bustling mayor of a small town', while his successor, General Dorrego, on negligible evidence, was described as corrupt and unpatriotic. On the other hand, his views on Commodore William Brown were of uncritical admiration.

His more youthful colleague in Rio de Janeiro, the Honourable Robert Gordon, was no less well connected, being the son of Lord Haddo and brother to the Earl of Aberdeen. But, rather than being a cosmopolitan man of fashion, he was a tenacious and serious-minded Scot who was frequently forced to bring Ponsonby's over-imaginative interpretations of events down to earth. This was Gordon's third diplomatic post and he was stimulated by the challenges of the assignment – which included not only leading the Imperial Government towards a peace based on the creation of an independent buffer state in the Banda Oriental, but also tying up the loose ends of the independence settlement in terms of a commercial treaty which maintained the privileged position of Britain's trade and an agreement which would bring to an end the Brazilian slave trade. Scenically, the lush green hills, rocky headlands and gleaming beaches of Rio de Janeiro seemed more agreeable than the damp mudflats and low treeless landscape which were Ponsonby's lot. But, the heat and humidity of the Imperial capital rapidly undermined Gordon's health, and only the cool breezes and tranquillity of his residence at the Bay of Botafogo enabled him to survive the climate.

The appointment of these grand personages put an immediate stop to any actions by the two consuls-general, Woodbine Parish and Henry Chamberlain. British diplomatic activity was therefore muted from the beginning of 1826 when news of the nominations of Ponsonby and Gordon arrived. Not that much could have been done. Both sides were pushing the war forward in the expectation of victory – the Emperor Pedro determined to extinguish what he saw as an ungrateful rebellion, President Rivadavia using the war as an opportunity to strengthen the authority of the Central Government and promote patriotic enthusiasm for it.

Lord Ponsonby was the first to arrive. The plan was that he should sail first to Rio de Janeiro to press on the Imperial Government the chosen British solution to the dispute – namely, the voluntary withdrawal of Brazil from the Banda Oriental (in return for financial compensation) and the establishment of the province as an independent buffer state.[2] He was then to go on to Buenos Aires to persuade the Government there to accept the same solution.

As planned, the envoy sailed into the Bay of Guanabara on HMS *Thetis* on 26 May 1826 together with his suite, personal effects and a bevy of servants. Although the Court was in official mourning following the death of King João VI, talks began immediately with the Foreign Minister, the Marquis of Inhambupe, members of the Council of State and, ultimately, with the Emperor himself. They went on for three months. Ponsonby avoided being drawn into the rights and wrongs of the dispute and stuck to Brazil's need for a compromise solution based, desirably, upon the creation of an independent Banda Oriental. The continuation of the war, he argued, would lead to intervention by other South American republics in support of Buenos Aires to the ruin of monarchical Brazil. Inhambupe, bland and courteous, seemed sympathetic to the idea, but the Emperor was adamantly opposed. Ponsonby pointed out bluntly that the Brazilian solution – peace on the basis that the area would remain under Imperial control but with Montevideo available to Buenos Aires as a free port – was 'pointless', and threatened that, while remaining neutral, Britain 'would favour the belligerent who shall have shewn the ready disposition to bring about a ... just termination.'[3] But aristocratic plain-speaking had no effect, and when Ponsonby boarded the frigate *Doris* to continue his voyage at the end of August, he had achieved little. On reaching Montevideo, the envoy, his suite, personal effects and servants were transferred to the shallower draught corvette *Ranger* and eventually arrived at Buenos Aires on 16 September.

By this time, Rivadavia had been President of the United Provinces for seven months. His main energies during this period had been devoted to imposing a unitarian model on the republic and undermining the regional centres of power. The old Provincial Government of Buenos Aires had been immediately abolished, and by July, a pliant National Congress was working on a new constitution which was clearly intended to establish the supremacy of the Central Government. Fierce rumblings of opposition were already to be heard from the provincial landowners and *caudillos* who objected to both the measures themselves and the petty and insensitive way they were being implemented. However liberal his economic and social ideas, in office Rivadavia adopted a style so haughty and vain that even foreign diplomats were shaken.[4] The previous governor of Buenos Aires, General Las Heras, was treated with shocking discourtesy and the Ambassador in London was sacked for daring to criticize the President. Rivadavia seemed oblivious both to the hostility he was provoking and to the power of his federalist opponents. He saw the conflict with Brazil as a useful way of strengthening Central Government influence and of stimulating patriotic enthusiasm. Rivadavia therefore pursued the war with enthusiasm, 'managing' the news by minimizing every setback and trumpeting every triumph in his 'unitarian' mouthpiece the *Mensagero Argentino*. By August, there were 20,460 Argentinian troops of all arms in the Banda Oriental, all eager for the fray and under a new commander, General Alvear.[5]

Lord Ponsonby presented his credentials on 19 September 1826. Guards of honour were inspected, gun salutes fired and, escorted by a high-ranking general, he was conducted to the presidential presence in a coach drawn by six spirited horses. Rivadavia realized the political kudos to be gained from having an ambassador who was a British peer and was making the most of it. Then, the talks began. Rivadavia, still expecting victory by harassing the Empire at sea and by invading its southernmost province of Rio Grande do Sul, rejected the Brazilian proposals out of hand. Then, when Ponsonby offered a British guarantee of freedom of navigation on the Plate as a sweetener, Rivadavia attempted to manoeuvre him into declaring open support for the Buenos Aires position and guaranteeing any territorial arrangement a peace treaty might contain. For a fortnight, he attempted by the most obvious of tricks to achieve his objective while Ponsonby became increasingly annoyed. Eventually, on 9 October, the British envoy lost patience, wrote a private note emphasizing his country's neutrality, and ended the talks.[6] They had not got very far, and their very existence had fuelled the suspicion of observers, notably US Consul Forbes who was obsessed with the idea that the real motive of British mediation was to obtain control of the Banda Oriental for itself.[7] Ponsonby then directed his efforts at the Foreign Minister, General de la Cruz, and for the next four months steadily pressed him to accept British mediation, hinting that the independence of the Banda Oriental should be its basis. By this time, Ponsonby had become certain that this was the only solution as his intelligence reports increasingly showed that Lavalleja and his followers were as hostile to Argentinian rule as they were to that of Brazil. At last in February 1827, General de la Cruz agreed to his proposals.

Meanwhile, on 13 October 1826, the Honourable Robert Gordon had arrived in Rio with his entourage and effects on board the 74-gun *Ganges*, flagship of a new commander-in-chief, Rear Admiral Sir Robert Otway. He got to work on the Imperial Government straight away, gravely stressing the dangers of the war, the need for peace, and the wisdom of Britain's chosen solution. When the Emperor sailed south to Rio Grande do Sul, Gordon went too, remorselessly pressing the same arguments. On his return he continued the campaign with the Minister of Foreign Affairs in the new Government, the Marquis of Queluz. By February Gordon, with a degree of wishful thinking, had come to the conclusion that his persistence had worked, and that the Emperor was weakening in his opposition to the idea of an independent Banda Oriental. He therefore presented the peace proposals which Ponsonby had already sent on behalf of Rivadavia's Government.[8]

Encouraged by Gordon's guarded optimism, Ponsonby increased the pressure in Buenos Aires, even revealing to General de la Cruz that an independent Uruguay was Britain's preferred option. Eventually, Rivadavia's ministers were won over. News in

February and March of the victory of the Argentinian Army at Ituzaingú, the annihilation of the Brazilian Third Division at Juncal and the defeat of the Brazilian expedition to Patagonia, increased their confidence. But in April, the destruction of Brown's squadron at Monte Santiago brought a note of realism. There was also disturbing news of disputes between Lavalleja and the Argentinian Army command. General Alvear was convinced that only trained professionals could take Montevideo, and he was keen not only to absorb the Uruguayan irregulars into his army but to subject them to military discipline. The proposal provoked such horror that, instead of exploiting their advantage after Ituzaingú by advancing into Rio Grande do Sul, the troops turned to plunder, rustling Brazilian cattle on an enormous scale. The hostility to Buenos Aires was not lost on Rivadavia's ministers and at the end of April 1827, de la Cruz wrote to Ponsonby to say that they were now willing to enter into peace talks as long as the envoy was 'properly' received in Rio de Janeiro, and the basis of the negotiations was the independence of the Banda Oriental. Ponsonby reassured the Foreign Minister on both points.

Argentina's leading 'dove', the former minister, Manuel José Garcia, was chosen to be the peace envoy. Armed with instructions that he should push for the incorporation of the Banda Oriental into the United Provinces, but could settle for the establishment of the province as a separate state, Garcia boarded HMS *Heron* in April and headed optimistically for Rio de Janeiro. But on arrival, Garcia learnt the uncomfortable truth. The Emperor Pedro certainly wanted peace but he was still opposed to the independence of the Banda Oriental! It is hard to say whether the British ambassadors had misrepresented his willingness to compromise, or whether the defeats at Ituzaingú, Juncal and Patagonia had hardened his attitude. Gordon certainly felt that 'the success of the negotiation has been impaired by recent events ... the Emperor is less easy to deal with in defeat than in victory.'[9] Whatever the reason, it was impossible for Garcia to achieve his objective. He did his best, but being personally dismayed by the disastrous financial consequences of the war on Argentina, allowed himself to be outmanoeuvred. The draft peace treaty which Garcia signed on 24 May bore little resemblance to his instructions. It required Buenos Aires to acknowledge Brazilian sovereignty over the Banda Oriental – merely obliging the Emperor to find a just solution to its problems – laid down that Brazil should be compensated for the actions of Argentinian privateers, and committed both countries to freedom of navigation on the Plate under the guarantee of Great Britain.

Likewise, the peace proposals hardly reflected Gordon's instructions from London. Indeed the terms were so much in Brazil's favour that he felt embarrassed at his role in the talks and, on 8 June, wrote to Canning to explain what had happened.[10] But by the time the packet *Eclaire* reached England with the despatch, there was a new Foreign Secretary. Lord Liverpool had suffered a stroke in March, and after a struggle for power between the Duke of Wellington and Canning, the latter had emerged triumphant as Prime Minister with Lord Dudley as Foreign Secretary. George Canning was therefore feeling relaxed and wrote back to Gordon on 8 August 1827 to reassure and congratulate him – after all, peace was peace whatever the terms. It was the last letter he wrote. The following day, to the dismay of liberal opinion in Britain, Canning was dead.

Garcia returned to Buenos Aires with his draft treaty on 21 June in the *Heron* to be met with a storm of protest, personal vilification and war hysteria. In three consecutive editions, the English-speaking *British Packet and Argentine News* published the whole of the correspondence. The settlement was denounced as an act of betrayal and an affront to national honour. Printed placards appeared in the streets denouncing both Garcia and the role played by the British. Hostility rose to fever pitch. Ponsonby's residence was stoned by a mob, and feeling against the British became so great that HMS *Forte* was summoned to stand by in case of trouble.

For Rivadavia, Garcia's return could not have come at a worse – or better – time. Opposition to his centralizing policies and to his overbearing vanity suddenly reached a head when, on 7 June, every Argentinian province rejected his new constitution and denounced both the National Congress and the Central Government. Fighting for his political life, Rivadavia tried to regain popularity by orchestrating the wave of patriotic antagonism to the peace proposals. Then – expecting to be reappointed on a wave of nationalistic fervour – he overplayed his hand and resigned. He was disappointed. His enemies seized the opportunity, voted decisively that he should go – and he went. In the months that followed, the Rivadavia system was firmly dismantled and power returned to the provincial governments. The Congress and the central administration were abolished, and in August, the Province of Buenos Aires was reconstituted with General Manuel Dorrego once more as Governor. Technically, the United Provinces had ceased to exist. There was immediate uncertainty among diplomats as to whom they were now accredited, but Dorrego assured them that, by consensus, Buenos Aires would continue to be responsible for foreign affairs on behalf of the Argentine Republic. Ponsonby and the others took a pragmatic view, and things went on as before. Ponsonby attempted to reactivate the Garcia proposals with the new Foreign Minister, but in a rapidly changing political situation one thing remained depressingly certain – there was no further chance of peace during 1827.

But the fierce opposition to the Garcia peace proposals was not matched by any enthusiasm to continue the war. The provincial *caudillos* had never been much interested, and the keenness of the urban middle classes had been blunted by the economic hardships which had fallen almost exclusively upon them. Economically, Buenos Aires had been almost shattered by the cost of the war and the impact of the Brazilian blockade. Government income nowhere matched expenditure, state debt was increasing by leaps and bounds and the value of the peso had fallen from 45 to only 15 English pence. In the Banda Oriental, the army went unpaid. The infantry were in rags, the cavalry without horses. Administratively too, it took weeks for the Buenos Aires Government to sort itself out. In Lord Ponsonby's view, General Dorrego, its head, and General Balcarte, now Minister for Foreign Affairs, were 'in the mood for peace but had no-one had any idea how to obtain it'.[11] As a result, they continued with the war the best they could.

Commodore William Brown, however, had no doubts. He was always ready for a fight. No sooner had the peace proposals been rejected in August, than he launched another foray, sailing from Buenos Aires in the *Sarandí* for Martim Garcia. Detected and pursued by the blockading squadron, he was bottled up in the nearby port of San Juan for a week before a shift of wind and a diversion by the gunboat *11 de Junio* enabled him to escape and return home. Six weeks later, on 24 September, he was out again. Leaving Buenos Aires with Francisco Segui's brig *General Balcarce* and the schooners *8 de Febrero*, *9 de Febrero* and *Maldonado*, he headed up river. Impatient with the slow sailing of his companions, Brown and the *Sarandí* left them behind and pushed ahead, appearing alone off Montevideo flying the American flag. The Imperial brig *29 de Agosto*, on patrol outside, was not fooled and after an exchange of fire sailed back to summon assistance from the frigates *Piranga* and *Isabela* anchored in the port. If they had managed to get within range, the two massive Brazilian frigates could have blown the *Sarandí* to pieces, but to Brown's enormous relief, the wind dropped and he was able to make his escape before the Brazilians could catch him.

But in their commodore's absence, the other Argentinian ships had run into trouble. As the flotilla cautiously approached the enemy base at 3.40 am on 27 September, a large anchored frigate suddenly loomed in the darkness. Certain that it was Brazilian, the *Maldonado* fired a shot which struck her rigging, then turned with her companions to escape. The frigate promptly hoisted two lights, weighed anchor and made sail to follow. In the gloom, the Argentinians could make out the shape of the larger warship steadily overhauling them and could hear her clearing for action as she did so. By the time dawn began to lighten the sky the frigate was well within range and coming on fast. Wildly, the Argentinians loosed off four more shots, then realized to their horror that the pursuing vessel was not flying the green and yellow of Brazil but the red ensign of the British Navy. The frigate was HMS *Thetis*.

Her commander, Captain Bingham, had realized from the beginning that the incident had been a mistake and had refrained from replying (though his assessment was that with one broadside he could have sunk three out of his four rash attackers).[12] As dawn broke, the Argentinian ships hove to and sent boats to the *Thetis*. Tomas Espora, as senior officer, offered his apologies for the mistake, which Bingham accepted. The incident was over. Brown rejoined the flotilla and together the ships returned to Buenos Aires. The cruise had not been a success. Indeed it seemed to have lacked both purpose and organization. And when Francisco Segui described the events in a letter to a friend, he was careful to ask that nothing was leaked to the newspapers since negative publicity of this kind 'would not be to the taste of our commander!'[13]

CHAPTER 19

RIO DE JANEIRO:
TAKING STOCK

The Brazilian Government was taken by surprise by the Argentinian rejection of the peace terms. After the arrival of Manuel Garcia in Rio de Janeiro, it had relaxed its war effort. Now it had to put new energy into hostilities. Its first problem was political. The second session of the Legislative Assembly, which had opened in May 1827, had already begun to reflect a hostility to the Government. Ministers acted with lofty disdain, rarely appearing in person and rejecting the notion that they should be subject to scrutiny and criticism. The Assembly's anger had been further provoked when it was revealed that two treaties with the British – one on commerce, the other guaranteeing the abolition of the slave trade within three years – had been settled in the recess without any kind of reference to them. This had in fact been a deliberate ploy by Ambassador Robert Gordon to minimize opposition to the terms he had been sent to Rio to secure. Ministers made the situation worse by sending details of the *fait accompli* to the Assembly for comment. Delegates accepted the commercial treaty with its low import duties as a 'reward' for Britain's role in securing Brazilian independence, but there was anger at the overhasty abolition of the slave trade which was denounced as a ploy to destroy Brazilian agriculture in the interests of British colonial produce.

The acrimony overflowed into naval affairs. Delegates not only used the setbacks of the war as sticks with which to beat the Government, but began to drag their feet in agreeing the Navy's Estimates for the coming year. These had been delivered in the form of a *Relatório* on 26 May by the Minister of Marine, the Marquis of Maceió. It showed that although the naval forces of the Empire consisted of 65 armed ships, 22 packets and transports, 7813 sailors, 309 sea officers, 210 civilian officers and 2267 marine artillerymen, the number was still inadequate to win the war.[1] Additional funds were needed for the purchase of half a dozen additional men-of-war to make up for the losses of Juncal and Patagonia and for the crews to man them.

In the Assembly there was a general acceptance of the need for expansion, but the temptation to embarrass the Government was too great. The leader of the republican left, Clemente Pereira, was scathing in his criticism of the Navy's commanders, dwelt at length on its reverses and ignored its successes. Deputy Vergeiro, a radical firebrand from São Paulo, railed against the 'proven incapacity' of ministers and bitterly criticized the Navy's failure to defeat the enemy or exterminate privateers, contrasting it with their success in rounding up neutral merchantmen. Deputy da Silva Maia demanded – and received – copies of all orders which had been issued relating to the blockade. Another alluded to the fates of Admiral Byng and General Whitelock – the one shot, the other disgraced for military failure – hinting darkly that Brazil too should make examples. There was little in terms of defence or answer from the Emperor's ministers to these scurrilous and often unfounded attacks.

Nevertheless, the debates showed that many delegates fully understood both the disadvantages which followed when a nation with an enormous merchant marine went to war with a country which had none, and the navigational difficulties faced by the Imperial Navy in the Plate. Even Deputy Cunha Mattos, in a series of otherwise highly critical speeches, summarized the situation in perceptive terms:

> Let me say here what is really occurring. A Buenos Aires vessel can do greater harm to Brazil than a Brazilian ship can do to Buenos Aires. The Argentinians have no merchant marine and as a result can spread their forces and their privateers across a vast ocean. We, unfortunately, cannot do the same. ... We blockade their ports, and for this need a great number of ships. And as the

mouth of the Plate is so wide and its depth so variable we need ships of all sizes to maintain the blockade. Mr President, the enemy has been able to take advantage of this by the tactic of fighting in the shallows. And as their crews are more skilful than ours, their lighter vessels are able to avoid contact with our larger ones and so gain the advantage. Their crews are better than ours because they are attracted by the money to be made from raiding the great commerce of Brazil. ... Buenos Aires has no merchant marine [the capture of] which would attract foreigners into our service, with the result that many of our ships have had to sail with crews which are inexperienced and so deficient in numbers that the government has been forced to embark land artillerymen to compensate. ... We also need to realise that the gains of commerce raiding have enabled the enemy to sustain the costs of the war. To maintain our honour and dignity at sea, we must maintain a large naval force![2]

Cunha Mattos was right. The conflict between Brazil and Argentina was a classic confrontation between a maritime power trying to control the seas and a non-maritime state attempting to deny its use to its opponent. But however convinced he and his colleagues may have been of the need for a large Brazilian Navy, they were slow in doing anything about it. Months dragged on in petulant discussion. But the failure of the peace initiative brought a new sense of urgency. On 1 August, the Minister of Marine instructed Pinto Guedes to resume hostilities against Buenos Aires, promising to provide all the force, money and supplies he needed. The admiral was ordered to 'rigorously prevent all communication with that Republic ... burning all vessels which are shown to be employed in that purpose to whosoever they belong', to seal off Buenos Aires by sinking ships loaded with rocks in the channel, and to attack the vessels sheltering in the Inner Roads in a series of lightning strikes.[3]

Good as his word, in September and October, Maceió asked the Assembly for an additional 400 contos (£60,000) and an extension of credit to purchase the new ships Pinto Guedes needed. Not only had the losses of Juncal and Patagonia to be made up, but the Navy had suffered an additional setback when the 50-gun frigate *Dona Paula* ran itself aground off Cape Frio on 1 October chasing the Argentinian cruiser *Congresso*. But once again in both the Assembly and its committees, there was much talk but little action. Maceió even appeared twice in person to argue his case, but it made no difference. To fill the financial gap, the Government invited voluntary donations to help fund the Navy. The Emperor took the lead on 21 September by giving one-twelfth of the Imperial income as a gift and half as much again as a loan. A few – but not many – patriotic citizens followed suit. In a letter printed in the *Diário Fluminense* to encourage the others, Pedro's mistress, the Marquesa de Santos, donated a conto of reis and a loan of 40 milreis monthly. Commodore Jorge de Brito, Lobo's second-in-command at the Battle of Corales, gave up an eighth of his salary.

With the promise of more money, the Imperial Navy acquired nine more ships, seven of which were purchases and two prizes. In accordance with Pinto Guedes' requests, most were vessels at the larger end of the scale, able to confront Argentina's new generation of big privateers with a chance of success.[4] They included the 400-ton merchantships *Robert Fulton* and *Aristides*, bought for a total of 208 contos (£42,000) and converted into the corvettes *Maria Isabela* (28 guns) and *Bertioga* (20). Both vessels were given British crews and commanders – respectively Captain John Pascoe Grenfell, now returned fully restored after sick leave in England following the loss of his arm at Lara-Quilmes, and Commander George Broom, the hero of Juncal – and immediately began to distinguish themselves. Of the remainder, four were fitted with 16 guns and became respectively the 200-ton brigs (or brigantines) *Imperial Pedro* (formerly *Bolivar*), *Constança* (formerly *República del Paraguay*), *15 de Agosto*, and *13 de Maio*, while the fifth became the schooner *Bela Maria*. Refurbished and armed, all were at sea by the end of 1827. Their numbers were supplemented by the addition of the privateer *Pampeiro*, taken off Cape Frio on 27 March by the new frigate *Isabela* on its way to the Plate, and by the Buenos Aires cruiser *Patagones* (originally the Imperial brigantine *Escudeira*) recaptured by the immediately operational *Imperial Pedro* after a fierce action off Bahia which left 15 of its Argentinian crew dead including its commander, the Englishman George Love.

In their embassies, British Ambassadors Ponsonby and Gordon were equally dismayed by the failure of the Garcia peace initiative. Both attempted to get the process moving again, but the stumbling block continued to be the acceptability of the independence of the Banda Oriental. In October, Lord Ponsonby confessed that 'he was almost certain that if left to themselves, His Imperial Majesty and the Republic ... will never come to any understanding.'[5] But the continuation of the war raised other problems. Not only were British ships being interfered with by Brazilian blockading cruisers and by Argentinian privateers, but the conflict was having a serious effect on trade. Between July and December 1825, British goods entering Buenos Aires had been worth £455,000.[6] By the last quarter of 1827, the Brazilian blockade had reduced the value of British trade to a mere £18,750.[7] Likewise, the value of return cargoes of Argentinian exports to Britain had been cut from £325,000 to zero. As a result British merchants were forced to send all their profits home in warships or packets in the form of coin or bullion. In July 1827, this escape route was cut off when the Buenos Aires Government banned the export of bullion believing, rightly, that the merchants would now have to invest their profits locally either in land or in long-lasting products such as hides. Argentina certainly gained from the measure, but − as Ponsonby's protest indicated − it was a second serious blow to Great Britain. Not only had it lost an important export market, but now even the cash returns of British commercial enterprise were out of reach.

In Rio de Janeiro, the Hon. Robert Gordon was also worried by the economic effects of the war. What he found particularly galling was the fact that the two navies whose actions were destroying British commerce in the Plate were both substantially commanded and manned by British subjects. Reporting to London, he pointed out gloomily that the real war between Brazil and Buenos Aires was being fought at sea, that British trade was its principal victim, and that it was being both financed and fought by foreigners, principally Britons. Waxing eloquent on this theme in October 1827, he wrote:

It is not far from the truth to say that the war is now in point of fact betwixt Englishmen in direct contravention of the Laws of England [i.e. the Foreign Enlistment Act]. ... There are not less than 1,200 British sailors in the Brazilian Navy and it is with pain that I say that some of them are deserters from the Royal Navy. No ship enters here which does not lose many of her ablest seamen, nor can it be prevented for they are enticed away by their own countrymen. ... The commander of the Blockading Squadron in the River Plate is an Englishman and the commander of the Navy of Buenos Aires is the same. Their English crews when taken prisoner without hesitation join their countrymen in the service of the other side and not infrequently change back again.[8]

Although over-indulgent in his use of the term 'Englishman' to describe all subjects of King George whether born in England, Scotland or Ireland, Gordon (a Scot himself) was right. Ever since the secret recruiting campaigns of 1823 in London and Liverpool had supplied 450 reliable officers and sailors to man Cochrane's victorious fleets during the War of Independence, Brazil had come to rely heavily on British seamen. More and more were recruited into its service. In July 1825, the newly purchased *Dona Paula* sailed with 200; four months later, the *Piranga* carried 150 more when it returned to Brazil following Lord Cochrane's dramatic dash to Portsmouth; and, in early 1826, the two steamships *Correio Brasileiro* and *Correio Imperial* brought another 50 men.

The Imperial Government was also tempting British and American seamen to desert their ships in Brazilian ports – a constant source of complaint by ambassadors and naval officers. But although Brazilian pay and conditions were attractive, the demand for men was so great that voluntary enlistment proved inadequate. The Imperial Navy, like others before it, had therefore been forced to turn to impressment. Consequently, the British Embassy had spent months in vigorous protest against the forced recruitment of British subjects at the dockside and from prizes taken at sea. In May 1827, its efforts were at last crowned with success and 70 impressed British sailors were released from the Plate Squadron for repatriation. But, as Gordon reported to London with scarcely disguised annoyance, as soon as the men reached Rio de Janeiro, 60 had promptly re-enlisted in the Brazilian Navy to get the recruitment bounty![9] The result of all this was that by 1827, 1000 of the Imperial Navy's 7813 seaman were British, mostly serving with officers of the same nationality on selected warships like the *Piranga*, *Independência ou Morte*, *Caboclo* and *Itaparica*.

The nationality of the Imperial Navy's officer corps reflected the same pattern. Between 1823 and 1825, the Brazilian Government had recruited 59 British officers, or aspirant officers, many with Royal Navy experience. Some subsequently died or were dismissed, but they had been easily replaced, and the Brazilian Navy List for 1827 still contained the names of 58 officers of English, Scottish or Irish origin. As a result, in 1827, one-fifth of the 290 'active' officers of the Imperial Navy, and one-third of those employed at sea, were British – 1 commodore, 8 captains, 10 commanders and 39 lieutenants. The contribution of these experienced men to the Imperial war effort was indeed important. All were in the front line during the war with Buenos Aires and, in 1827, they commanded 14 of the Imperial Navy's 46 major warships.[10] The number of officers from other foreign nations was small by comparison, amounting to eight Danes, nine Frenchmen and only two Americans. American citizens were obviously less comfortable in the monarchical trappings of Brazil than their British and European counterparts.

But as Ambassador Gordon had indicated, reliance on foreign officers and seamen fighting for pay had its perils for both sides. The officers were inevitably a mixed group with variable professional abilities. Some may have had undistinguished careers, often because of drink, while others were outstanding as tacticians and leaders of men – but the loyalty of both to the cause of Brazil or Argentina was total whether they were serving on short-term contracts or committing themselves to a naval career in an adopted homeland. The casualty list and the numbers of escaped prisoners-of-war both testify to this. The only exceptions occurred in 1827 – in May, when Lieutenant John Clark and the 24 man crew of the Argentinian gunboat *No 12* turned their ship over to the Brazilian authorities in Colonia; and in September, when the commander of the *Maria Theresa*, Sublieutenant Robert Mackintosh, seized control of his schooner with the help of Argentinian prisoners and deserted to Buenos Aires.[11] Mackintosh sold it to the Government and set himself up in business with the proceeds.

With the seamen, however, things were different. They did their duty well enough, but their modest pay and short engagements generated little in terms of deep loyalty. There were few instances of a ship fighting to the last man – once the superiority of one vessel had been established, the crew of the other were inclined to surrender without further struggle. And when the financial interests of the crews clashed with their duty, it was the former which tended to win. There were numerous instances of ships captured by Argentinian privateers being carried into Brazilian ports by their prize crews – presumably in order to receive the whole value of the cargo instead of the share which would have been awarded by a Buenos Aires Prize Court. And in August 1827, the crew of Gunboat *No 3* took advantage of the absence of her captain to hand the ship over to the Brazilian blockaders off Salado. Likewise, if they were made prisoners of war, foreign seamen often preferred (as in Patagonia following the Brazilian defeat) to switch their allegiance rather than undergo a period of unpaid imprisonment. However, many only pretended to change sides in order to find an opportunity to rejoin their comrades. The privateer *Oriental Argentina*, for example, was seized off Rio de Janeiro by former Brazilian seamen who had changed sides in Patagonia then turned over to the Imperial authorities. Some officers tried the same trick. Sublieutenant Robert Steel, captain of the armed yacht *12 de Outubro*, pretended to change sides after Juncal and got himself in trouble with both sides. Sublieutenant Jean Graumont, captured in the *Isabela Maria* in July, enlisted in the Argentine privateer *Niger* under an assumed name, waited his opportunity, then carried a prize into Florianopolis and rejoined the Brazilian Navy. Others like Lieutenant George Broom of the *Bertioga* took the more daring route and promptly escaped.

While Gordon concluded his despatches in the British Embassy, the Legislative Assembly at last concluded its discussions on the Naval Estimates, and on 14 November 1827, agreed to the Government's proposals. But the Emperor was tired of his ministers' feebleness and their inability to control the legislature. A week later he sacked the lot. In their place he appointed a government of real talent – men of liberal views, most Brazilian-born, some members of the Assembly itself. Foreign observers were impressed and were fully in favour of the changes. The new Chief Minister was Senator Pedro de Araujo Lima – later to serve as Regent to the infant Pedro II and destined, as Marquis of Olinda, to dominate conservative politics in mid-century. The Minister of Finance was the brilliant Deputy for Bahia, Miguel Calmon, while the Foreign Ministry was given to the Marquis of Aracaty, a much respected and amiable figure whose Swedish father had been ennobled in the Portuguese royal service. As the Minister of Marine, the Emperor appointed a familiar naval personality, Commodore Diogo Jorge de Brito, a man whose professional standing – it was hoped – would enable him to act as an ideal intermediary between the sailors in the field and the politicians in Rio de Janeiro.

CHAPTER 20

CONGRESSO AND *GENERAL BRANDZEN*: THE RISE AND FALL OF THE PRIVATEER

The strategy of General Dorrego's Government in Buenos Aires was, once again, to concentrate on attacking Brazilian sea-borne commerce by using privateers. This would, it believed, do the greatest damage to the Empire at the smallest cost. In theory, following the battles of Juncal, Patagonia and Monte Santiago, the Argentinian Navy had grown to 16 armed ships plus 13 gunboats and armed yachts,[1] needing 80 sea officers, 120 warrant officers and 1400 petty officers, gunners and men. But these figures were misleading. Only the corvette *Ituzaingú* in Patagonia and the brigs *Congresso* and *General Balcarce* in Buenos Aires, were capable of doing any serious mischief to the bigger and more numerous warships of the Brazilian Navy. The other vessels were just too small. To keep the National Squadron in being was therefore a waste of money – which the Government could not afford – and of manpower – which it could use better elsewhere. As a result, most of its ships were laid up, leaving both officers and men free to command and man a new wave of privateers. To challenge the blockade and defend Buenos Aires, a small flotilla under Commodore Brown was kept operational, but – to increase the damage inflicted on Brazilian trade – the *Ituzaingú*, the *Congresso* and the brigantine *Patagones* were used as State-owned commerce raiders manned by naval personnel. The *Juncal* was sent off to buy munitions, leaving first for Chile under John Halstead Coe in July, then sailing for the United States under Fournier in January 1828.

During the second half of 1827, the new-style 'official' privateers proved their worth. The *Patagones* only managed to take one major prize before its interception and capture by the *Imperial Pedro* but, in a cruise between Bahia and Rio de Janeiro, the *Ituzaingú* seized a handsome total of 10 vessels, four of which got safely home to make Commander William Mason a rich man. But even more spectacular was the voyage of the *Congresso* under Cesar Fournier, specially commissioned as a naval captain for the purpose in spite of vigorous protests from British Ambassador Lord Ponsonby because of his action in seizing the *Florida*.[2] Fournier was a man of daring and resource whose head buzzed with schemes to annoy the enemy, some of them sound, others ridiculous. One was to raise Brazil's German mercenary troops in rebellion; another to kidnap the Emperor while he was walking in Rio's Jardim Botanico. As a privateer captain his record was brilliant, and under his command, the *Congresso* cut a swathe of destruction from Cape Frio to Rio Grande, terrorizing the Brazilian coasting trade and gaining 24 prizes, most of them small coasters. Stealing out of Buenos Aires in September, Fournier made for Cape Frio and immediately took the trading smacks *Senhora de Cabo* and *Melania* loaded with rice, flour and coffee. On 1 October he was spotted by the 50-gun *Dona Paula*, and it was during the ensuing chase that the Brazilian frigate ran herself aground on a shoal. Still lurking in the vicinity a week later, the *Congresso* met the four-gun Imperial steamship *Correio Brasileiro* (built in Liverpool as the *Hibernia*) on her way to Cape Frio to pick up survivors and opened fire, scoring a hit on one of her paddlewheels. The steamer turned and ran for Rio and it was only the timely appearance of the frigate *Paraguassú*, escorting a convoy, which caused the Argentinian brig to bear away and disappear over the horizon.

Judging the waters off Rio de Janeiro to be too dangerous for comfort, Fournier turned south-west and made for the coast, registering foreign merchantships and avoiding enemy warships as he went. For three weeks, the *Congresso* prowled the waters between Ilha Grande and Santa Catarina, terrorizing the coasting trade. The Argentinian brig was like a pike among minnows, seizing anything that floated. No vessel was too small – even oared launches and smacks carrying a few sacks of coffee were taken and, edging close inshore on 20 October, the *Congresso* even seized four canoes, one of which was a pleasure boat described in the *Diario* as 'beautifully fitted out and brightly painted with four negroes and a small girl'.[3] Only the largest vessels were kept as prizes. The *São Antonio Brillante* carrying dried meat was taken and sent to St Barthélemy in the French West Indies where Buenos Aires had established a prize agency under an Englishmen called Winsey. The *Bom Jesus* carrying rum, coffee and tobacco and the *Visconde de São Leopoldo* with dried meat and hides were sent back to Salado – already buzzing with rumours of Fournier's activities. It was even said that he had captured the frigate *Thetis* in the Bay of Bahia,[4] even though he had not been within five hundred miles of the place! On 29 October, he took the largest prize of all, the 142-ton *Armonia dos Anjos* carrying wine and dried fruit, and decided it was time to sail south for home. On 5 November, the *Congresso* entered the murky waters of the Plate Estuary and headed up river. Later that day she passed Salado and Punto Indio and made for the southern channel to Buenos Aires. Fournier had only to evade the Brazilian blockading squadron to reach home and a hero's welcome.

Meanwhile, the privateering war was reaching its climax. From the resumption of the war in mid-1827 to its end in 1828, 29 commerce raiders put to sea. They included five representatives of the new wave of big ocean-going privateer – the *Bonaerense* and *Triunfo Argentino* commanded by the Frenchmen Jean Soulin and François Villard, the *Presidente* and *Presidenta* under the Americans Thomas Allen and Robert Beazley, the *Sin Par* of the Irishman John King and the *Vencedor de Ituzaingú* commanded by the Spaniard Jaime Costas. In 1828, they were joined by the 200-ton 11-gun brig *Niger* commanded by the American John Halstead Coe. The crews were predominantly from France, Britain, the United States, Spain and Latin America, the proportion reflecting the nationality of their captain.

Their numbers were augmented by veteran privateers of older, smaller vintage, ships like Fisher's *Union Argentina*, Henderson's *General Mancilla*, Antonio Cuyas' *Vengadora Argentina* (now renamed *Rayo Argentino*) and Fourmantine's *Oriental Argentina*, its crew now augmented by a group of British seamen who had changed from the Brazilian side after the disaster in Patagonia. This time the Argentinian privateers ranged further than the Brazilian coast and were to be found in the Caribbean, near the Canaries and off the coast of Angola. Inexorably the bag of seizures began to rise. Ocean-going merchantmen, coastal smacks and schooners, mail-packets, immigrant ships, slavers – all found themselves boarded and liable to be sent back to Argentina under prize crews. Beazley in the *Presidenta* took two slave transports off the coast of Angola and was heavily fined for sending them to St Barthélemy for sale instead of to Argentina and liberty. Brazilian naval transports were special targets, and, on 26 October, the *Presidente* attacked and captured the armed brig *Ururão* and the storeship *Santissa* with supplies and money for the garrison in Montevideo.

Audacious as they were, the Argentinian commerce raiders were careful to avoid the escorted convoys which were now a feature of Brazil's southern seas and to keep well clear of patrolling Imperial warships. But sometimes they were unlucky. The *Rapido* was taken by the frigate *Dona Paula* off Cape Frio in July, and the schooner *Esperanza* by the corvette *Maria Isabela* in November. In August, the *Estrella del Sur* confidently attacked the Imperial gunboat *Grenfell* off the mouth of the Plate but was promptly boarded and captured in its turn. At the end of the year the *Rayo Argentino* (renamed once more as the *Cazador*) was driven ashore and wrecked. Fourmantine's luck was no better. When the *Oriental Argentina* damaged itself after running aground near Rio de Janeiro in November, the British seamen who had switched their allegiance so readily in Patagonia promptly changed it back again and handed the brig over to the Imperial authorities.

The most dramatic and successful voyage was, however, that of the *General Brandzen*. Originally the *Sylph*, the brig was purchased by Vicente Casares for £5500 (or 87,000 pesos) in June 1827 and issued with Letter of Marque no 148. At the end of the month, eight guns were loaded by the Artillery Park – two long 12-pounders, four medium 8-pounders and two 12-pounder carronades. It seems unlikely that this was the total armament of a ship so large. Brazilian sources claim that the *General Brandzen* carried 'eight guns a side'[5] – twelve long guns and four carronades – and this, taking into account both her size and behaviour seems to be closer the truth. Surprisingly, command was given to an untried American, George De Kay. De Kay was a 25-year-old New Yorker, who had gone to sea at an early age and had voyaged extensively in the Mediterranean, Atlantic and the Caribbean. His association with South America had began in 1824 when, finding his ship detained in Chile, he had joined the patriot side, seeing action at the siege of Callao. Eventually – after, it was said, having his offer of service turned down by the Brazilian authorities – he arrived in Buenos Aires and, after a brief period in the privateer *Presidenta*, found himself in command of the *General Brandzen*.

Armed, and with a crew of 111 officers and men, the privateer weighed anchor on 23 June 1827, and slipped unobserved down the channel between the coast and the Chico Bank. Two days later she sighted the rocky headland of Cape Santa Maria and headed for the open sea. The excitement began almost immediately when the sails of two vessels lifted over the horizon, one with three masts, the other two. They proved to be the Imperial lugger *Principe Imperial* of 14 guns and the schooner *Isabela Maria* of 5 guns. De Kay headed directly for the first, came within range, and fired a broadside, intending to carry the vessel by boarding. But the *Principe Imperial* did not wait. After a brief exchange of fire, the lugger bore away and disappeared over the horizon, leaving her smaller consort to her fate. In his report on the incident, Admiral Pinto Guedes was acid in his condemnation of *Principe Imperial*'s lack of courage, comparing it unfavourably with the spirit which had been shown by the *Grenfell*.[6] By nightfall, the schooner was on its way to an Argentinian prize court under Lieutenant William Stabb. Her officers and men were taken on board the privateer, her commander, Lieutenant Voiget, being later transferred to HMS *Beagle*, encountered at sea on 6 July.

The *General Brandzen* headed north along the Brazilian coast, avoiding Imperial naval units, registering foreign merchantmen and flying French or American flags as a ruse to lure suspicious vessels within range. Off Rio Grande do Sul at the end of July she seized one prize, the *São Antonio Vencedor*, burned another and released two more after looting them of naval stores. In early August the privateer passed Cape Frio, took the *Invencível*, then registered and released two Portuguese ships with prisoners. Ten days later, sailing north with the prevailing easterly winds on her starboard beam, the *General Brandzen* sighted three vessels ahead sailing in company. Instead of attempting to escape, they promptly raised the Brazilian flag and continued their approach. They proved to be the merchant brigs *Princeza*, *Flor de Verdade* and *Aurora*, the first two lightly armed for protection. De Kay immediately hoisted the blue and white of Argentina and stood towards them, exchanging fire as soon as they came within range. The Brazilians suddenly realized their mistake and scattered, the damaged *Princeza* striking her colours in surrender, while the *Flor de Verdade* turned south and the *Aurora* fled north. The *General Brandzen* set off in pursuit of the largest ship, the *Flor de Verdade*, overtaking it after an hour and forcing it to surrender. The *Aurora* by this time had disappeared over the horizon, followed rapidly by the *Princeza* which had rehoisted its colours and taken the opportunity to escape. The *Flor de Verdade* was soon on its way to St Barthélemy with a prize crew under William Pearce while the privateer continued northwards.

In the weeks that followed, the *General Brandzen* took three more Brazilian smacks. One, the *Minerva*, was released with prisoners, the others, the *Estandarte Venturoso* and *Fiesca* were detained as prizes. But now, the privateer was running short of water. On 20 August therefore, the *General Brandzen* sailed boldly into the tiny Bahian haven of Camamú flying French colours, surprised and sank the floating battery guarding the anchorage, and refilled her water casks. Then, she turned seawards again and headed north for Pernambuco.

As a result of requests from nervous members of the Legislative Assembly, the approaches to the port of Recife were guarded by a small naval flotilla headed by the brig-of-war *Cacique* commanded by Captain George Manson. Manson had been one of the first foreign officers to be recruited into the Imperial Navy back in 1822 and had already gained considerable fighting experience, having served in Lord Cochrane's flagship during the blockade of Bahia, the capture of Maranhão and the suppression of the Pernambuco rebellion the following year. He, his second-in-command, Sublieutenant Charles Yell, and a number of the crew of 120 were British. His ship, the 270-ton *Cacique*, was slightly larger than the *General Brandzen* and carried two 9-pounder cannon as chase guns and sixteen 18-pounder carronades. In close action it was a formidable armament. News that a powerful Argentinian privateer was in the area therefore caused no alarm, and Manson put to sea confident in his ability to find the intruder and teach him a lesson.

The fatal encounter took place on 9 September 1827. As the dawn mists began to lift, the lookouts on the *General Brandzen* sighted a white speck on the leeward horizon between the privateer and the land. Both ships maintained their courses, and by noon the identity of the *Cacique* was confirmed. No-one would have blamed George De Kay if he had turned and disappeared over the horizon. It was not the job of a privateer to fight a regular warship of the Imperial Navy and his ship's company was down to some 75 men as a result of the need to provide prize crews for his six captured ships. But De Kay's Irish-American daring was a match for Manson's British confidence, and the two ships plunged forward on converging courses with neither side flinching. At 3.30 pm the *Cacique*'s port side battery burst into thunder and smoke and the action began. But to Manson's dismay, the shot went high, cutting up the privateer's rigging but missing the hull. With the distance between the ships rapidly shortening and the *General Brandzen* beginning to return fire, the *Cacique* tacked and fired its starboard broadside. But the same thing happened – all the shot went high and none struck home on the enemy's hull. Manson's subsequent report blamed the ineptitude, or indeed disaffection, of his crew.[7] Whatever the reason, the *Cacique* had now lost its major advantage in the contest and was reduced to peppering the enemy with musketry from a platoon of German troops being carried as marines. Meanwhile, De Kay saw his chance. Swiftly turning the *General Brandzen* before his opponent could re-load, he brought his ship into juddering contact with the *Cacique*, fired a broadside and boarded the brig in the thick eddying smoke. After 25 minutes of desperate fighting, it was all over. The Imperial ensign came down from the peak and Manson surrendered his sword on the brig's blood-stained quarter deck. Six of his men had been killed and 17 wounded, three – including Sublieutenant Yell – mortally. Half the *Cacique*'s crew had run below when the privateer had come alongside, but those who remained on deck had given a good account of themselves in the struggle, killing one of the *General Brandzen*'s men and wounding 14, including De Kay himself.[8]

Hove to and rolling in the swell, the survivors patched up the rigging and tended to the wounded; then the *General Brandzen* and *Cacique* with a prize crew on board under a British sublieutenant calling himself John Gray (his real name was Nelson), headed north. De Kay wanted a quiet voyage as far as the Caribbean where he hoped to find rest and supplies. But it was not to be. On 16 September, the prisoners on the *Cacique* tried to retake the ship, but were overpowered by the prize crew. The two ringleaders, Robert Samson and Charles Bowen, were shot out of hand. But worse was to follow. Gray was obsessed with the notion that the Brazilian sailors were planning another revolt and, two days later, called the men one by one to the quarter deck demanding to be told of the conspiracy. When they refused to talk, he shot them one by one in cold blood. A member of the boat's crew from the *General Brandzen*, sent to investigate the noise, said that Gray was 'in a state of drunken madness'.[9] He claimed that a fight broke out when they tried to restrain him and that the brutal sublieutenant fell overboard. Brazilian sources claim that he was thrown into the sea by a black Brazilian sailor he had tried to shoot. Whatever the truth of the matter, Gray was drowned. A boat was launched, but in such an inefficient manner that it promptly sank, drowning some of its crew. Only prompt action by the *General Brandzen* prevented further loss.

De Kay sorted out the mess, appointed a prize master to replace Gray and, after burying Sublieutenant Yell at sea with military honours, ordered the *Cacique* to New York. Meanwhile the *General Brandzen* headed for the West Indies, reaching the island of St Eustacius on 13 October. Seven of the prizes had already arrived and were being sold in the various islands by the Argentinian Agent Winsey. In St Barthélemy the business was handled by local merchants Haddock and Dinsay, in St Eustacius by the firm of Martin and Richardson.[10] The Dutch authorities received the Argentinians with courtesy, watered the privateer and offered provisions while De Kay helped fit-out and man a number of small privateers. Then, the *General Brandzen* headed north once more to join the *Cacique* in New York, where she received a hero's welcome from a press and a population which was wholly on the side of their fellow republicans in Buenos Aires. There – in spite of frenzied protests from the Brazilian Chargé d'Affaires[11] – the two Argentinian ships were refitted and their depleted crews were brought up to strength with American recruits. Whilst in New York, De Kay stayed with his brother, a local physician who was married to the daughter of Henry Eckford, the great American shipbuilder. After two weeks, on 2 January 1828, they were ready for sea once more, and with De Kay flying the flag of a commodore in the *Cacique*, the two vessels left their anchorage, rounded Sandy Hook and headed back for the River Plate via the Azores, Madeira and the Canary Islands.

The return voyage was largely uneventful. Dozens of neutral vessels were stopped and inspected. Off the Canaries, the brig *Hector* bound for Rio carrying cannon had its cargo removed but was then allowed to proceed. In mid-Atlantic, the *Sacramento* was taken and sent to St Barthélemy with a prize crew under Lieutenant Clarke after 6000 pesos in gold and silver had been removed from its hiding place in the water casks. Then the *Cooperação* and

Príncipe were seized and packed off to Salado. In May, now approaching the Brazilian coast, the two ships stopped the British merchantmen *Eliza* and *George Canning*, removing canvas from the first and copper plates from the second on the grounds that they were contraband of war. Then, on 2 June, off Cape Frio they met and were boarded by a boat's crew from HMS *Ganges*, flagship of Rear Admiral Otway. De Kay swore that he had not interfered with any British vessel and was allowed to go on his way.[12] In the middle of June, the Argentinian privateers left the blue rollers of the Atlantic and entered the brown shallows of the River Plate. De Kay moved back to take command of the *General Brandzen*, while the *Cacique* was ordered to Patagonia under Lieutenant Cunningham. One year after leaving these waters, George De Kay was back at his point of departure. He had only to run the Brazilian blockade of Buenos Aires to successfully complete a cruise which is still remembered as one of the most daring enterprises in the early years of the Argentinian Navy.

With deeds as dramatic as these, the war against Brazilian commerce reached its climax. In the last half of 1827, privateers seized 142 Brazilian ships, of which 59 were destroyed and 45 reached a prize court to make rich men of their owners and crews.[13] The Imperial Government was seriously worried – and they were not the only ones. At the end of May, Captain Jaime Costas in the Argentinian privateer *Vencedor de Ituzaingú*, hunting in the sea routes off Cape Frio, had suddenly begun to seize foreign merchantmen. One, the Hamburg-based *Gertrude Wilhelmina*, was recaptured; the second, the British *Daphne*, was turned over to the Brazilians by its prize crew; the third, the brig *Huskisson*, was taken and carried off to Patagonia. Apart from a crate of swords and lances, her cargo consisted of nothing that could be defined as contraband,[14] but it was remarkable nonetheless since it included a tiger, a jackal, an orang-utan, a hyena, a boa constrictor, a pair of leopards and some zebras, all bought by a Mr Brooks for Rio de Janeiro zoo.[15] The seizure of the *Huskisson* resulted in a sharp British protest to the Argentinian authorities.[16] More was to follow. In July, the British vessel *Pacific* was stopped at sea by the privateer *Congresso* which not only illegally removed large quantities of canvas, cordage, wine and brandy, but had the cheek to leave a receipt![17] Next month, the *Ann*, outward-bound from Liverpool and becalmed off Montevideo was boarded and looted by the oared launch *Convención Argentina* commanded by the Catalan Pepe Onzas.[18] Then, in September, the American brig *Ruth* carrying a cargo of flour was seized by the *Rayo Argentina* off Santos and sent back to Buenos Aires with a prize crew. (This was not, of course, the same *Ruth* which had been taken by the Brazilians in 1826.) The result was panic among the foreign mercantile community at what seemed to be a new and uncontrolled turn in the privateering war.

The foreign naval commanders, however, knew exactly what to do. In June 1827, Rear Admiral Otway deployed his cruisers along the coast, ordering his captains to recapture any British merchantmen taken by Argentinian privateers and to arrest any of the latter found in possession of 'plundered' goods.[19] In particular, the squadron was instructed to find the *General Brandzen* and arrest De Kay for the outrages on the *Eliza* and *George Canning* and for deceiving Otway as to his activities. HMS *Cadmus* was sent off to Patagonia to find the *Huskisson* and the notorious Jaime Costas in the *Vencedor de Ituzaingú*. HMS *Forte* caught up with *Convención Argentina*, arrested Pepe Onzas (according to Otway, 'a man of abominable character') and 14 of his men ('most desperate and savage characters'), and released the *Ann*.[20] Other nations were provoked as privateers became more foolhardy. In July, a brig flying the flag of Buenos Aires had the impudence to fire into the French frigate *Surveillante* off Rio de Janeiro, wounding her captain. Admiral Lamerant swore to sink two Argentinian corsairs as a reprisal and ordered three of his squadron to sea for that purpose.[21]

The Government of Buenos Aires was assailed by a storm of protest. Even their ally, the American Consul Forbes joined in, pointing out that on seizing the *Ruth*, the commander of the *Rayo Argentino*, Antonio Cuyas, had declared that the whole of the coast of Brazil was now under blockade and that all American ships carrying flour to the Empire would in future be arrested.[22] Dorrego quickly dealt with the situation. In September, to prevent a repeat of the *Ann* incident, the Government cancelled the Letters of Marque given to all privateers of less than 25 tons and promised to consider banning all seizures in the Plate Estuary.[23] Then to its own astonishment, it was revealed that secret instructions recently given to Argentinian privateers had indeed put the whole of the Brazilian coast under blockade and authorized them to seize 'provisions of whatever kind bound for the said ports.'[24] It was under this rule that the *Huskisson* and the American flour ships had been taken. There was an international outcry. Dorrego and his ministers promptly revoked the instruction and offered profuse apologies. But the incident marked a watershed. As it had with the Brazilian blockade, foreign protest put the brakes on Argentinian privateering at the peak of its effectiveness.

CHAPTER 21

BRAZIL RENEWS THE OFFENSIVE

The first priority of the new Brazilian Government was to accelerate the war. They had seen the Garcia peace proposals flatly rejected and were determined to force the Argentinians back to the negotiating table. The army in the south was reinforced and, in November 1827, the cautious General Lecor was restored to command. No-one believed he had the energy to win the war, but there was equal confidence that he would never lose it particularly with a gifted Englishman, Major General Brown, as Chief of Staff. In naval matters, the defeats of 1827 at Juncal and in Patagonia, and the economic impact of the privateering war had shaken the Government's nerve. The Emperor and his ministers mistakenly decided to become directly involved.

On 3 December 1827, Minister of Marine Commodore Diogo de Brito, wrote at length to Pinto Guedes. The Emperor and the Government had full confidence in their Admiral, he said, but needed to know the size, state, condition and manning of the Plate squadron and of all existing proposals for operations against the enemy. Pinto Guedes was asked for full information. Likewise, they were convinced that a bombardment of the city of Buenos Aires was both possible and desirable. They urged the Admiral to consider such a plan, at the same time as undertaking 'the most rigorous blockade ... and all possible hostilities to keep the enemy in a constant state of alarm.'[1] As inducements to extra effort, decorations were promised to successful officers and pensions and bonuses for the men. But then the natural caution of the politician took over. Pinto Guedes was told to act with 'circumspection' so as to ensure that 'we incur no further losses without inflicting as much if not more damage on the enemy.' A fortnight later, the Minister wrote again. In case the Admiral had misunderstood the reference to 'rigorous blockade', Diogo de Brito repeated the need to treat neutral ships with kid gloves. The wording of the letter was aggressive, but the content merely repeated the weak compromise forced on Brazil by France and the United States – namely, that ships breaking the blockade could only be seized if their logs showed that they had been previously warned of its existence, or if they refused to stop when ordered to do so. Such a position was unavoidable, he wrote, as the protests of foreign powers had been 'of a nature so imperious ... that they almost amounted to a declaration of war'.[2] Sitting in the great cabin of his frigate, Admiral Pinto Guedes read these despatches with as much annoyance as he had felt when reading the criticism of the Legislative Assembly in the newspapers. In a series of pungent replies – written at almost daily intervals – he told his superiors in Rio exactly what he thought. He deplored the political weakness which had caused the Brazilian Navy to abandon the doctrine of strict blockade; he narrated at length the successes and failures of the last year attributing credit or blame where it was due; and he listed with satisfaction the losses which had been inflicted on Argentinian shipping since he took command.[3]

Pinto Guedes gave as good as he got. He also pondered on the political situation. He was bitter in his criticism of the English, claiming that they were encouraging Lavalleja's ambitions; that they 'had never lost their desire to meddle in the River Plate in spite of the reverses they suffered (in 1806)'; and that they intended to dominate an independent Uruguay. Rear Admiral Otway had made this clear from the first moment of his arrival.[4] Pinto Guedes was also struck by the independent line now being taken by the Uruguayans, and by their growing hostility to Buenos Aires. As a result, he was convinced that an independent Banda Oriental would be entirely free of Buenos Aires influence, and that this would be a better option for Brazil than the continuation of a damaging and expensive war. He was surprised when Diogo de

Brito revealed that the Government was thinking along the same lines.[5]

In the military sphere, Pinto Guedes focused on his Government's pet project – the bombardment of Buenos Aires. Rumours of the plan had been carried in the Rio newspapers and it was soon common talk among the inhabitants of Buenos Aires as they gloomily looked out at the distant white sails of the Brazilian warships patrolling the horizon. Their own ships were safely secured within the port or beached under the protection of the batteries, and the city's defences, although strengthened, were not expected to offer much resistance.[6] For his part, Pinto Guedes, began to assemble the small ships needed for such a raid, asked Rio for 18-pounder guns to arm them, and promised to give ample notice of any attack so that diplomats and other foreigners would be able to flee the city in time. But first, he tried a dummy run. On 1 February 1828, the *Liberal*, *Caboclo* and *Rio da Plata* with the schooner *Dona Paula* and the gunboats *Grenfell* and *1 de Dezembro* suddenly left their anchorage and began to advance menacingly on Buenos Aires. The larger vessels stayed in the channel, but the three smaller ones crept nearer through the muddy water, then opened fire with their single 18-pounders. But the range was too great to do significant damage and stormy weather forced the attempt to be abandoned. A naval bombardment was more difficult than had been thought. Nevertheless, preparations went on until the beginning of April, when the Imperial Government wrote to say that it had accepted British mediation in finding a settlement and felt obliged to cancel such a provocative attack.[7]

Meanwhile the Imperial Navy tightened the blockade. At the mouth of the river was Pinto Guedes with his force of brigs and heavy frigates. Off Salado was a second force under the veteran Captain João de Bottas. And, blocking the channels in sight of Buenos Aires itself, lay the inshore squadron commanded by the intrepid James Norton. It was still possible for vessels to sneak out to sea when the wind blew foul and the blockading warships were blown off station, or when the river was shrouded in fog or darkness, but getting back safely was another matter. On 6

December 1827, the *Congresso*, arriving in the Plate with the prize *Armonia dos Anjos* after its epic commerce raiding cruise, attempted to get up river to the safety of Buenos Aires. Unfortunately for Fournier, his ships were intercepted by Norton's blockading squadron, then escorting a convoy to Colonia. The Brazilians immediately gave chase and the privateer, edging too close to the shore, ran aground at Ensenada. Next day, leaving his two biggest vessels to mind the convoy, Norton transferred his flag to the gunboat *Grenfell* and attacked the cornered ships with his six remaining schooners and gunboats. All day long the *Congresso* was pounded with a steady and overwhelming fire from the *Grenfell*, *Bela Maria*, *Dona Paula*, *1 de Dezembro*, *Victoria de Colonia* and *Esperada* until, by early afternoon, the brig was a total wreck with 24 dead and 11 wounded. Seeing that destruction was inevitable, Fournier launched what remained of his boats and rowed ashore with the survivors, leaving his ship, his surgeon and his wounded to the Brazilians. Meanwhile, in Buenos Aires, Commodore Brown was hastily organizing a flotilla to go to the rescue. But at 4 pm two columns of thick smoke to the south-east told him it was too late. The Brazilians had boarded the *Congresso* and the prize and, having removed the wounded, had put both to the torch. To most observers, Fournier had put up a doughty defence and had been justified in abandoning the *Congresso*. But Brown, angry, frustrated and perhaps resentful of the fact that command of a national ship had been given to a temperamental privateer, typically thought otherwise. With little justice and much pique, he claimed that the defence had been poor and that 'Fournier was more interested in saving his coffers, which contained a rich booty, than in fighting, and was the first to abandon that handsome brig'.[8]

In the months which followed, the bag of privateers and prizes captured or destroyed by the Brazilian Navy steadily grew larger. On 16 November 1827, the Salado squadron gave chase to the *Presidente* and three of its prizes – the *Ururão*, *Santista* and *Bonzado*. The privateer managed to escape but the prizes were taken by the Brazilians and burned. Two weeks later, the *General Mancilla* and the *Federal Argentina* were spotted, driven ashore and destroyed. In

January 1828, the *Bravo Colonel Oliveira* suffered the same fate. In March, the *Niger*, returning after a profitable voyage in which it had almost captured the new corvette *Maria Isabela*, commanded by Captain Ignacio Maia, was overhauled by the brig-of-war *Caboclo* (Captain William James Inglis), raked with cannon fire and forced to surrender in full sight of the cheering ships of the Salado squadron. The Brazilian Navy soon had such control over the Plate that it could afford to send detachments to patrol the waters off Rio Grande do Sul and Patagonia. In April, Buenos Aires lost the *Honor*, in May, the *Feliz*. In August, the Brazilians dealt another blow by destroying the incoming *Empresa* and burning – as a lesson to neutrals on what would happen if they overstepped the mark – the two blockade runners it was escorting, the American *Hussar* and the British *Lord Eldon*.

But the greatest blow to Argentinian morale was the destruction of the *General Brandzen*. The privateer arrived back in the Plate after her legendary voyage on 16 June 1828 and was navigating the Chico Bank heading for the safety of Buenos Aires when she was spotted by Norton's lookouts. The inshore squadron consisted of six ships at this time – the corvette *Bertioga* (Commander George Broom), the captured brig *Niger* (Lieutenant Thomas Craig), the brigantine *2 de Julho* (Sublieutenant William MacErwing) and the schooners *9 de Janeiro* (Sublieutenant John Williams), *19 de Outubro*, (Sublieutenant Augusto Leverger) and *União* (Sublieutenant Cecil Browning). The Brazilians gave chase, the faster sailing *Niger* and *9 de Janeiro*, to which Norton had moved his flag, taking the lead. Fleeing for her life, the *General Brandzen* stood too close to the southern shore, slid onto the mud and was stranded beneath the battery at Punta Lara. The *9 de Janeiro*, impetuously following, did the same. The Brazilian schooners surrounded the helpless privateer and began a relentless bombardment. Within hours, the *General Brandzen* was a wreck with 20 dead and wounded. De Kay and his men abandoned ship, rowed ashore and reinforced the artillerymen in the battery. Under heavy fire, the Brazilians boarded the privateer, captured the 14 members of the crew who remained and set it afire. Then, they withdrew. But the victory was not without loss. Nine men had been killed, nineteen wounded and four captured – including the commander of the *9 de Janeiro* who had been taken when he stayed to burn his ship. Among the seriously wounded was James Norton himself, who was rushed bleeding to the *Bertioga* where his arm was amputated. Pinto Guedes reported that with typical heroism Norton had made light of the injury, saying, 'I have lost my right arm but am content since it was in defence of Brazil and the Emperor. I am ready to return and risk my life for the same cause ... and trust it will not be long delayed!'[9] Norton was awarded an annual pension of 800 milreis (£200) for his heroism and was back in command within three months.

With the privateering war in decline, the Argentinian Government used more of its own ships as commerce raiders. In June the schooners *Sarandí* and the *Federal* put to sea under Captain George Bynon – now officially second-in-command of the Argentinian Navy – and took seven prizes, but otherwise the policy was not a success. In April, the *Union*, leaving with the *8 de Febrero* under Captain Tomas Espora to support a campaign being waged by small boats for control of Lake Mirim on the eastern coast of the Banda Oriental, was caught and destroyed. The following month the *8 de Febrero* itself was intercepted on its return by the Salado squadron and captured to rejoin the Brazilian Navy under its original name of *Dona Januária*. Espora's defence was so spirited, and his reputation with his enemies so high, that Pinto Guedes immediately exchanged him and Lieutenant Antonio Toll with flattering compliments for Captain William Eyre, who had been captured at San Blas, and Lieutenant Leal Ferreira, who had languished in captivity since the capture of the *Leal Paulistana* in the first year of the war.

By the middle of 1828, the Brazilian convoy system and the tightening of the blockade in the Plate had inflicted serious losses on the Argentinian commerce raiders. The odds on success were diminishing and crews were increasingly reluctant to take the risk. Officers and men were less easy to find, and behaved with greater caution when they put to sea. The big ocean-going privateers continued their deprivations and took 50 more ships, but half of the 13 new privateers which put to sea in 1828 took no prizes at all. Only the schooner *Empresa* and the *Niger* had any luck, seizing nine vessels each. Meanwhile, the bag of Brazilian captures continued to rise. Indeed, over two-thirds of the Argentinian privateers which put to sea in the last twelve months of the war were wrecked, captured or destroyed, while none of the three state commerce raiders survived at all. For Argentina, the price of their heroic attacks on Brazilian sea-borne trade in blood, men and ships was both heavy and punishing.

Locked up in the Inner Roads of Buenos Aires, Commodore William Brown was faced with a hopeless task. Under his command he had only the one surviving brig, the *General Balcarce*, five schooners – *Maldonado, Guanco, Uruguay, 29 de Diciembre* and *9 de Febrero* – and 14 tiny gunboats and yachts capable of nothing but port defence. But it was impossible to man all these vessels simultaneously. The reverse in Argentina's fortunes was having its effect on recruitment. The supply of foreign seamen was drying up and the Navy was forced to rely more and more on reluctant South American conscripts and on pressed men from the local gaols. The effect on the morale and size of its crews was predictable. In September 1827, recruits had seized the *29 de Diciembre*, murdered its Captain Smith and deserted en masse. The following January, the crew of the *Guanco* did the same when it became separated from the rest of Brown's squadron after a brief Argentinian foray into the river in pursuit of the Brazilian privateer *Mosquito*. And, in August 1828, came the shame of the mutiny on the *Nuevo 25 de Mayo*.

With his Government giving priority to privateering and his ships easily outnumbered by the enemy, Brown's capacity for offensive action was limited. He was forced to confine his activities during 1828 to the defence of Buenos Aires and to a series of very limited objectives outside. Sometimes it was to escort outgoing privateers or warships on special missions – in January, the *Juncal* with Fournier heading for the United States; in February, the *Bonaerense*; in August, the state commerce raiders *General Rondeau*, *Argentina* and *Gobernador Dorrego*. In February and April, he left port to protect incoming privateers or blockade runners from the pursuing Brazilian Navy. On 18 June, he sailed with 12 schooners and gunboat to rescue the *General Brandzen*. Unfortunately he arrived a day too late and in the ensuing skirmish lost one more vessel to the Brazilians – gunboat *No 4*, whose captain not only surrendered but freely handed over the signal book.

On each occasion Brown's tactic was the same – to sail into the estuary, secure the objective without delay and then get back, frequently over the shallows, before the Brazilians could arrive. Sometimes it worked, sometimes it didn't. On 17 February, for example, an Argentinian force of 12 schooners and gunboats left the Los Pozes anchorage under the command of Nicolas Jorge to help the incoming American brig *Sicily*. Seeing the movement, Norton headed west from his blockading position, switched his flag from the corvette *Carioca* to the *Caboclo*, then to the lighter draught *Dona Paula*, and led his force of two brigs and six schooners and gunboats into the attack. The Argentinians got back safely to port, but in the chase two of their vessels were lost – gunboat *No 11* which was captured and the *Guanco*, which ran aground and was wrecked. The *Sicily* was taken but burned by the Argentinians before the Brazilians could remove it.

General Dorrego and the Argentinian Government were aware of the problem. They made desperate attempts to buy the bigger ships Brown needed to break the Brazilian stranglehold. In December 1827, Captain Robert Ramsay in London was ordered to send out at least one of the vessels he was in the process of fitting-out. But the letter came too late. Having received neither funds nor instructions for months, Ramsay had stopped his search for a ship-of-the-line, had discharged the men he had recruited and was in the process of selling the *Asia* in order to pay for the cost of maintaining the frigate *Chapman* – now renamed *Congresso*.[10] A few months later he heard that the British Government had roundly rejected his request for permission to join the Argentinian Navy.[11] Wearily, he gave up his assignment, a disappointed man.

They were just as unlucky in the United States. Fournier and the *Juncal* arrived in Baltimore in March and promptly purchased a corvette which he called *25 de Mayo*. Forced to leave in haste by Brazilian diplomatic protests, he headed for the Caribbean where he bought a Danish brig which he renamed *General Dorrego*. But the return voyage ended in disaster. Having successfully passed the Canaries and the Cape Verde Islands, in September 1828 the three ships were nearing the South American coast when they were hit by a hurricane. The fury of the storm was so great that both the *25 de Mayo* and the *Juncal*, with Fournier aboard, perished. Only the *General Dorrego* was left to carry out a successful privateering campaign in the Atlantic and the Caribbean which lasted up to – and after – the end of the war.

And so, as the Argentinian naval effort weakened, that of Brazil continued to grow in strength. There were problems. Naval expenditure far outstripped the amounts voted and the pay of the Plate squadron fell woefully into arrears. Pinto Guedes took strong action against any crew that protested, raised loans at a frightening rate of interest in Montevideo, and complained bitterly to the Imperial Government that the same practice had been the ruin of the Portuguese Navy.[12] It also caused an increase in the number of deserters. Against local advice, Pinto Guedes sent shore patrols to round them up, but they had little success. The only result was the tragic murder of Captain Alexander Anderson of the *Maranhão* who was stabbed in a scuffle. But in terms of warships, the Imperial Navy was able to replace its losses and still had 65 armed vessels in commission with 12,000 officers and men.[13] More and more were deployed to the south. Commodore Brown and the Argentinian Government struggled with ingenuity and skill against the inevitable, but by the middle of 1828, the Brazilian Navy had secured military dominance in the River Plate.

PART VI: ENDGAME

CHAPTER 22

THE ROAD TO PEACE

In Rio de Janeiro, the Honourable Robert Gordon was nonplussed by the rejection of the Garcia peace proposals in July 1827. Both he and Lord Ponsonby in Buenos Aires were at a loss as to what to do next. But meanwhile, there was another important problem to occupy Gordon's attention. This was the question of British prizes taken during the blockade of the River Plate. The concessions forced on the Brazilian Government had satisfied foreign objections as to the conduct of the blockade, but there remained the question of what to do with the prizes which had already been taken by the Imperial Navy. By the middle of 1827, the majority of these ships had been moved to Rio de Janeiro, and it was to the capital that the focus of diplomatic attention now turned.

The weakening of the Brazilian Navy's enforcement of the blockade had been caused by the objections of France and the United States. Robert Gordon's first task in tackling the prize issue was therefore to ensure that the new rules were applied to the ships of every nation impartially. The second was to insist that they were applied retrospectively to all vessels captured since the beginning of the war. If this were agreed, then the majority of prizes would be released immediately. The Brazilian Government seemed anxious to settle and, in September 1827, the Minister of Foreign Affairs, the Marquis of Queluz, provided reassurance on both counts. But it was a slow business, and it soon became clear that whatever the intentions of the Government, the Superior Prize Court was still applying the old rules. It could only implement its policy by intervening directly and overriding the Court's decisions.[1]

With eight British, five French, one Danish, one Swedish and three American prizes afloat in Rio harbour awaiting a decision,[2] Gordon pressed the Imperial Government to release the vessels which were his responsibility. These were the *Utopia*, *Atlantic*, *William and Henry*, *Ann*, *George*, *Henry and Isabella*, *John* and *Stag*. An accomplished diplomat, he did not think it would be difficult in spite of his secret knowledge that if judged according to English prize rules, they would all have been condemned.[3] At first all went well with pressure being equally applied by the American, French and British legations. The Imperial Government wanted to solve the problem, and obtained the agreement of the Assembly that it should be sorted out by the Council of State. But then the question of indemnities arose. It was not just a matter of releasing the prizes but of making cash payments which would (in Gordon's view[4]) restore the ships to the condition in which they were taken, compensate owners for lost or spoilt cargo, meet the costs of port, docking and customs charges and repay all prize court expenses. The price tag made ministers nervous and, to cover themselves, they decided in October 1827, that no further action could be taken until the financial claims had been examined by a special 'Junta Consultativa'. The foreign ambassadors settled down to wait.

For months nothing happened. The three powers responded in different ways. The French relied on diplomatic horse-trading aimed at a reciprocal agreement on blockading, but let it be known that a powerful naval force was on its way to back their negotiations with muscle. The Americans – still benefiting from the momentum created by Condy Raguet and with no sign of his replacement, William Tudor – exerted gentle pressure. The British, believing the assurances given to Gordon of 'the most positive promises of speedy and ample justice',[5] waited confidently for a solution.

But there was no time for Robert Gordon to relax for, suddenly, the possibility of peace presented itself. To the Ambassador's astonishment, the Emperor's speech at the closure of the Legislative Assembly in November 1827 contained the hint that a settlement was possible on the basis of an independent Banda Oriental which would not form part of the Argentine Confederation. The Brazilians, like the British, had noted Lavalleja's separatist ambitions and his increasing hostility to Buenos Aires, and were coming to the conclusion that the creation of a friendly buffer-state was the best deal they were likely to get. Gordon seized his opportunity, presented a 'Project' to the Brazilian Government and was able to report in the middle of February 1828 that the Emperor had agreed to British mediation aimed at restoring peace on the basis of an independent Uruguay![6] The news was immediately sent to Lord Ponsonby in HMS *Thetis*, which dropped off an embassy secretary in the Banda Oriental on the way to secure the agreement of General Lavalleja.

In Buenos Aires, British credibility had been shaken by the failure of the Garcia initiative, and in December 1827, Lord Ponsonby was incensed to learn that General Dorrego's Government had approached Colombia as a possible mediator! But the following month, the new Foreign Minister, General Juan Balcarte, formally requested British mediation aimed at a peace settlement based on the creation of an independent Uruguay. Studying the political situation in the Banda Oriental, the Argentinians had come to exactly the same conclusion as their counterparts in Rio de Janeiro. This was exactly what the British envoy wanted to hear. The news was sent to Rio on 12 February 1828, but to make sure that the Imperial Government played ball this time, it was accompanied by details of a bizarre plot aimed – so Lord Ponsonby claimed – at the assassination of the Emperor Pedro! According to Ponsonby, General Dorrego was its principal architect; the Marquis of Aracaty was secretly involved; armaments were being assembled in the United States; and Argentinian privateers were cruising off São Paulo ready to pounce.[7] Rear Admiral Sir Robert Otway, then off Maldonado with the *Ganges* and *Cadmus*, hurried back to Rio de Janeiro at Ponsonby's behest to save the Braganza dynasty. The information was so secret that it could not be committed to paper, and Flag-Lieutenant Paget was forced to ride 400 miles across the Banda Oriental to receive it personally![8] Admiral Otway was not amused to find the Brazilian capital in a state of peace and tranquillity. There was no sign of any plot, he reported in tart terms to the Admiralty, who asked the Foreign Office with equal asperity what their ambassador thought he was up to. In the British Embassy, Gordon was equally annoyed. He did not believe a word of Ponsonby's wild inventions, and told the Imperial Government as much. Fortunately, the embarrassing affair soon blew over as the Brazilian and Argentinian governments, spurred on by the two British envoys, began to push the peace process forward.

The possibilities of peace did not, however, obscure the long-running saga of the prizes taken in the River Plate. Anxiously, the foreign ambassadors waited for the Junta Consultativa to produce the expected solution. But in May 1828, Robert Gordon was dismayed to hear that instead of merely finding excuses to release the captured ships, the Junta Consultativa had re-opened the whole question.[9] Then he heard rumours that the Brazilian Government had already agreed to pay compensation for French and American ships taken during the blockade! Gordon wrote immediately to Foreign Minister Aracaty, demanding the settlement of British prize demands and putting forward a solution – basically, the release of all ships and the use of the customs dues owing to compensate their owners. It was, as he pointed out, a fair proposal which would involve the Brazilian Government in no extra cost.[10] But the compromise was rejected. Gordon was too late. The Emperor had already made up his mind and, on 21 May 1828, issued a decree settling the matter. By its terms, all captured neutrals were eligible for compensation and six more prizes were to be released, but eight remained condemned. These were the British vessels *George*, *Henry and Isabella*, *John* and (in Montevideo) *Cocquito*; the French *Jules*, (in Montevideo) *Salvador* and *Courier*; and the American *Matilda*. Gordon protested vigorously but got nowhere.

Then, a fortnight later came an unpleasant distraction. The recruiting campaign which Colonel Cotter had launched in Ireland had been blessed with success, and during the Brazilian summer of 1827–8, three immigrant ships had arrived from Cork carrying 3000 men, women and children. Unfortunately, the unscrupulous Cotter had tricked them into thinking that they were coming to Brazil as immigrant farmers and not as mercenary troops. To their dismay, on arrival the men were herded into barracks, forced to train as soldiers and submitted to the most severe military regime. Robert Gordon tried to intervene but his protests were ignored.[11] The explosion came on the night of 11 June 1828. Incensed by the savage punishment of one of their number, a German mercenary battalion in Rio de Janeiro mutinied and, joined by the now desperate Irishmen, took violent control of the city. Brazilian artillery and infantry units were immediately deployed against the mutineers, joined by 500 French sailors and 224 Royal Marines from HM Ships *Ganges*, *Forte* and *Sapphire*. The redcoats were given the honour of guarding the São Cristovão Palace and the person of the Emperor. With the foreign units holding the ring, the Brazilian Army ruthlessly suppressed the mutiny, the black troops singling out the Irish, whom they despised as 'white slaves', for particularly brutal treatment.[12] The Brazilian Government was stunned by the outbreak and decided to repatriate the unfortunate Irish. In the middle of July, under the supervision of the first lieutenant and purser of the *Ganges*, the remaining men, women and children were loaded onto transports and sent back home. It was a satisfactory outcome, although as Gordon sadly reported, of the 3000 who had arrived, only 1400 had survived to return.[13] The Brazilian Government came out of the affair no better. With the exception of the Marquis of Aracaty, all the ministers were dismissed or resigned and were replaced by the fifth administration in as many years.

For the Emperor Pedro, the mutiny could not have happened at a worse time. He had other things on his mind. Not only did the peace process need his attention, but there were disturbing developments in Portugal. For a year, the two brothers Pedro and

Miguel had been negotiating warily over the succession. Miguel had declared his willingness to marry his eight-year-old niece, and become Prince Consort in accordance with his brother's great scheme, but only if he were made Regent first. Pedro had taken him at his word, and in February 1828, Miguel had duly arrived in Portugal to swear allegiance to the new liberal constitution. But things immediately began to go wrong. Forces within the country which were politically reactionary or resentful of the Brazilian connection, rallied round Miguel. Supporters petitioned him to take the throne. The two houses of parliament were stalemated between absolutists and constitutionalists until, in April, the more liberal Assembly was ominously dissolved. In Rio de Janeiro, Pedro strove to avert a crisis by fulfilling his side of the bargain. First he abdicated the throne of Portugal in favour of Maria da Glória. Then on 5 July 1828, the young Queen boarded the frigate *Imperatriz* with the Marquis of Barbacena and headed for Europe escorted by the *Dona Francisca*. The idea was that Dona Maria II, as she now was, should go to Vienna to greet her grandfather, the Emperor of Austria, then, with his backing, head for Lisbon to claim her crown. Barbacena, meanwhile, would search the courts of Europe for a suitable bride for his newly widowed Emperor. Pedro could only hope that he had acted in time.

Fortunately, on the question of peace with Argentina, things were going according to plan. With the main point now agreed, it was not difficult to settle the minor details, and on 6 August 1828, two Argentinian envoys, Generals Guido and Balcarte, arrived in Rio on the British packet *Redpole* to finalize the settlement. But no sooner had they left Buenos Aires than General Dorrego had second thoughts. Encouraged by a successful attack on the Province of Missiones on the Rio Grande do Sul border, interpreting the Rio mutinies as the beginnings of a military collapse, and encouraged by the purchase of four warships using a national subscription launched by Commodore Brown,[14] Dorrego told his delegates to harden their terms.

Guido and Balcarte respectfully refused to obey. It was clear to them that the mutinies had had no impact on Brazilian military capability and, witnesses as they were of the bustle and strength of

Brazil's principal naval base, they realized that adding a handful of ships to Brown's squadron would make no difference to the Imperial Navy's dominance of the River Plate. They were right. Shortages of munitions and dockyard facilities in Buenos Aires doomed the initiative from the start, and the ships could only be manned by emptying the local gaols. When three of the new ships attempted to break out in August, the *Gobernador Dorrego* was promptly captured by the blockading squadron, while the *Argentina* under William Granville was so badly damaged that it limped no further than Carmen de Patagones and stayed there. Only the *General Rondeau* commanded by John Halstead Coe managed to escape for a commerce raiding cruise to West Africa and the Caribbean.

Guido and Balcarte stuck to their original instructions and, on 27 August, finally signed a preliminary convention of peace. The main provision was the creation of an independent Uruguay, with subsidiary arrangements for the framing of a constitution, elections, an amnesty for all concerned, and the evacuation of the area by all military forces. There had been, however, a change in the cast list which enacted the final stage of the drama. The Honourable Robert Gordon, surrendering at last to ill health, sailed for Europe in the midst of the negotiations to become British Ambassador to Lisbon. It was therefore his replacement, Lord Ponsonby, arriving in Rio de Janeiro in the middle of August, who had the satisfaction of seeing the completion of the task to which the two envoys had devoted so much energy, sound and fury. In early September, the British packet *Nocton* sailed south for Buenos Aires with the peace terms, to be followed a fortnight later by HMS *Heron* carrying the Argentinian delegates themselves.

Meanwhile in Buenos Aires, the final confrontation of the war was taking place. Ignorant of the progress of Argentinian ratification, on 26 September 1828, Commodore James Norton appeared with 18 ships of the Brazilian blockading squadron in a demonstration off Buenos Aires. There was the flagship *Niterói*, the brigs *Pirajá*, *Caboclo*, *Maranhão*, *29 de Agosto*, *Constança*, *Feliz*, *Niger* and *Rio da Plata*, the brigantines *Dona Januária* and *2 de Julho*, the lugger

Principe Imperial, the schooners *Dona Paula, Itaparica, Rios, União, Bela Maria,* and the recommissioned prize *Gobernador Dorrego.* Most were veterans of the war in the River Plate and were familiar sights to the citizens of the Argentinian capital as they looked across the river. True to form, Commodore Brown anchored what ships he had aggressively across the narrow channel leading to the anchorage of Los Pozes, then sent Tomas Espora under flag of truce to tell the wary Norton that at that very moment, an Argentinian convention was meeting to endorse the peace proposals.

The final act took place three days later. The schooner *Sarandí* sailed out of the Inner Roads flying a white flag to officially inform Commodore Norton that the agreement had been ratified and that peace between the two countries was now a reality. The *Sarandí* then raised the green and yellow flag of Brazil to her main truck and fired a 21-gun salute, while the *Niterói* hoisted the blue and white ensign of Argentina and replied in like manner.[15] Next day, Norton formally lifted the Brazilian blockade. The long and damaging war between the Empire of Brazil and the Republic of the United Provinces of Argentina was over.

Then came the ceremonial. On 4 October, two Argentinian delegates left Buenos Aires in the *Nuevo 25 de Mayo* under the command of George De Kay to formally exchange the instruments of ratification in Montevideo. They were respectively, 84-year-old Brigadier General Miguel Azcuenaga and Commodore William Brown – the two carefully chosen to epitomize the past and present traditions of the Republic. Diplomatically, all went well. But no sooner were Captain De Kay and the delegates ashore than the crew of the *Nuevo 25 de Mayo* seized the ship, killed the second-in-command and any loyal hands who resisted them, took her up river and deserted ashore en masse in the boats. It was a sad reflection on the state of the Argentinian Navy at the end of the war, its strength and morale undermined not so much by enemy action but by the exaggerated emphasis placed by the Government on privateering. Admiral Pinto Guedes promptly supplied prisoners-of-war to man the vessel, and the *Nuevo 25 de Mayo* returned to Buenos Aires discreetly escorted by Captain

Grenfell in the Brazilian corvette *Maria Isabel* to ensure there was
no further trouble.[16]
    In both capitals the arrival of peace was marked by masses in
the cathedrals, gun salutes from the forts and ships of war,
celebrations and junketing. Pedro needed something to celebrate,
for the news from Portugal was uniformly bad. Egged on by his
diminutive and malevolent mother, the Queen Dowager Carlota,
Miguel had torn up the constitution, declared Pedro's succession
void, and seized the throne. On 15 July 1828, ten days after Queen
Maria II had sailed from Rio, Miguel was proclaimed King and the
country was plunged into civil war. Within months, his supporters
had taken control of peninsular Portugal, driving thousands of
liberals into exile. Only the island of Terceira in the Azores
remained loyal to the young Queen. In November, the *Dona
Francisca* returned to Rio to report that Barbacena had accordingly
changed his plans and was heading for England seeking safety and
assistance. Pedro could only wait anxiously for further news.
    Back in the River Plate, messages were being sent to the mili-
tary commanders on both sides to end the state of war. The
Sarandí and *18 de Enero* sailed for the coasts of Rio Grande do Sul
and Patagonia to spread the news and summon home any privateers that were still operational. Prisoners on both sides were
exchanged. In November, the Argentinian Army began to leave
the Banda Oriental. The Brazilians did the same. On 3 December,
Imperial troops withdrew from Colonia and, a week later, the first
contingent of 1800 officers, men and families sailed from Montevideo for Rio de Janeiro. The evacuation continued for another
two months until, on 3 April 1829, the green and yellow flag of the
Empire was lowered from the citadel of Montevideo for the last
time. A naval rundown reflected the military withdrawal. Admiral
Pinto Guedes returned with the bulk of his force to Rio de Janeiro
where Pedro's advisers were already discussing how Imperial
warships could be used to help the young Queen Maria. Eight
vessels were left to safeguard Brazilian interests in the River Plate
– the brigs *Maranhão* and *Pirajá*, the brigantine *Dona Januária*, and
the schooners *Rio da Plata*, *Bela Maria*, *Itaparica*, *Despique Paulista*

and *1 de Dezembro*. Command was given to the veteran expert in the area, Captain Jacinto Senna Pereira.

On the Argentinian side, what remained of the National Squadron was reduced to a handful of brigs and schooners. The bulk of its officers and men were given their discharge. In October, William Brown relinquished his post as commander of the tiny force, having had the satisfaction of being promoted to the specially created rank of Brigadier General – that is, Rear Admiral. Brown emerged from the war with an enormous reputation among friends and enemies alike. His outstanding energy and bravery made it easy to overlook his weaknesses – particularly his propensity to take perilous risks and his short-tempered habit of constantly finding fault with his subordinates. One of General Balcarte's last acts of the war was to write to Brown from Rio de Janeiro on 31 August 1828, telling him that:

> I have heard with the greatest of pleasure in many gatherings of important people, tributes to my friend the Admiral of the Argentinian Squadron and expressions of praise and even admiration occasioned by your gallant conduct during the present war. The newspapers at this place constantly speak of you, and always with admiration. ... This is the highest honour that can be given to great men and particularly to great patriots like my good friend Admiral Brown.[17]

Admiral Rodrigo Pinto Guedes was not so lucky. In Rio de Janeiro he was seen as being responsible for both the defeats and the victories of the war. Ministers made him the scapegoat for the international hostility caused by the blockade, and opposition newspapers criticized him as a means of embarrassing the Government. And unlike his Argentinian counterpart, he had received no support from a propaganda campaign aimed at magnifying the Imperial Navy's achievements and minimizing its setbacks. Commodore Brown returned home to promotion and praise; Admiral Pinto Guedes to a court martial. The charges against him focused on the defeats at Juncal and in Patagonia, and on his detention and treatment of 18 named neutral ships seized as prizes during the blockade. Pinto Guedes and his friends produced a long and eloquent defence which was published in the form of a pamphlet.[18] On 25 June 1829, after a three-month trial, the charges against the Admiral were predictably, and justly, dismissed.

CHAPTER 23

SETTLING ACCOUNTS

With the peace process well on the road to success, Robert Gordon turned his attention back once more to the prize dispute. By June 1828, it had become clear that the Brazilians intended to settle the prize issue on a 'divide and rule' basis, dealing with each nation separately and offering reciprocity as the basis of the solution.[1] In other words, Britain, France and the United States were to be treated in the same way that they would treat Brazil in the same situation. Thus British ships detained during the blockade of the River Plate would be dealt with severely, while French and American vessels would be treated leniently! With French and American acceptance of this solution, the Emperor was standing firm.

This was exactly what Gordon had tried to avoid, and he pressed the Brazilian Government to reverse the decision. But his efforts were suddenly undermined by a shift in his own Government's position. For years the British had backed the Brazilian blockade, but the weakening of the rules and the resulting expansion of American trade had caused the Government to think twice. Assailed by protests from merchants and shipowners, ministers decided that they could no longer penalize British trade by observing the blockade. They merely needed a plausible excuse to abandon it. In February 1828, the merchants of Glasgow were promised that the Government would make enquiries into the efficiency of the blockade 'in the expectation that the results ... will justify it in asserting its invalidity and remonstrating against its continuance.'[2]

City chambers of commerce, Lloyd's of London and private individuals provided evidence. A list of ships arriving and leaving

Buenos Aires was produced to 'prove' that the Brazilian blockade was ineffective. It was shown that 16 ships had arrived between June and September 1827 – the fact that only four had been merchantmen was not commented on. Another informant discussed the navigational problems of the River Plate. He described the sandbanks, the irregular currents, the hazards of sailing at night, and the Brazilian Navy's habit of anchoring at sunset which gave skilful seamen the opportunity of avoiding the blockade after dark. Finally he described the shallows before Buenos Aires and the concentration of Brazilian ships to the west of the Ortiz Bank, which effectively left the upper part of the river open. In these circumstances he argued, it was physically impossible for any navy to maintain a complete blockade of the Plate.[3]

The British Government accepted the information at its face value. It neither checked its accuracy nor considered whether a blockade had to be 100 per cent effective to be legal. It wanted to be convinced, and it was convinced. In April 1828, Robert Gordon was sent his orders in the packet *Hobart*. He was to tell the Brazilians that although his Government had supported the blockade from the beginning in spite of the damage done to British trade, 'recent facts have shown ... that the blockade is neither so actively nor so uniformly enforced' as to make it acceptable and, 'for reasons not gone into, the commerce of the River Plate is virtually open to vessels of a certain description while it is completely closed to English merchantmen.' As a result, the British Government now considered the blockade to be 'inefficient, ineffectual and therefore illegitimate' and was no longer prepared to observe it.[4] On 4 June, the Ambassador passed on the bad news.

A week later, Gordon tried to raise the prize issue again. He received no reply. Neither did repeated requests in the month which followed. Then, on 12 July, the long-awaited French squadron arrived in Rio de Janeiro. With the thunder of salutes rolling round the mountains and the smoke of cannon fire drifting lazily into the blue sky, Rear Admiral Roussin in the 84-gun *Jean Bart*, with the frigates *Magicienne*, *Nymphe*, *Arethuse* and *Terpsicore*, the corvette *Isis* and *Cygne*, the brig *Railleuse* and two store ships, passed between the Sugar Loaf and the Fort of Santa Cruz into the bay and dropped anchor in the glittering water before the city. It was an impressive display of naval power. Robert Gordon noted gloomily that by contrast the only British warship in evidence was one tiny brig-of-war.[5] Delighted by the demonstration, French Ambassador Gabriac, whose negotiations were already well advanced, eagerly assured his hosts that the presence of the French squadron implied no threat and that it was there to provide any service the Brazilian Emperor might wish.

On 30 July, Aracaty replied at last to Gordon's repeated notes on the prize question. But there was nought for the Ambassador's comfort. The Minister confirmed that the sentences on the *George*, *Henry and Isabella*, *John* and *Cocquito* must stand but, using a classic diplomatic delaying tactic, said that the matter would now be referred to London via the Brazilian Ambassador, Gameiro Pessoa, Baron Itabayana. This was an ingenious excuse. As Aracaty courteously explained, Gordon's imminent departure for Lisbon made further talks in Brazil pointless as he would be unable 'to follow the thread' of the negotiations.[6]

All Ambassador Gordon could do was to pack his bags and watch the more successful diplomatic efforts of other powers. And Lord Ponsonby, arriving in Rio de Janeiro to replace him in August, could do little more. In September, he reported glumly that the Franco-Brazilian Treaty of Commerce and Amity had been amended to cover blockades and that the French Government now accepted the blockade of the River Plate as legitimate! In return, the Brazilians had agreed to release the remaining French prizes and pay compensation and legal costs (with interest) on all vessels. The new US Chargé d'Affaires, William Tudor, had likewise been successful. Arriving in June 1828, he had tried a new American tactic – courtesy and moderation. Tudor found that the financial claims which Condy Raguet had pushed with such vigour were based on exaggerated values and fake wage bills. In his opinion, there had been few flagrant injustices. Most of the detained ships had clearly been blockade runners and the American claimants had 'notoriously been doing everything in their power to aid the Buenos Aireans'.[7] The result of Tudor's new style

was that the Brazilian Government not only granted the USA the
same terms they had given to France, but made no stipulation
about future blockades. Indeed, when the terms of an American-
Brazilian commercial treaty were announced in July 1829, the US
interpretation of the law of blockade was enshrined in clauses 17
and 19![8]

In London, the Foreign Office waited for the promised approach from the Brazilian Ambassador on the prize issue. None
came. Then it received Ponsonby's report of the favourable
settlements reached with the French and the Americans. There
was a sharp reaction. On 10 November 1828, Ponsonby was
ordered to show the iron fist by demanding compensation for the
four captured ships. If no reply was received within 30 days, he
was to give notice that warships of the British South America
Squadron would seize Brazilian vessels up to the value of the
compensation owed.[9]

With aristocratic disdain, Lord Ponsonby delivered the ultimatum. In fact he went further, and in a lengthy note dated 20
January 1829, threatened naval reprisals unless *all* British claims
were settled, even for ships that had been released. In a preliminary interview Aracaty had hinted at the way forward, stressing
that the agreements with France and the United States had been
based on mutual concessions and complaining that Britain merely
made one-sided demands.[10] But Ponsonby failed to take the point.
With flat-footed insensitivity he seemed to believe that threatening
notes repeating at excessive length the justice of his case were all
that was needed.

The situation was made worse by the deteriorating situation in
the River Plate. Frustrated at the number of foreign merchantmen
– now including British vessels – which were trying to run the
blockade in the last months of the war, Admiral Pinto Guedes had
resorted to high-handed tactics. Four British ships – *Hellesponte*,
Unicorn, *Liberator* and *Resolution* were seized without being warned
off first, and the *Nestor* – an Argentinian prize recaptured by the
Imperial Navy – was improperly detained. In August 1828, the
Brazilian Navy captured an Argentinian privateer and burned the

two merchantmen, the British *Lord Eldon* and the American *Hussar*, she was escorting. Then, with the creation of an independent Uruguay at the end of the year, the Brazilians began to evacuate Montevideo, taking with them the prizes still in the harbour. In December, the *Nestor* set sail for Rio de Janeiro escorted by the frigate *Niterói* and was seized by HMS *Tribune*, acting under somewhat confused orders.[11] The Imperial Government was furious. Orders were sent for the cargoes of the *Hellesponte* and *Unicorn* to be sold to avoid another British seizure, and for the captain of the *Niterói*, Francis Clare, to be court martialled.

In London, the new Foreign Secretary, Lord Aberdeen, had been watching Ponsonby's antics with alarm. Orders were immediately sent for the *Nestor* to be handed back to the Brazilian authorities together with a reprimand for Ponsonby's threat of reprisals.[12] But it was too late. In March 1829, the Marquis of Aracaty had written a note deploring the unfriendly and bullying tone of Ponsonby's demands but eventually accepting that Brazil had no choice but to comply. Typically, Ponsonby replied with a justification of enormous length demanding a total of £475,000 in compensation. Then, disregarding the appalling atmosphere he had created, he merely reported to London that Aracaty had agreed to settle all prize claims.[13] A mixed commission of two British and two Brazilian members was then appointed to settle the matter.

The Brazilian horse may have been led to water, but it was another matter to make it drink. The Imperial Government was resentful of Ponsonby's high-handed actions and was deeply disappointed by the British Government's attitude to events in Portugal. In Canning's day, quick military action had stifled an early Miguelite outbreak. But he was dead, and the new ministry under the Duke of Wellington made it clear to Barbacena that its position on Miguel's coup was one of strict neutrality. It not only refused to intervene, but actively prevented Queen Maria's supporters from buying arms and mounting an invasion of the Azores using four ships and emigré troops which Brazilian agents had raised – and paid for – for the purpose. The frigate *Isabela* had been specially manned by British sailors and sent to Europe under Norton to be on hand for such an attempt.[14]

On 16 October 1829, the *Isabela* and the *Imperatriz* returned to Rio carrying Queen Maria and a crestfallen Barbacena. Also on board was a new bride for the Emperor, Amelia de Leuchtenberg. Alas, the royal houses of Europe had shied away from supplying a consort for the wayward Pedro, and Barbacena had had to settle for Amelia – granddaughter of Napoleon's first wife Josephine and, therefore, step-grandchild of the great Emperor himself. The wedding took place amid pouring rain the following day.

The new coolness between Britain and Brazil, and the financial crisis in which the Empire found itself as a result of the war, made a prize settlement even more difficult. The question of claims, valuations, deterioration, port charges, demurrage, losses and wages were complicated enough. But it soon became clear that the Brazilian commissioners, reflecting the mood of the Government and of the Legislative Assembly, were dragging their feet, and using any excuse to delay a settlement.[15] An exhausted Lord Ponsonby withdrew from the scene to be replaced as ambassador by the moderate Arthur Aston, but it made no difference. By the beginning of 1831, the Brazilians had already reached agreement with the Americans and the French, and had paid compensation in Treasury bills to the tune of 243 contos of reis (£32,400) and 409 contos (£54,000) respectively.[16] But of the 26 British claims, none had even been considered.

It was ironic that France and the United States, whose opposition to the blockade of the River Plate had done so much to undermine Brazil's war effort, should secure such a prompt and generous settlement. In the case of the United States, it was even more remarkable given the support afforded to fellow republicans in Argentina during the war and the sarcastic hostility of the public and the press to the Imperial cause. Britain, on the other hand, which had supported the blockade and had been instrumental in helping Brazil to end the war, received little but obstruction. In all likelihood, the Emperor felt that he had been pushed around too much. The unpopularity of the treaties on commerce and the slave trade, Gordon's dour nagging and Ponsonby's fanciful plots, the one-sided nature of British prize demands, and their refusal to take action against Miguel's coup in Portugal, all proved to be too much. Pedro had decided to make a stand – and this was it. As the post-war political and economic situation in Brazil deteriorated, so the delays went on. Ministers seemed afraid to ask the Assembly for funds to pay British prize claims – now greater than 3000 contos (£406,240). The nervous Brazilian commissioners repeatedly resigned. Documentation was incomplete. There were disputes over insurance valuations and the amounts claimed. Then in March 1831, came a political upset. The charismatic but increasingly autocratic Emperor Pedro had been losing popularity since the heady days in which he had led Brazil in its dramatic fight for independence. Now, there was growing discontent at the loss of the Banda Oriental, at Brazil's disappointing performance in the conflict, and at the financial mess the war had created. An increasingly virulent Brazilian press began to complain about the Emperor's obsession with the dynastic problems of Portugal, hinting that he was Portuguese by inclination as well as by birth. Then, in 1831, the dismissal of a popular ministry provoked the last in a succession of a political crises and a night of bottle-throwing. But this time, Pedro had had enough. On 7 April, he suddenly abdicated in favour of his five-year-old Brazilian-born son and sought refuge on HMS *Warspite*. A week later, he transferred to HMS *Volage* and sailed from Rio de Janeiro bound for Europe and exile, accompanied by Queen Maria II in the French warship *La Seine* and escorted by the Imperial Navy's latest frigate, *Dona Amelia*, commanded by Captain William Eyre. Pedro's remaining years were spent fighting for the cause of his daughter until his premature death in 1834 at the age of 35.

With the Emperor's departure from Rio de Janeiro, the last vestiges of Portuguese influence were removed, and native Brazilian rule was firmly established through a three-man Regency and a powerful Assembly. One of Ambassador Aston's fears was that the anti-foreign feeling that had accompanied the crisis would halt the progress made on claims. A six-month deadline was imposed.[17] But he need not have worried. The new regime was not only determined to settle, but strong enough to do so. Pedro de Araujo Lima – destined, as Marquis of Olinda, to dominate Brazilian politics for half a century – became Foreign Minister and determined to clear up the prize issue once and for all. He quickly reached agreement with Aston and the claimants, and squared his own colleagues. The Mixed Commission speeded up its proceedings and, in November 1832, was able to report that its labours were at an end. The Legislative Assembly then formally approved compensation of up to 4717 contos (£628,933) in Treasury bills payable over three years. The total award covered 21 British ships and five British cargoes carried in other vessels.[18] During 1833, detailed individual claims were agreed one by one until at last, on 20 September 1834, it was all over and the British Ambassador was able to write to Palmerston, 'I rejoice to inform your Lordship that the whole of the sums due by the Brazilian Government for the liquidation of British prize claims have now been paid!'[19]

CHAPTER 24

REVOLUTION AND
REPARATIONS

The petitions with which merchants and shipowners bombarded the British Government during 1827 and 1828 were not only concerned with the conduct of the Brazilian blockade. There was a growing wave of protest against the activities of Argentinian privateers and, as time went on, increasing fears that they were getting out of control. It was said that blank Letters of Marque could be bought by anyone who wanted them. One informant told Lloyd's that they were being sold openly in Baltimore for as little as $70.[1] In fact the problem was exaggerated. There was no evidence of any wholesale commissioning of privateers in foreign ports. Lord Ponsonby knew of only one which had been licensed overseas,[2] although Rear Admiral Otway reported that a number of small commerce raiders had been fitted-out in the West Indies.[3] But there were more and more examples of British ships being intercepted, even fired into, on the High Seas. Some – like the seizure of the *Albuera* carrying 600 barrels of gunpowder to Brazil – were legitimate. But others were not. In March 1828, the *Gaspee*, carrying only a general cargo, was taken by the notorious Jaime Costa in the *Vencedor de Ituzaingú*, now called *Bolivar*. That same month, the *George and James* carrying American wheat was seized by the *Triunfo Argentino* but was wrecked on its way to port. In September, the *Helvellyn* was seized by the *Gaviota*. In each case, the privateers helped themselves to gear and property.

And there was worse. Some ships were taken and looted by vessels flying the Argentinian flag which refused to disclose their identity. In February, the *Morning Star* bound for England from

Ceylon carrying coffee and 24 soldiers with their families was plundered by a fast, black-painted ten-gun brig. In April the *Sunbury* was attacked by a yellow six-gun ship manned by Italians and Spaniards. Orders were sent to British naval commanders and consuls to identify and seize these pirates.[4] As a result, when HMS *Black Joke*, on anti-slavery patrol off West Africa, was fired on by the schooner *Presidente* in August, she promptly pursued and captured the privateer which lost 20 wounded and 6 dead including its English captain Prouting.[5] Lieutenant Ohm and 39 survivors were taken to England to be tried – and acquitted – of piracy. The following month in the West Indies, HMS *Victor* seized *Las Damas Agentinas*. Her officers and crew were less lucky: most were found guilty and hanged. Other nations also began to take a strong line. The *Presidenta* was detained by the Dutch authorities in Curaçoa, while the United States Navy seized the *Federal*.[6] When the end of the war came, the Argentinian Government seemed reluctant to cancel existing privateering commissions, but pressure from Woodbine Parish and Colonel Forbes ensured that this was done in March 1829.

Argentinian privateers may have been getting out of hand, but the Government in Buenos Aires acted with as much speed as was possible under the circumstances. Whereas Brazilian prize court proceedings dragged on for years, in Argentina the question was settled more promptly. In 1827, the *Florida* was restored within four months of its detention by Fournier. In June 1828 the *Gaspee* was given back to its owners after three, only those parts of the cargo classified as contraband being confiscated. In December, the same verdict was delivered on the *Albuera*. In March 1829, the owners of the *Triunfo Argentino* were ordered to pay full compensation for the loss of the *George and James*.[7] The only delays were over the *Huskisson* (because of an appeal by the *armadores*) and the *Dove* (whose ownership had to be proved), but these were released at the end of 1828.

Foreign governments and diplomats had hoped that the arrival of peace in the River Plate would inaugurate a period of economic and political stability. They could not have been more wrong. The rot began in December 1828 with a sudden military coup against the Government of Buenos Aires, inspired by unitarian supporters of Rivadavia and executed by General Juan Lavalle, commander of the Argentinian troops recently returned from the Banda Oriental. Dorrego withdrew into the interior pursued by Lavalle, was defeated, captured and shot out of hand. This single act, and the events which followed from it, introduced a legacy of bitterness and brutality into Argentinian politics which lasted for decades. Foreign observers and Argentinian leaders alike were shocked – including Admiral Brown who had been left in charge of Buenos Aires. The country relapsed into bloodshed and civil war. Not even a brief visit from the hero General San Martin could stop it. For a year, the unitarians and the federalists led by the *gaucho* leader Juan Manuel Rosas fought it out until, in December 1829, Rosas emerged triumphant. Lavalle with many of his followers fled to Uruguay. Others – including Balcarte, Iriate and Aguirre – were arrested and exiled. Rivadavia had read the signs earlier and had already sought refuge in France. Disappointed, Admiral Brown withdrew from the scene and returned to his trading ventures.

The representatives of the foreign powers in Buenos Aires – Parish for Britain, Forbes for the United States and Mandeville for France – attempted to remain neutral in the turmoil. But unwisely, French citizens took a leading part in forming a military unit to defend the city – against, of course, the federalists. Thus, when Rosas seized control he promptly took advantage of the fact that there was no Franco-Argentinian treaty to give them protection and threatened to enlist them all in the national army. In May 1829, Mandeville withdrew in a huff to Montevideo accompanied by hundreds of French citizens, while others found themselves arrested. Bourbon arrogance did the rest. On 21 May, 'to avenge French honour' the Vicomte de Venancourt, commanding the frigate *Magicienne*, attacked nine Argentinian ships in the Inner Roads, seized the *General Rondeau, Rio Bamba, Cacique, 11 de Junio* and four gunboats, and burnt the brigantine *Argentina* down to the waterline.[8] In the turmoil of the times, the Argentinians could do nothing to prevent it.

The restoration of order by the apparently moderate Rosas was generally welcomed – more so since he appointed the experienced Manuel Garcia and Tomas Guido to be his principal ministers. In the British legation, Woodbine Parish reported the settlement with relief and turned his attention back to the outstanding problems left by the war. The issue of the enormous repayments due on the Baring loan of 1824 was clearly beyond the financial capacity of the new Government. Parish therefore concentrated on the question of compensation for British vessels captured by Argentinian privateers. On this issue, General Guido, now responsible for foreign affairs, proved positive and in September 1829 agreed that the whole question should be referred to a mixed commission made up of equal numbers of Argentines and local British merchants.[9] The first case to be examined was that of the *Huskisson* – now officially released, but in fact a wreck with its cargo looted and its livestock dead. The commissioners wrangled over what seemed to be an open and shut case for four months before Parish intervened and reached a direct agreement with Guido that the owners should be awarded an indemnity of £5000. For good measure, Mr Brooks was later given £2000 in compensation for his lost zoo animals.[10]

But Parish had been worried by the 'tedious and unsatisfactory' nature of the proceedings and, taking advantage of Argentina's internal preoccupations, managed to persuade Guido to transfer the whole business to London. So in July 1830, it was agreed that the question of indemnities would be settled by one British and one Argentine commissioner – respectively the lawyer Michael Burke and the new Ambassador Manuel Moreno – with Danish diplomat Bourk acting as arbitrator when necessary. There were six cases for adjudication – the *Concord*, *Ann*, *Albuera*, *George and James*, *Helvellyn* and the cargo of the *Huskisson*.[11] The Argentinians seemed unworried by the financial aspects of the situation. The commerce of Buenos Aires had almost returned to pre-war levels, but with the peso being exchanged at only one-sixth of its old rate and the value of exports in sterling being less than a quarter of the 1825 figure,[12] the Government was desperately short of hard currency. Nevertheless, it was confident that it would be able to meet all claims by selling the warships *Asia* and *Congresso* which Ramsay had bought on its behalf during the war.

The commissioners began their work in October 1831 with the collection of documents and claims. There were minor disagreements over the more difficult cases – notably the *Ann* and the *Concord* – but proceedings went smoothly. The only snag occurred when a distraught Moreno heard that although Ramsay's agents, Hullet Bros, had sold the two warships for £19,000, the amount was less than they were owed for buying them in the first place![13] But in July 1834, the last case was agreed and the commissioners concluded their work. In all, compensation of £23,501 was awarded – £12,650 for the cargo of the *Huskisson*, and £10,850 for the five other merchantmen.[14] Substantial claims for losses of British property carried on captured Brazilian vessels were disallowed. Thus, the cavalier behaviour of Argentinian privateers towards British ships during the war cost their Government over £30,000 in indemnities.

Fortunately, the solution of the privateer problem was not compromised by the first sign of tension over what in Britain are called the Falkland Islands, and in Argentina the Malvinas. One of the first acts of Rosas' Government was to appoint an entrepreneur merchant called Luis Verner as Governor of the Islands. On the instructions of London, Woodbine Parish lodged a protest, but the matter was not pursued. But two years later, both nations took steps to assert their claims. In December 1832, the *Sarandí* arrived with a party of settlers and was in the process of founding an Argentinian penal colony, when HMS *Clio* hove into sight, sent the *Sarandí* packing and raised the Union Jack over the islands. There was a storm of protest from Buenos Aires at what was regarded as an exercise in naked power,[15] but apart from diplomatic objections there was little the Argentinians could do about it. The issue has lingered on to poison relations between the two states, but the dispute did not prevent a just settlement to the claims resulting from the war with Brazil.

But the British were not the only nation to have suffered from the activities of Argentinian privateers. American ships had also been interfered with and, in 1828, Consul Forbes had prepared a claim for damages amounting to 57,000 pesos – that is, £4285 at the current low rate of exchange. But neither Forbes's local prestige nor the modesty of the amount cut any ice with the Argentinians. And the political turmoil of the times, combined with a crudely handled dispute over American fishing and shooting rights in the Falklands in the early 1830s, did not make them any more disposed to help. The commissioners handling the British compensation question refused to consider American vessels, and the claim was repeatedly presented to the Argentinian Government without the slightest effect. In November 1834, American warships were sent to Buenos Aires to demand compliance.[16] But the threat only increased local stubbornness, and successive American consuls failed to make any progress. By 1851, only three of the claims had been liquidated – and these were for incidents during the independence period rather than during the war with Brazil.[17] So by an irony of fate, just as sympathetic Britain received worse treatment in relation to merchantmen taken by the Brazilian Navy, so the supportive Americans were the losers in terms of compensation for the activities of Argentinian privateers. But with these solitary exceptions, by the middle of the 1830s, all the international loose ends remaining from the war between Brazil and the United Provinces had been securely tied.

EPILOGUE

The creation of Uruguay to act as a buffer between the two powers was the most visible result of the 1825–8 war between Brazil and the Argentinian Provinces. But the conflict did nothing to stabilize the situation in the River Plate, and the strains it imposed on the two participants caused political turmoil in both. In Brazil, the overthrow of Emperor Pedro in 1831 was followed by a deliberate weakening of the powers of the Central Government by the Regency which coincided with – and helped bring about – a resurgence of local nationalism. The result was a spate of regional rebellions. There was the 'Cabanos' in Pernambuco 1832–5 and in Pará 1835–6; the 'Sabinada' in Bahia in 1837–8; the 'Balaiada' in Maranhão in 1839–40; and the 'Farrapos' in Rio Grande do Sul and Santa Catarina which dragged on from 1835 to 1845. Only the mystique of the Brazilian monarchy and action by the Army and the Imperial Navy kept the country together until 1840, when Pedro II was prematurely proclaimed Emperor at the age of 15 and the centre began to regain its former powers.

In Argentina, the war put a temporary end to the dream of a liberal, progressive state on the River Plate. Blindly backed by the rural *gauchos* and the urban lower classes, rule by the 'moderate' General Rosas rapidly took on the form of a brutal dictatorship which lasted for 21 years. There were benefits. Argentina's southern frontier was pushed back, there was increased immigration, a secure economic environment and resulting expansion. But in other aspects the regime was conservative and oppressive, bigoted in terms of religion and hostile to foreigners. A consummate politician, Rosas adopted a remote – even genial – style, while his followers imposed a totalitarian regime punctuated by intermittent purges. Meanwhile, Uruguay was signally failing to perform the role of a buffer state. Indeed the two factions which began fighting for power reflected the traditional rivalries of the region. On one side were the conservative *blancos*, led by General Oribe and backed by Rosas and Argentina; while on the other, were the liberal *colorados* led by Fructuoso Rivera who became a rallying point for anti-Rosas elements whether they were Argentinians fleeing from persecution, or foreign powers, notably France. In fact French hostility was such that they had actually blockaded Buenos Aires from 1838 to 1840. Only intervention by the British Foreign Secretary, Lord Palmerston, put a stop to it. In Uruguay, Rivera successfully got rid of his mentor, Lavalleja, to become the country's first president. Then, in 1838, he maintained his reputation for treachery by overthrowing his elected successor, Oribe, and plunging Uruguay into open civil war. In 1841, Rosas began to help Oribe in earnest, sending a steady stream of troops to Uruguay and ordering Admiral William Brown with a naval squadron to blockade Montevideo, where Rivera – backed by units of resident Italians and Frenchman, and supported by a small flotilla commanded by the Italian patriot Garibaldi – was being loosely besieged by his rival.

This devil's brew was made worse when the French began to provide Rivera with arms and direct military support, and when Palmerston was replaced as British Foreign Secretary in 1841. His successor, the Earl of Aberdeen, tried to impose a settlement on the warring parties while at the same time favouring Rivera. The result was a foreign policy disaster which led to the British Squadron in the Plate, assisted by the French, breaking the Argentinian sea blockade of Montevideo, and eventually seizing the entire Argentinian Navy. Returning to office in 1846, Palmerston put an end to this folly and reverted to strict neutrality. Then, in 1851, the Brazilians, now free from internal rebellion, decided to put a stop to Rosas' ambitions in Uruguay and Paraguay once and for all. They had maintained a watching brief in the Plate for years; now they acted in support of a revolt in Entre Rios by sending an army under its finest general, and a fleet commanded by Vice Admiral John Pascoe Grenfell, who penetrated the fortified passage of Tonelero and delivered the troops to the enemy's rear. The nine-year-long siege of Montevideo was lifted and Oribe defeated. Within a year, Rosas was overthrown and fled to exile in England, where – according to Woodbine Parish – he ended his career as a modest and well respected Hampshire country gentleman. But that was not the end. It took 15 years for the unitarian idea to triumph and for Argentina to develop as a single country, while Uruguay's instability continued unabated. It only took the emergence of a heavily armed and paranoid Paraguay to make the mixture volatile and to cause, in 1865, the cataclysmic War of the Triple Alliance.

Against this disturbed and politically confused background, the veterans of the 1825–8 war attempted to continue with their lives and careers. It was not easy. In Brazil the Government of the Regency believed not only in decentralization, but in political realism and cuts in expenditure. Brazil was recognized for what it was – a continental country of vast resources and regional tensions which had the sea as an easy but vital means of control, communication and trade. The logic of this position was ruthlessly applied to the Brazilian Navy. By 1832, it had been cut to one-fifth of its former size, boasting no more than 17 warships, the largest of which was a medium-sized frigate, with only 1500 officers and men.[1] Its success in the independence campaign and in the war with Buenos Aires was forgotten, and the Navy was recast into the role it would occupy for the next two decades – that of regional policeman and coastguard. And when it eventually went to war, first against the Rosas in 1851–2, and as part of a triple alliance with Argentina and Uruguay against Paraguay, its field of glory lay not on the ocean but in seizing control of the great internal rivers of South America. This abrupt change in the Navy's role and fortune caused hardship among its officers. Promotion was effectively frozen, and foreign officers who had not returned home at the end of their contracts were dismissed unless they had fought actively in the War of Independence. By 1835, only 22 of the 270 names in the Brazilian Navy List were British.[2]

But the Navy was still needed to control the spate of internal rebellions. In 1836, the number of ships in commission was increased to 30 but a rapid expansion in manpower proved as difficult to achieve as it had been in 1823 and 1826. As before, the Government recruited in Britain and found over 100 men in the Orkneys and Shetland.[3] Coincidentally, the arrangements were made by Marquis de Barbacena who had carried out the original 1823 recruitment and was back in London attempting to renegotiate the unfavourable trade treaty. The Brazilian Navy was prominent in the suppression of all the outbreaks. And so were its remaining British officers. William James Inglis was in command of the naval station during the rebellion in Pará and ·was killed during its early stages. Commodore John Taylor led the force which restored order, assisted by Captains William Eyre, George Manson and Bartholomew Hayden. In the south, it was likewise Commodore John Pascoe Grenfell who directed the naval units deployed against the 'Farrapos', having Captains William Parker and George Broom under his command.

The names of six British officers stand out in Brazilian naval history at this time, many of them settling in the country, marrying local ladies and staying on to be entrusted with important commands and to reach the highest ranks of the Navy. James Norton, the hero of the blockade of Buenos Aires, was promoted commodore but died prematurely in 1835 at the age of 46 on a voyage to New Zealand to purchase wood for yard-arms. Commodore John Taylor was at last forgiven by the British authorities,[4] and was restored to active duty in 1833. He commanded the forces which fought the Pará rebels in 1836, held a series of important administrative posts, then retired to his coffee plantation at Cantagalo near Rio and died as a vice admiral in 1855.[5] Bartholomew Hayden remained in almost continuous employment, commanding the anti-slavery Squadron of the East, and fighting the rebels in Pará in 1836. He died a commodore in 1857.[6] George Broom of Juncal fame was in command of the blockade of Laguna in 1839 during the 'Farrapos' rebellion when Garibaldi evaded the vigilance of the

Brazilian patrols and escaped to find greater glory in Montevideo and Italy. He died as a commodore in 1860 at the age of 63.[7]

The most distinguished of these men was John Pascoe Grenfell. From the beginning to the end, his career was spectacular and his abilities and personality were admired by all who met him. After losing his right arm in the Battle of Lara-Quilmes he returned to duty, fought the 'Farrapos' in the late 1830s, was in charge of the naval stations in southern Brazil during the 1840s; and in 1851–2 commanded the Brazilian sea forces during the war with Argentina, achieving a famous victory at Tonelero.[8] Grenfell died as an admiral in 1869, having spent his later years as Brazilian Consul General in Liverpool. It was in that capacity and as his Government's chief representative, that he attended the funeral of his old chief, Lord Cochrane, in Westminster Abbey in 1860.

The longest and steadiest career, however, was that of William Parker. Born in Dumfries, Parker, was 22 years old when he enlisted in the Brazilian service. Following the end of the Buenos Aires war, he remained in command of warships and small squadrons until 1844, and was a participant at the victory of Tonelero. In the 20 years that followed, he successively commanded Brazil's three main naval stations – Rio Grande do Sul, Bahia and Rio de Janeiro – and retired as an admiral in 1867. Parker died in Montevideo at the age of 82 in 1883,[9] the last British survivor of the Buenos Aires war.

For officers in the Argentinian service, the political confusion of the times made life even more problematic. After the war, the Navy was cut to the bone, and it was only in 1841 that Rosas revived it, appointing William Brown once more to command. Many of the veterans of the Brazilian war promptly rejoined to take prominent roles in the blockade of Montevideo and in the fighting in the Plate and the Paraná between 1841 and 1844. Tomas Espora, William Granville and Leonardo Rosales took no part, having died of natural causes in the interim, but John King, William Bathurst, Francisco Segui, Nicolas Jorge, John Gard and Antonio Toll all distinguished themselves in these campaigns, while Commandant-General Zapiola and Commissioner Goyena retained their posts at the head of the Navy. Other officers, however, fell foul of the Rosas purges, and were either assassinated – like Francisco Lynch, the port commander of Buenos Aires – or fled to Uruguay. There, ironically enough, many found themselves fighting in Rivera's Uruguayan Navy against Admiral Brown and their former Argentinian comrades. Thus Brown's principal opponent in the 1840s was John Halstead Coe at the head of a squadron of ships whose commanders included Malcolm Shannon, Robert Beazley and William Mason, while the privateer Fourmantine was prominent among the Frenchmen defending Montevideo.[10] The confusion of the times was reflected in the fact that both Coe and Fourmantine rejoined to fight for post-Rosas Argentina in the 1850s. One absent veteran was George De Kay of *General Brandzen* fame. After the war he left to try his luck with Cochrane in Greece, later returning to New York where he adopted the self-appointed title of commodore. There, in 1847, he borrowed the USS *Macedonian*, filled it with food and took it on a mercy mission to help relieve the famine in Ireland. It was a generous and much acclaimed humanitarian gesture, but so incompetently organized that the financial consequences contributed to his early death two years later.[11]

But the period also saw the apotheosis of Admiral William Brown. Briefly offered command of Oribe's Uruguayan squadron in 1838 before the latter's overthrow, he was recalled to the colours by Rosas in 1841 at the age of 64 and, once more, was instrumental in recreating the Argentinian Navy. He had lost nothing of his old skill and flare, and carried out an aggressive campaign in the Plate against Rivera until his ships were disgracefully seized by the British and the French in 1845. Thereafter, he devoted himself to business and family matters, writing his memoirs, and even managing to visit his place of birth in Ireland. He died in 1857 acclaimed as a national hero, the father of the Argentinian Navy and the architect of its early victories. Since then, the reputation for daring, bravery, skill and success which was so remarkable during his lifetime has burgeoned to give him an almost legendary stature. It is not for nothing that one of his innumerable biographies describes him as 'the Nelson of the River Plate'.

In Argentina, the Brazilian war is celebrated as a glorious episode in the history of the Republic, a time when the nation and the Navy not only put up a dogged defence against the enormous power of the Brazilian Empire, but fought back with a series of dramatic and daring offensives against their more numerous foes. In modern times, the Argentinian Navy continues to celebrate it in the naming of its ships – the *25 de Mayo*, *General Belgrano*, *Gránville*, *Drummond*, *Segui* and, of course, the *Almirante Brown*. In Brazil on the other hand, outside the ranks of a group of naval enthusiasts, there is little interest in either the heroic aspects of the Buenos Aires conflict or in its fascinating strategic and international context. David always has a better press than Goliath, and the political rivalries of the time have obscured – even distorted – the Imperial Navy's achievements. Few have tried to put the record straight. Early Brazilian naval history tends to focus on the independence campaign and on the wars against Rosas and Paraguay. It is here that the nation and the Navy finds its heroes. And in Britain there is an even more profound lack of knowledge on the conflict, in spite of the serious political and economic problems it caused at the time, the challenges it posed for the Royal Navy, and the fact that officers and men from England, Scotland and Ireland played such a prominent and distinguished part on both the Brazilian and Argentinian sides. Hopefully this book will do something to fill the gap.

BRAZILIAN ARMED NAVAL VESSELS, DECEMBER 1825

Note: Asterisk indicates ships at the Plate

NAME	GUNS	COMMANDER
line		
Pedro I	74	Commodore F.M. Telles
frigates (6)		
Piranga	64	Capt. James Shepherd
Dona Paula	50	Capt. J.C. Pritz
Imperatriz *	50	Capt. L. Barroso Pereira
Paraguassú	44	Capt. Matheus Welch
Thetis	36	Capt. D.M. de S. Coutinho
Niterói	36	Capt. James Norton
corvettes (5)		
Carioca	18	Capt. F.R. de L. Pinto
Liberal *	22	Capt. A.F. Salema Garcão
Maceió *	18	Capt. A.J. de Carvalho
Maria da Glória *	26	Cmdr T. de Beaurepaire
Itaparica *	22	Cmdr E. Barbosa
brigs (12)		
Caboclo	16	Sublieut. F.P. de Carvalho
Maranhão	18	Cmdr F. Rib. de Castro
Liguri	16	Lieut. J.Q. de Santana
Beaurepaire	18	Lieut. V.M. Boisson
Cacique	16	Cmdr George Manson
Guarani	14	Lieut. James Nichol
Independ ou Morte	16	Cmdr William Eyre

NAME	GUNS	COMMANDER
Pirajá *	18	Cmdr Bartholomew Hayden
29 de Agosto *	18	Lieut. J.R. Gleddon
Rio da Plata *	10	Lieut. Alex W. Anderson
Real Pedro *	10	Cmdr F. Mariath
Real João *	10	Lieut. José de F. Ribeiro

brigantines (6)

Atlanta	10
2 de Julho	10
Dona Januária *	14
Pará *	8
Empreendador	8
Leopoldina	12

schooners (19)

Maria Theresa *
Conceição *
6 de Fevereiro *
Isabela Maria *
Maria da Glória *
Dona Paula *
Infante D. Sebastião *
Itaparica
Alcantara
Providência
1 de Dezembro
Carolina
(with Flotilla of the Uruguay)
Oriental *
Camões *
Dom Alvaro da Costa *
Imperial/R Unido *
Mameluka *
Maria Isabela *
Isla de Flores *

Plus
Gunboats = 16
Armed launches = 8
Transports = 8
Mail-packets = 13
Lugger = 1
Cutter = 1

Total = 96

APPENDIX B

ARGENTINIAN SHIPS
11 JUNE 1826

ORDER OF BATTLE

TYPE	NAME	GUNS	COMMANDER
gunboat	*No 1*		J.B. Nogueira
corvette	*25 de Mayo*	28	Cmdr Tomas Espora
gunboat	*No 2*		Lieut. A. Erezcano
corvette	*Congresso Nacional*	18	Lieut. W.R. Mason
gunboat	*No 5*		Sublieut. A. Richitelli
brig	*República Argentina*	16	Lieut. William Clark
gunboat	*No 10*		M.J. Martinez
brig	*Independencia*	22	Lieut. William Bathurst
gunboat	*No 3*		Sublieut. A. Zupitch
gunboat	*No 11*		Sublieut. Fran. Segui
gunboat	*No 12*		Sublieut. Pedro Natal

CONVOY TO COLONIA

TYPE	NAME	GUNS	COMMANDER
brig	*General Balcarce*	14	Lieut. Nicolas Jorge
schooner	*Sarandí*	9	Lieut. J.M. Pinedo
schooner	*Rio de la Plata*	1	Lieut. Leonardo Rosales
schooner	*Pepa*	1	Lieut. V.F. Dandrcys
gunboat	*No 8*		Sublieut. José Monte
gunboat	*No 9*		Sublieut. J. Maximin

Note: Details from *Estado General de las Tripulaciones y Tropa que existe Abordo de la Escuadra y demás destinos del Servicio*, Buenos Aires, 13 May 1826, printed in Carranza, *CNRA*, vol IV, p 189.

ARGENTINIAN SHIPS
JANUARY 1827

MARTIM GARCIA

NAME	GUNS	COMMANDER
brigs		
General Balcarce	14	Lieut. Francisco Segui
schooners		
Sarandi	9	Lieut. John H. Coe
Maldonado	8	Lieut. Francis Drummond
Guanco	10	Lieut. Henry Granville
Union	14	Lieut. Malcolm Shannon
Pepa	1	Lieut. C. Silva
Uruguay	7	Lieut. W.R. Mason
gunboats		
no 1		J.B. Nogueira
no 2		George Clark
no 3		Sublieut. A. Zupitch
no 5		Sublieut. Archibald Smith
no 8		A. Mendez
no 9		Sublieut. J. Maximin
no 10		Sublieut. John Lee
no 11		Sublieut. John Clements
no 12		Sublieut. Henry Wildblood
launch 3		—

BUENOS AIRES

NAME	GUNS	COMMANDER
corvette		
Congresso Nacional	18	Sublieut. Gerald Fisher
brigs		
República Argentina	16	Lieut. William Clark
Independencia	22	Lieut. William Bathurst

Note: Details from *Extracto de la Officialidade y Tripulantes que existen Abordo de los Buques de Guerra em frente de Martim Garcia el 20 de Enero de 1827,* printed in Carranza, *CNRA,* vol IV, p 227.

NOTES

AGN   Arquivo General de la Nacion, Buenos Aires
AN   Arquivo Nacional, Rio de Janeiro
BN   Bibliotéca Nacional, Rio de Janeiro
PRO   Public Record Office, London

CHAPTER 1

1. *Report of Trade of the River Plate sent by the Chairman of the British Committee to Consul Woodbine Parish*, July 1824, PRO, FO 6/4.
2. J. Whitaker to Woodbine Parish, 1 January 1832, PRO, FO 354/8.
3. Woodbine Parish to Canning, 22 June 1825, PRO, FO 6/9. Correspondence between Brazilian Consul Sodré and Garcia, 30 April and 2 May 1825, quoted in Lucas A. Boiteux, 'A Guerra da Cisplatina', *Revista Maritima Brasileira*, July–September 1956, chap VI, p 570.

CHAPTER 2

1. Chamberlain to Canning, no 39, 6 April 1825, PRO, FO 13/9. Silvestre Rebello (Washington) to Carvalho e Melo, 26 October 1824, *Archivo Diplomático da Independência*, vol 5, Ministério de Relaçoes Exteriores, Rio de Janeiro, 1922.
2. Chamberlain to Canning, no 42, 15 May 1825, PRO, FO 13/9.
3. Lobo's instructions, 20 May 1825, printed in Boiteux, 'A Guerra da Cisplatina', chap IX, p 596.
4. Correspondence between Lobo and Garcia, 5, 6, 7 and 8 July 1825, printed in Henrique Boiteux, *Os Nossos Almirantes,* (ONA), vol 1, Imprensa Naval, Rio de Janeiro, 1925, pp 120–3.
5. Lobo to Paranaguá, 24 July 1825, AN, XM 292 and printed in Boiteux, 'A Guerra da Cisplatina', chap X, p 607.
6. Lobo to Paranaguá, 17, 31 August and 7 September 1825, AN, XM 292 and printed in Boiteux, 'A Guerra da Cisplatina', chap X, pp 611–12, chap XI, p 833.

7. Lobo to Paranaguá, 15 July, 31 August, 2 September 1826, printed in Boiteux, 'A Guerra da Cisplatina', chap XIX, pp 255–7.

CHAPTER 3

1. See Appendix A, based on the report of Vilela Barbosa to the Assembly, 30 June 1826, adjusted using Ministry of Marine correspondence, and Rio de Janeiro British Consular and *Diário Fluminense* shipping reports.

2. Chamberlain to Canning, no 35, 15 March 1825, PRO, FO 13/8.

3. Correspondence between Carvalho e Melo and Silvestre Rebello (Washington), January 1824 to March 1825, *Archivo Diplomático da Independência*, vol 5.

4. Gameiro (London) to Vilela Barbosa, nos 16 and 34, 6 August and 19 November 1825, AN, XM 453.

5. Brian Vale, *Independence or Death! British Sailors and Brazilian Independence 1822–5*, Tauris Academic Studies, London, 1996.

6. *Almanack do Rio de Janeiro 1825*, BN, Rio.

7. Woodbine Parish to Canning, 20 July 1825, PRO, FO 6/9.

8. Gordon to Dudley, no 26, 1 October 1827, PRO, 13/39.

9. Chamberlain to Santo Amaro, 3 December 1825 and reply of 4 December, PRO, Adm 1/30. Canning to Chamberlain, no 14, 28 February 1826, PRO, FO 13/21. Itabayana (London) to Santo Amaro, nos 84 and 86, 20 and 25 February 1826, *Archivo Diplomático da Independência*, vol 2.

10. Eyre to Chamberlain, (Secret), 24 December 1825, PRO, Adm 1/30.

11. Jorge de Brito to Paranaguá, 5 January 1826, printed in Boiteux, 'A Guerra da Cisplatina', chap XIX, pp 266–7.

12. Charles Darwin, *The Voyage of the 'Beagle'*, Everyman Edition, 1959, p 134.

13. See John Purdy, *The New Sailing Directory for the Ethiopic or Southern Atlantic Ocean*, R.H. Laurie, London 1845.

CHAPTER 4

1. Officer ranks in Brazil were those of the old Portuguese Navy, whereas Argentina used military titles at the time. In this book they are translated as their equivalents in the British Navy:

Britain	Brazil	Argentina
Admiral	Almirante	—
Vice Admiral	Vice Almirante	—
Rear Admiral	Chef-de-Esquadra	Brigadier
Commodore	Chefe-de-Divisão	Coronel Mayor
Captain	Capitão-de-Mar-e-Guerra	Coronel
Captain (less than 3 years)	Capitão-de-Fragata	Teniente Coronel
Commander	Capitão-Tenente	Sargento Mayor
Lieutenant	1º Tenente	Capitan Teniente
Sublieutenant	2º Tenente	Subteniente

2. Rear Admiral F.L. Morell, 'A Vida Abordo en la Guerra contra o Brasil, Capt. F. Eleta, 'El Poder Maritimo del Brasil y las Provincias Unidas', *Historia Maritima Argentina*, (HMA), vol IV, Departamento de Estudios Históricos Navales, Buenos Aires, 1988.

3. Presidential decree of 5 August 1826, printed in Angel J. Carranza, *Campañas Navales de la República Argentina*, (CNRA), vol IV, Ministerio da Marina, Buenos Aires, 1962, pp 170–1.

4. Argerich to Minister of War and Marine, 15 February 1825, printed in Carranza, *CNRA*, vol IV, pp 160–1.

5. Ramsay to Rivadavia, 27 October 1825 (Confidential), printed in Carranza, *CNRA*, vol IV, pp 173–4.

6. See J. de C. Ireland, *The Admiral from Mayo*, Edmund Burke, Dublin, 1995, for a readable English account of Brown's life illumined by the author's prejudices about monarchies and perfidious Albion.

7. Goyena to Minister of War and Marine, 13 May 1826, printed in Carranza, *CNRA*, vol IV, p 187. Of the 56 sea officers, 30 were British and American, and 6 of other European nationalities.

8. Woodbine Parish to Canning, no 5, 25 January 1826, PRO, FO 6/19.

CHAPTER 5

1. Woodbine Parish to Canning, no 5, 25 January 1826, PRO, FO 6/19.

2. Petition of the officers and crew of the *República Argentina* to the court martial, printed in Carranza, *CNRA*, vol IV, p 180.

3. *ibid.*

4. *ibid.*

5. *Defence of Azopardo, Beazley, Warnes and Mason*, Imprensa Hillier & Cia, July 1826, printed in Carranza, *CNRA*, vol IV, p 178.

6. Brown to Commandant-General J.M. Zapiola, 9 February 1826, AGN, VII-2-4-18, printed in Arguindeguy and Rodriguez, *Guillermo Brown. Apostillos a su Vida*, p 201, Instituto Browniano, Buenos Aires, 1994. Copy sent by Eyre to Croker, no 15 (Secret), 11 March 1826, PRO, Adm 1/30.

7. *Defence of Azopardo.*

8. Lobo to Paranaguá, no 76, 9 February 1826, AN, XM 292, and printed in Boiteux *ONA*, vol 1, pp 126–8.

9. See 6.

10. Brown's version of the whole event is given in his *Memorandum de las operaciones navales de la marina de la República Argentina desde el ano 1813 hasta la conclusion de la paz con el Emperador do Brazil en ano 1828*, printed in Carranza, *CNRA*, vol IV, pp 286–7.

11. Woodbine Parish to Canning, no 11, 12 February 1826, PRO, FO 6/19.

12. *Defence of Azopardo.* The full papers relating to the court martial are in AGN, VII-7-5-4.

13. Diogo do Brito to Paranaguá, 16 February 1826, printed in Boiteux, *ONA*, vol 2, pp 82–3.

14. Lobo to Paranaguá, no 76, 9 February, 1826, printed in Boiteux, *ONA*, vol 2, pp 82–3.

15. Admiral Visconde de Inhaúma, quoted in Boiteux, 'A Guerra da Cisplatina', chap XXI, p 300.

16. Lobo to Paranaguá, 16 February 1826, AN, XM 292, printed in Boiteux, 'A Guerra da Cisplatina', chap XXI, p 314.

17. Lobo to Paranaguá, no 76, 9 February 1826, AN, XM 292, printed in Boiteux, 'A Guerra da Cisplatina', chap XXI, p 314.

CHAPTER 6

1. Francisco Lynch, *Noticias del Puerto de Buenos Aires, 1826–8*, entry for 11 March 1826, AGN, VII-7-6-9, printed in Carranza, *CNRA*, vol II, p 271.

2. See captain's log of HMS *Jaseur*, 21 February 1826, PRO, Adm 51/3003.

3. J.R. Bamio, 'El Ataque a La Colonia del Sacramento' in *HMA*, p 192.

4. Lobo to Paranaguá, no 80, 28 February 1826, AN, XM 292 and printed in Boiteux, *ONA*, vol 1, p 130. Lobo's despatch is filled with excuses for his failure to engage the enemy (which he claims is superior in numbers) and renews his demand for extra frigates and brigs.

5. Mariath to Lobo, 26 February 1826, printed in Boiteux, *ONA*, vol 3, p 64.

6. Brown to Rodrigues and reply, 25 February 1826, printed in Boiteux, *ONA*, vol 3, p 61.

7. Rodrigues to Brown, 26 February 1826, printed in Boiteux, *ONA*, vol 3, p 62.

8. C.G. Zapiola to Ministro de Guerra y Marina, 1 March 1826, AGN, X-5-1-5, printed in Carranza, *CNRA*, vol II, p 290.

9. Bamio, 'El Ataque a La Colonia', *HMA*, p 200.

10. Mariath to Lobo, 3 March 1826, printed in Boiteux, *ONA*, vol 3, p 66.

11. Report published in the *La Gaceta Mercantil*, Buenos Aires, 7 March 1826, printed in *Documentos del Almirante Brown*, tomo II, Academia Nacional de la Historia, Buenos Aires, 1959, p 30.

12. *Diary of the Siege*, Archivo del Ministerio de Guerra de la República de Uruguay, printed in Carranza, *CNRA*, vol IV, pp 192–3.

13. Lobo to Paranaguá, 28 February 1826, AN, XM 292 and printed in Boiteux, *ONA*, vol 1, pp 130–1.

14. Lobo to Paranaguá, 12 March 1826, AN, XM 292 and printed in Boiteux, *ONA*, vol 1, pp 132–3

15. Rodrigues to Lobo, 10 March 1826, printed in Boiteux, *ONA*, vol 1, p 133.

16. Lobo to Paranaguá, 12 March 1826, printed in Boiteux, *ONA*, vol 1, p 133.

17. Lobo to Paranaguá, 14 March 1826, AN, XM 292 and printed in Boiteux, *ONA*, vol 1, p 135.

18. *La Gaceta Mercantil*, 10 March 1826.

19. Funeral Notice, *La Gaceta Mercantil*, 1 April 1826.

20. De la Cruz to Brown, 15 February 1826, printed in Bamio, 'El Ataque a La Colonia', *HMA*, p 205.

21. Boiteux, 'A Guerra da Cisplatina', chap XXVIII, p 497.

CHAPTER 7

1. Documents of the Comisario de Marina, dated 13 May 1826, AGN, X-5-1-5.

2. Captain's log of HMS *Doris*, PRO, Adm 51/3148.

3. Norton to Lobo, printed in Boiteux, *ONA*, vol 1, p 221.

4. *Memorandum de las operaciones navales de la marina de la República Argentina desde el ano 1813*, p 290.

5. Lobo to Paranaguá, 1826, AN, XM 292 and printed in Boiteux, *ONA*, vol 1, p 6.

6. *Relatório da Repartição dos Negocios da Marinha, 1828, (Annex)*, Bibliotéca do Serviço de Documentaçao da Marinha, Rio de Janeiro.

7. *Estado General de las Tripulaciones y Tropa que existe Abordo de la Escuadra y demás destinos del Servicio*, Comisario de Marina, Buenos Aires, 13 May 1826, printed in Carranza, *CNRA*, vol IV, p 189.

8. Lobo to Paranaguá, 27 March, 6 and 19 April 1826, AN, XM 292 and printed in Boiteux, 'A Guerra da Cisplatina', chap XXV, pp 515–7.

9. Letter of Capt. José M. Pinedo (in old age) to *La Nacion*, describing the campaign, printed in Carranza, *CNRA*, vol IV, pp 195–6.

10. The *Doris* was now anchored 3½ miles S.W. by S. of the cathedral. Captain's log of HMS *Doris*, PRO, Adm 51/3148.

11. *Memorandum de las operaciones navales de la marina de la República Argentina desde el ano 1813*, p 290.

12. C.F. Rebeldo da Gama to Lobo, 28 April 1826, printed in Boiteux, 'A Guerra da Cisplatina', chap XXV, pp 521–2.

13. Lobo to Paranaguá, no 103, 4 May 1826, AN, XM 292 and printed in Boiteux, *ONA*, vol 1, pp 137–8.

14. Brown to Zapiola, 3 May 1826, printed in Carranza, *CNRA*, vol IV, p 197.

15. *Cuaderno de Ordenes Jenerales del Ejército Nacional, 12 Agosto 1825 a 1 Octobre 1826*, printed in Carranza, *CNRA*, vol IV, p 194.

CHAPTER 8

1. Lobo to Paranaguá, 6 April 1826, AN, XM 292 and printed in Boiteux, *ONA*, vol 1, p 136.

2. The charges against Lobo are printed in Boiteux, *ONA*, vol 1, pp 144–5.

3. Lobo to Paranaguá, 3 August 1826, AN, XM 292 and printed in Boiteux, *ONA*, vol 1, pp 139–43.

4. Lobo to Paranaguá, 14 March 1826, AN, XM 292 and printed in Boiteux, *ONA*, vol 1, p 134. Pinto Guedes to Paranaguá, 20 August 1826, Boiteux, *ONA*, vol 2, p 16.

5. Pinto Guedes to Paranaguá, 9 August 1826, *ONA*, vol 2, p 11.

6. Hood (Montevideo) to Bidwell, no 21, 20 October 1826, PRO, FO 51/2.

7. Woodbine Parish to Bidwell, 1 December 1827, PRO, FO 354/8.

8. Minister of War and Marine to Ramsay, 13 March 1826, printed in H.R. Ratto, *Comodoros Britanicos en la Plata 1810–52*, Buenos Aires, 1945, p 112.

9. *Diario de operaciones de la Esquadra Nacional desde medio dia el 25 hasta medio dia el 26 del mismo*, printed in Carranza, *CNRA*, vol IV, pp 199–200.

10. Norton to Pinto Guedes, 15 June 1826, printed in Boiteux, 'A Guerra da Cisplatina', chap XXVI, p 554.

CHAPTER 9

1. Hood to Pinto Guedes, 28 May 1826, PRO, FO 51/3.

2. See Appendix B.

3. Norton to Pinto Guedes, printed in Boiteux, *ONA*, vol 3, p 11.

4. J.R. Senna Pereira, *Memórias e Reflexões sobre o Rio da Plata*, Rio de Janeiro, 1847.

5. The written advice of the Brazilian captains is printed in Boiteux, 'A Guerra da Cisplatina', chap XXVI, p 522.

6. Pinto Guedes to Paranaguá, no 21, 13 June 1826, printed in Carranza, *CNRA*, vol II, p 204.

7. C.G. de Marina to Ministro de Guerra e Marina, 29 July 1826 (list of ships and armament), printed in Carranza, *CNRA*, vol IV, p 205.

8. Woodbine Parish to Canning, no 29, 20 June 1826, PRO, FO 6/19.

9. Chamberlain to Canning, no 64, 29 June 1826, PRO, FO 13/23.

10. Pinto Guedes to Paranaguá, no 51, 11 August 1826, AN, XM 292 and printed in Boiteux, *ONA*, vol 2, pp 12–15.

11. Pinto Guedes to Paranaguá, no 23, 16 June 1826, printed in Carranza, *CNRA*, vol II, p 204.

12. Woodbine Parish to Canning, no 33, 20 July 1826, PRO, FO 6/19.

13. *British Packet and Argentine News*, quoted in Arguindeguy and Rodriguez, *Guillermo Brown*, pp 181–2.

14. *ibid.*

15. Pinto Guedes to Paranaguá, no 50, 3 August 1826, AN, XM 292 and printed in Boiteux, *ONA*, vol 2, pp 9–10.

16. Argentinian and Brazilian historians are in agreement as to the course of the battle of 30 July, and their interpretation is borne out by the log of HM Packet *Dove* which was in sight and gives details of time, wind and place of the action. PRO, Adm 51/3146.

17. Pinto Guedes to Paranaguá, no 51, 11 August 1826, AN, XM 292 and printed in Boiteux, *ONA*, vol 2, pp 12–15.

18. Woodbine Parish to Canning, no 35, 2 August 1826, PRO, FO 6/19.

CHAPTER 10

1. Woodbine Parish to Bidwell, 1 December 1827, PRO, FO 354/8.
2. *ibid.*
3. Chamberlain to Canning, no 72, 15 July 1826, PRO, FO 13/23.
4. Printed in Boiteux, 'A Guerra da Cisplatina', chap XIX, p 268, and attached to Gordon to Canning, no 19, 21 September 1827, PRO, FO 13/38.
5. Forbes to Lobo, 1 January 1826, printed in the *La Gaceta Mercantil* of Buenos Aires, 11 January 1826.
6. *La Gaceta Mercantil*, 12 January 1826. Woodbine Parish to Canning, no 5, 25 January 1826, PRO, FO 6/19.
7. Lobo informed Captain Sinclair of the *Doris* that his blockading force consisted of 43 vessels. Consul Hood in Montevideo, was able to identify 37 of these ships: the corvettes *Liberal, Maria da Glória, Itaparica* and *Macieó;* the brigs *Pirajá, 29 de Agosto, Real João, Real Pedro* and *Rio da Plata;* the brigantine *Pará;* the schooners *Maria Teresa, Liberdade do Sul, 6 de Fevereiro, Conceição, Oriental, Isabela Maria, Camões, Reino Unido, D. Alvaro da Costa, Isla de Flores, Maria da Glória, Mameluka, Dona Paula* and *Infante D. Sebastião;* the gunboat *Leal Paulistana;* with the frigates *Niterói* and *Imperatriz;* the brigs *Caboclo* and *Maranhão;* the brigantines *Independência ou Morte* and *Leopoldina,* with 6 schooners/armed yachts en route from Rio. (Hood to Canning, no 4, 8 January 1826, PRO, FO 51/3.) Hood omitted to mention the existence of the brigantine *Dona Januária,* the schooner *Maria Isabela,* the gunboats *Araçatuba* and *No 8,* and the launches *Montevideana* and *Atrevido.*
8. Lawrence A. Hill, *Diplomatic Relations between the USA and Brazil,* Duke University Press, 1932, p 44.
9. Correspondence between Canning and Sanderson, Anderson and Ravenscroft, August to September 1826, PRO, FO 13/34.
10. Woodbine Parish to Canning, no 3, 14 March 1826. PRO, FO 6/19.
11. The detained ships were the *Marquis of Anglesey, Druid, Henrietta, Elizabeth Ann, Perseverance, Volante, Trafalgar, Children* and *Hutton.*
12. Eyre to Croker, 6 May 1826, PRO, Adm 1/30.
13. Woodbine Parish to Hood, no 36, 2 August 1826, PRO, 51/2.
14. Chamberlain to Canning, 18 September 1826, PRO, FO 13/24.
15. Hood to Canning, no 12, 30 June 1826, PRO, FO 51/2.
16. Correspondence Hood–Pinto Guedes–Hood, 28, 29 May 1826, PRO, FO 51/2.
17. Hood to Bidwell, no 16, 8 September 1826, PRO, FO 51/2.
18. *Monarch, Jersey, Ann, William and Henry, Atlantic* and *Stag* (British); *Leonides* (US); *Le Courier, Junon* (French); *Fortuna* (Danish).
19. Laurio H. Destefani, 'Guerra de Corso Contra el Brasil' in *HMA,* p 296.
20. Court martial of Admiral Pinto Guedes, June 1829, printed in Boiteux, *ONA,* vol 2, pp 53–4.
21. Raguet to Henry Clay, 23 September 1826, *Despatches V,* quoted in Hill, *Diplomatic Relations between the USA and Brazil,* p 50.

22. Chamberlain (and Gordon) to Canning, July to December 1826, PRO, FO 13/24 and 13/26. Sir G. Eyre to Croker, no 45, 5 July 1826, PRO, Adm 1/30. Sir R. Otway to Croker, nos 34 and 50, 24 November and 7 December 1826, PRO, Adm 1/30.
23. Gordon to Dudley, no 19, 21 September 1827, PRO, FO 13/38. Ambassador de Gestas quoted in Boiteux, 'A Guerra da Cisplatina', chap XXXVII, p 334.
24. Woodbine Parish to Bidwell, 20 July and 31 December 1826, PRO, FO 6/19.
25. Woodbine Parish to Bidwell, 1 December 1827, PRO, FO 354/8.

CHAPTER 11

1. Ponsonby to Canning, no 22, 16 April 1827, PRO, FO 6/17.
2. Laurio H. Destefani, 'Apogeo y Decadencia del Corso en la Guerra contra el Brasil' in HMA, p 461.
3. Hon. Nina L. Kay-Shuttleworth, A Life of Sir Woodbine Parish, 1796 to 1882, London, 1910.
4. Destefani, 'Guerra de Corso contra el Brasil' in HMA, p 267.
5. Eyre to Croker, no 5, 26 January 1826, PRO, FO 1/30.
6. Parish to Bidwell, 15 April 1827, PRO, FO 6/20.
7. Ponsonby to Canning, no 38, 11 June 1827 (with enclosures). Parish to Bidwell, 15 July 1827, PRO, FO 6/20 and 6/17.
8. Ponsonby to Otway, 27 August 1827, PRO, FO 6/17.
9. Destefani, 'Apogeo y Decadencia del Corso' in HMA, p 461.

CHAPTER 12

1. Woodbine Parish to Canning, no 33, 20 July 1826, PRO, FO 6/19.
2. Chamberlain to Canning, no 96, 26 September 1826, PRO, FO 13/24.
3. Correspondence Rosales, Mason and Granville, 27 August 1826, AGN, X-5-1-5, printed in Carranza, CNRA, vol IV, pp 214–15.
4. Otway to Croker, no 35, 24 November 1826, PRO, Adm 1/30. Paranaguá to Pinto Guedes, 18 November 1826, printed in Boiteux, ONA, vol 2, p 20.
5. Chamberlain to Canning, no 97, 26 September 1826, PRO, FO 13/24.
6. Brown to Goyena, 25 December 1926, AGN III-57-4-3, printed in Arguindeguy and Rodriguez, Guillermo Brown, p 210.
7. The whole voyage is recorded in the captain's log of the Sarandí, AGN, X 5-1-5, printed in Carranza, CNRA, vol IV, pp 382–401.
8. Laurio H. Destefani, 'Cruceros de Guerra y Corso de Brown en 1826 con la Sarandí y la Ehacabuco' in HMA, p 319.
9. ibid.

CHAPTER 13

1. *Aviso* of 22 October 1826, printed in Boiteux, 'A Guerra da Cisplatina', chap XXX, p 752.

2. General Vila Bela to Pinto Guedes, 18 November 1826, printed in Boiteux, 'A Guerra da Cisplatina', chap XXXI, p 768.

3. Minister of War to Pinto Guedes, 5 February 1827, printed in Boiteux, 'A Guerra da Cisplatina', chap XXXII, p 16.

4. Hood to Gordon, 18 January 1827, PRO, FO 51/3.

5. Ramsay to Brown, 29 November 1826, printed in Arguindeguy and Rodriguez, *Guillermo Brown*, p 209. *British Packet and Argentine News*, 25 November 1826.

6. De la Cruz to Brown, 26 December 1826, AGN, X-5-1-5, printed in Arguindeguy and Rodriguez, *Guillermo Brown*, p 210.

7. Detailed movements in the port of Buenos Aires during the period can be found in *Diario de Noticias del Puerto de Buenos Aires* by Captain Francisco Lynch, AGN, VII-7-6-9.

8. See the detailed analysis given in P.E. Arguindeguy, 'El Juncal. Preliminares', in *HMA*, p 349. See also Appendix C.

9. Pinto Guedes to Paranaguá, 7 January 1827, printed in Boiteux, 'A Guerra da Cisplatina', chap XXX, p 752.

10. Ponsonby to Canning, no 3, 5 January 1827, PRO, FO 6/16.

11. Pinto Guedes to Mariath, 11 January 1827, printed in Boiteux, 'A Guerra da Cisplatina', chap XXXII, p18.

12. Letter in *El Mensajero Argentino*, 20 January 1827.

13. *Operaciones de la Escuadra Nacional*, no 1, printed by Imprenta del Estado, 19 January 1827.

CHAPTER 14

1. There is no single contemporary account which gives details of the Battle of Juncal. The best that can be done is to build up a picture from partial references in a number of sources, notably the *Apuntes de Familia of Francisco Segui*, AGN, VII-11-6-8, printed in Carranza, *CNRA*, vol IV, pp 235–7 and E. Senna (Pereira), *Guerra do Rio da Plata em 1825. O Libello Argentino e a Verdade Historica*, Rio de Janeiro, 1857.

2. Boiteux, 'A Guerra da Cisplatina', chap XXXII, p 33.

3. Brown to De la Cruz, 9 February 1827, printed in the *British Packet and Argentine News*, Buenos Aires, 17 February 1827, Arguindeguy and Rodriguez, *Guillermo Brown*, p 211.

4. Brown to De la Cruz, 10 February 1827, printed in the *British Packet and Argentine News*, Buenos Aires, 17 February 1827, Arguindeguy and Rodriguez, *Guillermo Brown*, p 211.

5. Pinto Guedes to Diogo do Brito, no 302, 23 December 1827, printed in Boiteux, *ONA*, vol 2, p 35.

6. Pinto Guedes to Diogo do Brito, 2 September 1827, printed in Boiteux, *ONA*, vol 2, p 28.

7. *ibid.*

8. Governor M.J. Rodrigues to Pedro Antonio Nunes (Port Commander of Montevideo), 12 February 1827, printed in Boiteux, *ONA*, vol 4, p 282.

9. Governor M.J. Rodrigues to Pedro Antonio Nunes, 14 February 1827, printed in Boiteux, *ONA*, vol 4, p 282.

10. Correspondence between Brown and the President of Entre Rios, 13–14 February 1827, AGN, X-51-5, printed in Carranza, *CNRA*, vol IV, pp 250–3.

11. The prizes were integrated in the Argentinian Navy under the following names *29 de Diciembre* (formerly *Oriental*), *8 de Febrero* (*Dona Januária*), *9 de Febrero* (*Bertioga*), *18 de Enero* (*12 de Outubro*), *30 de Julio* (*Brocaio*), *11 de Junio* (*9 de Janeiro*) and gunboats *6* (*Paranaguá*), *7* (*Cananea*), *4* (*Iguapé*) and *13* (*Paraty*).

12. Forbes to Clay, no 45, 8 March 1827, printed in P.E. Arguindeguy, 'El Combate Naval del Juncal', *HMA*, p 373. Ponsonby to Canning, no 13, 8 March 1827, PRO, FO 6/16.

13. Published in *La Gaceta Mercantil*, 10 February 1827. Neither received it, but were placed in a common prison in difficult conditions under police surveillance. Broom typically responded by escaping within a month. Senna Pereira followed four months later.

14. See footnote 12.

15. *British Packet and Argentine News*, 3 March 1827, printed in Arguindeguy and Rodriguez, *Guillermo Brown*, p 214.

16. Report of Minister of Marine Souza Coutinho to the Assembly, 26 May 1827, Bibliotéca da Marinha, Rio de Janeiro.

CHAPTER 15

1. Capt. Ben Morrell, *Narrative of Four Voyages*, 1822, quoted in Purdy, *The New Sailing Directory for the Ethiopic or Southern Atlantic Ocean*.

2. Pinto Guedes to Diogo do Brito, no 302, 23 December 1827, Boiteux, *ONA*, vol 2, p 34.

3. Archive of Admiral Tamandaré, *Subsidios para a História Marítima do Brasil*, Imprensa Naval, Rio de Janeiro, 1950, vol VIII, p 80.

4. Printed in E.G. Lonzieme, 'Intento Brasileño de Invasion el Territorio Argentino' in *HMA*, p 393.

5. For the national complexion of crews see Destefani, 'Guerra de Corso contra el Brasil' in *HMA*, pp 264–7.

6. Pinto Guedes to Maceió, 2 September 1827 and reply of 15 October 1827 (discussing the feasibility of court martialling the culprits), printed in Boiteux, *ONA*, vol 2, pp 29–30.

7. Darwin, *The Voyage of the Beagle*, pp 63–5.

8. Lacarra to Minister of War and Marine, 20 March 1827, printed in Carranza, *CNRA*, vol IV, pp 252–3. Hood to Canning, 18 April 1827, PRO, FO 51/3.

9. A complete list of captured personnel and materiel is attached to Lacarra's letter of 20 March 1827.

10. Ambrosio Mitre to Minister of Finance, 29 March 1827, printed in Carranza, *CNRA*, vol IV, pp 256–7.

11. Pinto Guedes to Diogo do Brito, no 302, 23 December 1827, Boiteux, *ONA*, vol 2, pp 34–5.

12. Maceió to Pinto Guedes, 17 April 1827, printed in Boiteux, 'A Guerra da Cisplatina', chap XXXVI, p 82.

13. John Armitage, *Historia do Brasil desde a chegada da família de Bragança em 1808 até a abdicação de D Pedro I em 1831*, (translation), Edições de Ouro, Rio de Janeiro, 1943, p 201.

14. Ponsonby to Canning, no 23, 10 April 1827, PRO, FO 6/17.

15. Pinto Guedes to Diogo de Brito, no 302, 23 December 1827, printed in Boiteux, *ONA*, vol 2, p 35.

16. Purdy, *The New Sailing Directory for the Ethiopic or Southern Atlantic Ocean*, p 289.

17. Eyre to Pinto Guedes, Buenos Aires, 29 November 1827, printed in Boiteux, *ONA*, vol 4, p 294.

CHAPTER 16

1. Ponsonby to Canning, no 2, 4 January 1827, and no 15, 9 March 1827, PRO, FO 6/16.

2. De la Cruz to Ramsay, 13 March 1826, printed in Ratto, *Comodoros Britanicos en la Plata 1810–52*, p 112.

3. Ponsonby to Canning, 4 December 1826, PRO, FO 6/13.

4. Ramsay to de la Cruz, 20 February, 14 March and 15 May 1827, printed in Ratto, *Comodoros Britanicos en la Plata 1810–52*, pp 121–2.

5. De la Cruz to Brown, 26 March 1827, printed in Carranza *CNRA*, vol II, p 438.

6. Gameiro to Vilela Barbosa, no 13, 9 July 1825 (with schedule of alterations made), AN, XM 453.

7. Hood to Gordon, 18 April 1827, PRO, FO 51/3.

8. Argentinian and Brazilian accounts of the battle are to be found in Laurio H. Destefani, 'Monte Santiago, una Heroica Derrota' in *HMA*, p 403, and Boiteux, 'A Guerra da Cisplatina', chap XXXV. Also printed in Carranza, *CNRA*, vol IV, pp 305–6. Also *Memorandum de las operaciones navales de la marina de la República Argentina desde el año 1813*, pp 305–6.

9. Ponsonby to Canning, no 24, 20 April 1827, PRO, FO 6/17. (Lieut. Col. MacDonald's report attached.)

10. Zapiola to Minister of War and Marine (with crew lists), 10 April 1827, printed in Carranza, *CNRA*, vol II, p 441.

11. Gordon to Ponsonby, April 1827, PRO, FO 13/37.

CHAPTER 17

1. Gordon to Canning, no 9, 27 November 1826, PRO, FO 13/26.
2. Hood to Bidwell, 4 November 1826, PRO, FO 51/2.
3. Faustinho (Washington) to Vilela Barbosa, 1 July 1825, AN, XM 210.
4. Sir Robert Otway to Croker, no 35, 24 November 1826, PRO, Adm 1/30.
5. Pinto Guedes to Hood, 31 January 1827, PRO, FO 51/2.
6. Sir Robert Otway to Croker, no 10, 3 February 1827, PRO, Adm 1/30.
7. Paranaguá to Pinto Guedes, 29 November 1826, printed in Boiteux, 'A Guerra da Cisplatina', chap XXXVII, p 330. Enclosed with Gordon to Canning, no 14, 21 February 1827, PRO, FO 13/36.
8. Hill, *Diplomatic Relations between the USA and Brazil*, p 48. Queluz to Silvestre Rebello (Washington), with enclosure, 6 April 1827, *Archivo Diplomático da Independência*, vol 5.
9. Hill, *Diplomatic Relations between the USA and Brazil*, p 55.
10. Woodbine Parish to Planta, 6 February 1827, PRO, FO 6/20.
11. Woodbine Parish to Bidwell, 31 July and 31 December 1827, PRO, FO 6/20.
12. Woodbine Parish to Bidwell, 31 July and 31 December 1827, PRO, FO 6/20. Ponsonby to Dudley, no 13, 4 December 1827, PRO, FO 6/19.
13. Hood to Bidwell, 11 January 1827, PRO, FO 51/2. Gordon to Canning, no 21, 3 April 1827, PRO, FO 13/37.
14. Hood to Bidwell, 20 October 1827, PRO, FO 51/3.
15. Ponsonby to Canning, no 29, 4 June 1827, PRO, FO 6/17.
16. Destefani, 'Apogeo y Decadencia del Corso' in *HMA*, pp 424–39.
17. *ibid*, p 425.
18. *Memorandum de las operaciones navales de la marina de la República Argentina desde el ano 1813*, p 308.

CHAPTER 18

1. Ponsonby to Lord Howard de Walden, 4 December 1826, PRO, FO 6/13.
2. Canning to Ponsonby, 28 February 1826, PRO, FO 6/12.
3. Ponsonby to Inhambupe, 11 August 1826, PRO, FO 6/12.
4. Woodbine Parish to Canning, no 12, 12 February 1826, PRO, FO 6/19.
5. Woodbine Parish to Canning, no 44, 5 September 1826, PRO, FO 6/19.
6. Ponsonby to De la Cruz, 9 October 1826, PRO, FO 6/13.
7. See Harold F. Peterson, *Argentina and the United States, 1810-60*, State University of New York, 1964, pp 90–2.
8. Gordon to Canning, no 12, 7 February 1827, PRO, FO 13/36.
9. Gordon to Canning, no 39, 10 May 1827, PRO, FO 13/37.
10. Gordon to Canning no 50, 8 June 1827, PRO, FO 13/37.
11. Ponsonby to Dudley and Ward, 27 August 1827, PRO, FO 6/18.

12. Log of HMS *Thetis*, 22–27 September 1827, PRO, Adm 51/3490. Bingham to Otway, 1 October 1827, quoted in Otway to Croker, no 153, 12 November 1827, PRO, Adm 1/30.

13. Printed in Boiteux, 'A Guerra da Cisplatina', chap XXXIX, pp 373–4.

CHAPTER 19

1. The major units in service in May 1827 were (asterisk indicates deployed in the Plate):

1 74-gun	*Pedro I*
9 frigates	*Imperatriz*,* *Piranga*,* *Dona Paula*,* *Niterói*,* *Principe Imperial*, *Paraguassú*, *Isabela*, *Thetis*, *Dona Francisca*
3 corvettes	*Liberal*,* *Carioca*, *Maceió*
12 brigs	*Independência ou Morte*,* *29 de Agosto*,* *Caboclo*,* *Pirajá*,* *Real João*,* *Urarão*,* *Rio da Plata*,* *Liguri*,* *Beaurepaire*, *Cacique*, *Maranhão*, *Guarani*
4 brigantines	*Pará*,* *2 de Julho*,* *Leopoldina*, *Atlanta*
16 schooners	*Maria Theresa*,* *Dona Paula*,* *Itaparica*,* *Rios*,* *Maria da Glória*,* *Providência*,* *Alcantara*,* *FCamarão*,* *Conceição*,* *1 de Dezembro*,* *Duas Estrellas*,* *9 de Janeiro*,* *Leopoldina*, *Carolina*, *Isabela Maria*, *12 de Outubro*
1 lugger	*Principe Imperial* *

There were also 1 cutter and 18 gunboats and armed launches. *Relatório do Ministro Souza Coutinho*, 26 May 1827, Bibliotéca da Marinha, Rio de Janeiro. Deployments given in Gordon to Canning, no 28, 6 April 1827, PRO, FO 13/37.

2. Substantial extracts from this and other speeches are printed in Boiteux, 'A Guerra da Cisplatina', chap XXXVIII, pp 353–60. Buenos Aires newspapers shared this view of the vulnerability of Brazil's commerce to privateering; see Monica B. Holm and Sandra M. Rabich, *El Bloqueo de Buenos Aires durante la Guerra con el Brasil (1825–28) atraves de la Prensa Porteña*, paper given at the II Simposio de Historia Marítima y Naval Iberoamericana, Chile, November 1993, p 426.

3. Maceió to Pinto Guedes, 1 August 1827, printed in Boiteux, *ONA*, vol 2, p 27.

4. Pinto Guedes to Maceió, 6 July 1827, printed in Boiteux, *ONA*, vol 2, p 26.

5. Ponsonby to Dudley and Ward, 15 October 1827, PRO, FO 6/19.

6. Woodbine Parish to Planta, 5 April 1826, PRO, FO 6/19.

7. Woodbine Parish to Bidwell, 31 December 1827, PRO, FO 6/20.

8. Gordon to Dudley, no 26, 1 October 1827, PRO, FO 13/39.

9. Gordon to Canning, no 21, 3 April 1827, PRO, FO 13/37.

10. British-commanded ships were the frigates *Principe Imperial*, *Thetis*, *Piranga* and *Dona Francisca* commanded by James Thompson, James Norton, Mateus Welch and Thomas Hayden; the corvettes *Liberal* and *Maceió* commanded by

Bartholomew Hayden and Alexander Reid; the brigs *Maranhão, Cacique, Caboclo* and *Independência ou Morte* commanded by Alexander Anderson, George Manson, William Inglis and Francis Clare; the schooners *Bela Maria, Duas Estrellas, Dona Paula* and *Conceição* commanded by William Parker, Richard N. Murphy, Thomas Reed and John B. Wilson. In addition, in the previous year James Shepherd (*Piranga*) and John Rogers Gleddon (*29 de Agosto*) had been killed, while William Eyre (*Itaparica*), Robert Steel (*12 de Outubro* yacht), George Broom (*Bertioga* schooner) and David Carter (*Duqueza de Goias*) had been captured.

    11. Pinto Guedes to Diogo de Brito, no 474, 7 September 1828, quoted in Boiteux, 'A Guerra da Cisplatina',.chap XXXVII, p 344.

CHAPTER 20

    1. On 1 May 1827, the Argentinian National Squadron comprised the following ships:

corvettes	*Chacabuco* (20 guns), *Ituzaingú* (formerly *Itaparica*) (20)
brigs	*General Balcarce* (14), *Congresso Nacional* (18)
brigantines	*Patagones* (formerly *Escudeira*), *8 de Febrero* (formerly *Dona Januária*)
schooners	*Sarandí, Guanco, Unión, Maldonado* (formerly *Leal Paulistana*), *Uruguay, Pepa, Juncal* (formerly *Constança*), *9 de Febrero* (formerly *Bertioga*), *29 de Diciembre* (formerly *Oriental*), *30 de Julio* (formerly *Brocaio*)
gunboats	*Nos 1, 2, 3, 5, 8, 9, 10, 11, 12, 6* (formerly *Paranaguá*), *7* (formerly *Cananea*), *4* (formerly *Iguapé*), *13* (formerly *Paraty*)
yachts	*11 de Junio* (formerly *9 de Janeiro*), *18 de Enero* (formerly *12 de Outubro*)

    2. Ponsonby to De la Cruz, 19 June 1827, PRO, FO 6/17.

    3. *Diario del Sargento Mayor D Cesar Fournier – 7 de nov a 7 de dec de 1827* (log of the *Congresso*), printed in Carranza, *CNRA*, vol IV, pp 217– 21.

    4. A. de Alzogaray, *Diario de Operaciones de la Escuadra Republicana: Campaña del Brasil 1826–8*, entry for 28 November 1827, Archivo General de la Nacion, República Oriental del Uruguay, Montevideo, 1934.

    5. Pinto Guedes to Maceió, 6 July 1827, printed in Boiteux, *ONA*, vol 2, p 26.

    6. *ibid.*

    7. Quoted in Boiteux, 'A Guerra da Cisplatina', chap XXXVIII, p 353.

    8. Medical report of Dr John Corbett printed in Carranza, *CNRA*, vol II, p 468.

    9. Otway to Croker, no 106, 20 August 1828, enclosing affidavit of carpenter's mate on the *General Brandzen*, PRO, Adm 1/31.

    10. Affidavit by William Foraty, Buenos Aires, 31 July 1828, PRO, FO 6/28.

11. Silvestre Rebello to Queluz, 4 December 1827, *Archivo Diplomático da Independência*, vol 5.

12. Otway to Croker, no 64, 7 July 1828, PRO, Adm 1/30.

13. Destefani, 'Apogeo y Decadencia del Corso' in *HMA*, p 445.

14. Woodbine Parish to Bidwell, 25 August and 10 November 1827, PRO, FO 6/20.

15. Letter of Sam Brooks Esq in Woodbine Parish to Bidwell, 1 December 1827, PRO, FO 6/20.

16. Ponsonby to Canning, nos 41 and 42, 2 and 27 July 1827, PRO, FO 6/18.

17. Hood to Bidwell, no 18, 12 September 1827, PRO, FO 51/3.

18. Ponsonby to Dudley, no 6, 27 August 1827, PRO, FO 6/19.

19. Otway to Croker, nos 80 and 106, 22 June and 27 July 1827, PRO, Adm 1/30.

20. Otway to Croker, no 141, 16 October 1827, PRO, Adm 1/30. Bruce to Palmerston, no 16, 5 April 1832, FO 6/36.

21. Otway to Croker, no 104, 31 July 1827, PRO, Adm 1/30.

22. Forbes to Moreno, 13 and 24 October 1827, quoted in Peterson, *Argentina and the United States*, p 92.

23. Ponsonby to Dudley, no 6, 27 August 1827, PRO, FO 6/18.

24. Woodbine Parish to Bidwell, 1 December 1827, PRO, FO 6/20.

CHAPTER 21

1. Diogo de Brito to Pinto Guedes, 3 December 1827, printed in Boiteux, *ONA*, vol 2, pp 31–2.

2. Diogo de Brito to Pinto Guedes, 17 December 1827, 16 February 1828, printed in Boiteux, *ONA*, vol 2, pp 38–41.

3. Pinto Guedes to Diogo de Brito, nos 301 and 306, 23 December 1827 and 6 January 1828, printed in Boiteux, *ONA*, vol 2, pp 33 and 39.

4. Pinto Guedes to Diogo de Brito, no 325, 21 January 1828, printed in Boiteux, *ONA*, vol 2, pp 33–6.

5. Diogo de Brito to Pinto Guedes, 17 February 1828, printed in Boiteux, *ONA*, vol 2, p 44.

6. Pinto Guedes to Diogo de Brito, no 290, 16 December 1827, printed in Boiteux, *ONA*, vol 2, p 33.

7. Diogo de Brito to Pinto Guedes, 8 April 1828, printed in Boiteux, 'A Guerra da Cisplatina', chap XLIII, p 56.

8. *Memorandum de las operaciones navales de la marina de la República Argentina desde el ano 1813*, vol IV, p 312.

9. Pinto Guedes to Diogo de Brito, no 449, June 1828, printed in Boiteux, *ONA*, vol 2, p 50.

10. Ramsay to Minister of War and Marine, 20 February and 21 May 1828, printed in Ratto, *Comodoros Britanicos en la Plata 1810–52*, p 112.

11. Correspondence between Home Department, Admiralty and Foreign Office, March to April 1828, PRO, FO 6/25.

12. Pinto Guedes to Diogo de Brito, 5 April 1828, printed in Boiteux, 'A Guerra da Cisplatina', chap XLIII, p 48.

13. *Relatório do Ministro da Marinha Diogo de Brito, 3 Maio 1828*, Bibliotéca da Marinha, Rio de Janeiro. Between May 1827 and May 1828, the Brazilian Navy had lost 12 of its major warships:

frigate	*Dona Paula* (wrecked)
corvettes	*Maceió* (wrecked)
brigs	*Cacique* (captured), *Ururão* (captured), *Independência ou Morte* (wrecked), *Real João* and *Rio da Plata* (both derelict)
schooners	*Conceição* (wrecked), *Maria Theresa* and *Isabela Maria* (both captured), *29 de Agosto* and *Rios* (both derelict)

but had gained 14:

frigate	*Defensora*
corvettes	*Bertioga* and *Maria Isabel*
brigs	*Duqueza de Goias*, *15 de Agosto*, *Imperial Pedro*, *13 de Março*, *Pampeiro* and *Niger* (both captured)
brigantines	*Patagonia* and *Dona Januária* (both recaptured), *Constança*
schooners	*Bela Maria*, *1 de Dezembro*

CHAPTER 22

1. Gordon to Dudley, no 19, 21 September 1827, PRO, FO 13/38.

2. i.e. the British *Utopia*, *Atlantic*, *William and Henry*, *Ann*, *George*, *Henry and Isabella*, *John* and *Stag;* the French *Courier*, *Junon*, *La Jenny*, *Jules* and *La Belle Gabrielle;* the American *Ruth*, *Leonidas* and *Mathilda;* the Danish *Fortuna* and the Swedish *Anders*.

3. Gordon to Canning, no 21, 3 April 1827, PRO, FO 13/37.

4. Gordon to Dudley, no 18, 21 September 1827, PRO, FO 13/38.

5. Gordon to Dudley, no 15, 13 February 1828, PRO, FO 13/47.

6. Gordon to Dudley, nos 14 and 18, 15 and 17 February 1828, PRO, FO 13/47.

7. Ponsonby to Dudley, 12 February 1828, PRO, FO 6/22.

8. Otway to Croker, no 20, 13 March 1828, PRO, Adm 1/30.

9. Gordon to Dudley, no 47, 6 June 1828, PRO, FO 13/47.

10. Gordon to Aracaty, 23 May 1828, PRO, FO 13/47.

11. Gordon to Dudley, no 35, 13 April 1828, PRO, FO 13/47.

12. Gordon to Dudley, no 54, 18 June 1828, PRO, FO 13/47. Otway to Croker, no 68, 14 June 1828, PRO, Adm 1/30.

13. Gordon to Dudley, no 58, 12 July 1828, PRO, FO 13/47.

14. The Hamburg ship *Matilde*, the American brig *Alison*, the French schooner *Hydra* and the American schooner *Fanny*. These were armed and renamed respectively the *Nuevo 25 de Mayo*, *General Rondeau*, *Argentina* and *Convencion*. The

French *Mandarine* had likewise be purchased in January and renamed *Gobernador Dorrego* (or *General Dorrego* – there is some inconsistency in the records).

15. Hector Tanzi, in *HMA*, p 500, says that it was the schooner *Maldonado* which carried the news and that Commodore Brown was on board. Unfortunately there is no other evidence – not even in Brown's own memoirs – for this charming story.

16. Pinto Guedes to Melo e Alvim, no 490, 12 October 1828, and quoted in Boiteux, 'A Guerra da Cisplatina', chap XLIV, p 58.

17. *Documentos del Almirante Brown*, tomo II, doc 113.

18. *Defenza do Almirante Pinto Guedes Barão do Rio da Plata perante o Conselho de Guerra*, Typographia Torres, Rio de Janeiro, 1829.

CHAPTER 23

1. Gordon to Dudley, no 2, 27 July 1828, PRO, FO 13/47.

2. Dudley to Gordon, no 7, 9 February 1828, PRO, FO 13/46.

3. Robert Pousell of Fulham to FO, 22 March 1828, PRO, FO 6/24.

4. Dudley to Gordon, no 16, 5 April 1828, PRO, FO 13/46.

5. Gordon to Dudley, no 59, 12 July 1828, PRO, FO 13/47.

6. Gordon to Dudley, no 6, 1 August 1828, PRO, FO 13/47.

7. Tudor to Clay, 28 September 1828, quoted in Hill, *Diplomatic Relations between the USA and Brazil*, p 60.

8. Aston to Aberdeen, no 4, 11 July 1829, PRO, 13/62.

9. Aberdeen to Ponsonby, 10 November 1828, PRO, FO 13/49.

10. Ponsonby to Aberdeen, no 9, 24 January 1829, PRO, FO 13/60.

11. Otway to Croker, no 150, 4 December 1828, PRO, Adm 1/31.

12. Aberdeen to Ponsonby, nos 5 and 15, 26 February and 20 June 1829, PRO, FO 13/59.

13. Ponsonby to Aberdeen, no 19, 26 March 1829, PRO FO 13/60.

14. Strangford to Aberdeen, no 3, 27 January 1829, PRO, FO 13/58.

15. Aston to Aberdeen, nos 1, 77 and 84, 6 October 1829, 17 August 1830, 4 September 1830, PRO, FO 13/69, 13/73 and 13/74.

16. Aston to Palmerston, no 62, 14 June 1831, with *Relatório da Repartição do Assuntos Estrangeiros, Maio de 1831*, PRO, FO 13/81.

17. Palmerston to Aston, no 18, April 1832, PRO, FO 13/91.

18. Fox to Palmerston, no 21, 20 September 1834, with *Relatório da Repartição do Negocios Estrangeiros, Abril de 1834*, PRO, FO 13/110. Compensation was paid for the British ships *Henry and Isabella, George, John, Ann, George and John, Cocquito, Atlantic, Stag, William and Henry, Dickens, Hellesponte, Liberator, Nestor, Hawk, Melpomene, Lord Eldon, Resolution, Unicorn, Utopia, Peruano* and – a remnant of the Pernambuco rebellion of 1824 – the *Rob Roy*, and for British cargoes on board the *Pioneer, Hussar, Sarah* and *Brutus* (US), and the *Fortuna* (Danish).

19. *ibid.*

CHAPTER 24

1. Report of Lieut. Claxton RN, 24 April 1828, PRO, FO 6/25.
2. Ponsonby to Dudley, 4 December 1827, no 12, PRO, FO 6/19.
3. Otway to Croker, no 128, 8 November 1828 (with enclosure), PRO, FO 6/28.
4. Foreign Office Instructions, 9 April 1828, PRO, FO 6/25.
5. Report of Lieut. W. Turner RN, 28 August 1828, PRO, FO 6/25. Petition of Lieut. Ohm, 5 May 1829, PRO, FO 6/28.
6. Destefani, 'Apogeo y Decadencia del Corso' in *HMA*, pp 447, 455.
7. Woodbine Parish to Bidwell, 15 June and 15 March 1829, PRO, FO 6/24 and 26.
8. Segui to Zapiola, 22 May 1829, AGN, X.1.4.6, printed in Arguindeguy and Rodriguez, *Guillermo Brown*, p 251. Woodbine Parish to Aberdeen, no 30, 2 June 1829, PRO, FO 6/27.
9. Woodbine Parish to Aberdeen, nos 42 and 45, 12 September and 10 October 1829, PRO, FO 6/27.
10. Woodbine Parish to Aberdeen, nos 7 and 28, 13 March and 25 September 1830, PRO, FO 6/30.
11. Woodbine Parish to Aberdeen, no 19, 26 July 1830, PRO, FO 6/30.
12. Woodbine Parish to Bidwell, January 1830, PRO, FO 6/31.
13. Bruce to Palmerston, no 21, 13 January 1834, PRO, FO 6/44.
14. Bruce to Palmerston, 4 July 1834, PRO, FO 6/44.
15. Gore to Palmerston, 14 February 1833, PRO, FO 6/500.
16. Hamilton to Palmerston, 11 December 1834, PRO, FO 6/41.
17. Peterson, *Argentina and the United States*, p 94.

EPILOGUE

1. The *Relatório da Repartição da Marinha, Maio de 1828*, shows the Brazilian Navy as having in commission 1 ship-of-the-line, 9 frigates, 20 brigs and brigantines, 21 armed schooners and gunboats, 1 lugger and 16 transports and packets. The *Relatório* for 1830 set the establishment for the following year as 2 frigates, 6 corvettes or brigs, 6 schooners and 6 transports and packets.
2. These were Commodores John Taylor and James Norton; Captains Mateus Welch and John Pascoe Grenfell; Captains (of Frigate) George Manson, Bartholomew Hayden, William Eyre, Stephen Clewley and William James Inglis; Commanders George Broom, William January and William Parker; Lieutenants James Wallace, David Carter, C.J. Appleton, R.N. Murphy, Richard Haydon, William MacErwing, Thomas Thompson and Charles Rose; and Sublieutenants J.H. White and Edward Newton. *Almanack da Marinha 1835*, BN, Rio.
3. London correspondence 1832–3, FO 13/131. Report from Rio, April 1833, FO 13/134.
4. Fox–Palmerston correspondence 1832–3, FO 13/99, 100, 109.
5. Boiteux, *ONA*, vol 2, pp 159–205.

6. Boiteux, *ONA*, vol 4, pp 243–64.

7. Boiteux, *ONA*, vol 3, pp 210–26.

8. Boiteux, *ONA*, vol 1, pp 193–264.

9. Boiteux, *ONA*, vol 4, pp 135–53.

10. D.A. Santillan, *Gran Enciclopedia Argentina*, 9 vols, Edoir SA Editores, Buenos Aires, 1956.

11. J.T. De Kay, *Chronicles of the Frigate 'Macedonian' 1809–1922*, Norton and Co, New York, 1995, pp 228–43.

BIBLIOGRAPHY

Alzogaray, A. de, *Diario de operaciones de la Escuadra republicana*. *Campaña del Brasil*, *1826–1827*, Archivo General de la Nacion, República Oriental del Uruguay, Montevideo, 1934

Archivo Diplomatico da Independência, Ministério de Relações Exteriores, Rio de Janeiro, 1922, vol 5

Arguindeguy and Rodriguez, *Guillermo Brown*. *Apostillas a su Vida*, Instituto Browniano, Buenos Aires, 1994

Armitage, John, *History of Brazil from the arrival of the Braganza family in 1808 to the abdication of D Pedro I in 1831*, 2 vols, London, 1836

Armitage, John, *Historia do Brasil desde a chegada da família de Bragança em 1808 até a abdicação de D Pedro I em 1831*, (translation), Edições de Ouro, Rio de Janeiro, 1943

Boiteux, Henrique, *Os Nossos Almirantes*, Imprensa Naval, Rio de Janeiro, vols 1–5, 1915–21

Boiteux, Lucas A., *A Marinha Imperial*, Imprensa Naval, Brasil, 1954

—— 'A Guerra da Cisplatina 1825–8', *Revista Maritima Brasileira*, 1956–7

Carranza, Angel J., *Campanas Navales de la República Argentina*, vols II and IV, Buenos Aires, 1962

De Kay, J.T., *Chronicles of the Frigate 'Macedonian' 1809–1922*, Norton and Co, New York, 1995

Documentos del Almirante Brown, Academia Nacional de la Historia, Buenos Aires, 1959

'Extratos do Arquivo do Almirante Tamandaré', *Subsidios para a História Maritima do Brasil*, vol VIII, Ministério da Marinha, Rio de Janeiro, 1950

Ferns, H.S., *Britain and Argentina in the Nineteenth Century*, Oxford University Press, 1960

La Guerra Contra el Imperio del Brasil, Departamento de Estudios Históricos Navales, Buenos Aires, 1979 (reproduces: *Diario de Noticias del Capitan del Puerto de Buenos Aires Coronel D Francisco Lynch 1825–28*)

'La Guerra Contra el Imperio del Brasil (1825–28)', (various authors), *Historia Maritima Argentina*, vol IV, Departamento de Estudios Históricos Navales, Buenos Aires, 1988

Hill, Lawrence A., *Diplomatic relations between the USA and Brazil,* Duke University Press, 1932

Holm, Monica B. and Rabich, Sandra M., *El Bloqueo de Buenos Aires durante la Guerra con el Brasil (1825–28) atraves de la Prensa Porteña,* paper given at the II Simposio de Historia Marítima y Naval Iberoamericana, Chile, November 1993

Humphries, R.A., *British Consular Reports on the Trade and Politics of Latin America 1824–26,* Royal Historical Society, London, 1940

Ireland, J. de C., *The Admiral from Mayo,* Edmund Burke, Dublin, 1995

Kaufmann, W.W., *British Policy and the Independence of Latin America,* Frank Cass & Co, New Haven, 1967.

Kay-Shuttleworth, Hon. Nina L., *A Life of Sir Woodbine Parish, 1796 to 1882,* London, 1910

Lynch, John, *Spanish American Revolutions, 1808–26,* W.W. Norton, New York, 1973

—— *Caudillos in Spanish America, 1800–1850,* Oxford University Press, 1992

Manchester, Alan K., *British Preeminence in Brazil: Its Rise and Decline,* Durham, NC, 1933

McLean, David, *War, Diplomacy and Informal Empire: Britain and the Republics of La Plata, 1836–1853,* British Academic Press, London, 1995

Peterson, Harold F., *Argentina and the United States 1810-60,* State University of New York, 1964

Purdy, John, *The New Sailing Directory for the Ethiopic or Southern Atlantic Ocean,* R.H. Laurie, London, 1845

Ratto, H.R., *Comodoros Britanicos en la Plata 1810–52,* Buenos Aires, 1945

—— *Biográfias Navales Argentinas – Almirante Guillermo Brown,* Buenos Aires, 1961

—— *Historia del Almirante Brown,* Buenos Aires, 1985

Rock, David, *Argentina 1516–1887. From Spanish Colonisation to the Falklands and Alfonsin,* I.B. Tauris, London, 1986

Santillan, D.A., *Gran Enciclopedia Argentina,* 9 vols, Edoir SA Editores, Buenos Aires, 1956

Senna (Pereira), Emilio, *Guerra do Rio da Plata em 1825. O Libello Argentino e a Verdade Historica,* Rio de Janeiro, 1857

Senna Pereira, J.R., *Memórias e Reflexões sobre o Rio da Plata,* Rio de Janeiro, 1847

Soares, Teixeira, *Diplomacia do Imperio no Rio da Plata,* Editora Brand, Rio de Janeiro, 1955

Vale, Brian, *Independence or Death! British Sailors and Brazilian Independence 1822–5,* Tauris Academic Studies, London, 1996.

Webster, C.K., *Britain and the Independence of Latin America 1812–30,* Oxford University Press and the British Council, 1944

INDEX

Note: Foreign officers of the Argentinian Navy are designated (A); of the Brazilian Navy (B)